CRITICAL
LEGAL STUDIES

D0875014

CRITICAL LEGAL STUDIES

Edited by
Peter Fitzpatrick & Alan Hunt

BASIL BLACKWELL

First published 1987
First published in USA 1987

Basil Blackwell Ltd
108 Cowley Road, Oxford, OX4 1JF, UK

Basil Blackwell Inc,
432 Park Avenue South, Suite 1503
New York, NY 10016, USA

British Library Cataloguing in Publication Data

Journal of law and society. — Vol. 14, no. 1
 1.Sociological jurisprudence —
 Periodicals   2. Law — Great Britain —
 Periodicals
 340'.115'0941   K370
 ISBN 0-631-15718-2

Library of Congress Cataloging in Publication Data

Critical legal studies
 Includes bibliographies.
 1. Law — Philosophy.   2. Sociological jurisprudence.
 I. Fitzpatrick, Peter.   II. Hunt, Alan.
 K235.C754 1987b   340'.1   87-10336
 ISBN 0-631-15718-2

Typeset by Cardiff University Press
Printed in Great Britain by Whitstable Litho, Kent

Contents

Critical Legal Studies: Introduction

PETER FITZPATRICK and ALAN HUNT

'Critical Legal Studies' has origins in the late 1970s with the work produced by the Conference on Critical Legal Studies in the U.S.A. Comparable groups and organisations were also created independently in France, Germany and a number of other countries. In Britain the Critical Legal Conference was formed in 1984.[1] There are considerable variations in the style, focus and method of work produced under the label of 'critical legal studies'. Critical legal scholarship has not formed clearly delineated 'national' varieties. This collection of work produced in the United Kingdom is presented as a contribution to the wider project of critical legal studies.

It is significant that critical legal studies has developed within specific organisational forms. This attests to a strong sense in which there is a general aspiration amongst participants to be a 'movement' within the field of legal studies. Yet, at the same time, as is evident from the essays presented in this collection, there is very considerable diversity. Indeed, that diversity is celebrated as a positive achievement to be nurtured and protected.

Critical legal studies draws heavily on the radical political culture of the period since the 1960s. It asserts the inescapability of commitment and rejects the aspirations of the preceding intellectual climate's search for value neutrality. Yet, at the same time, it seeks to avoid the vice of sectarianism which has so scarred radical politics during the same period. Critical legal studies seeks to provide an environment in which radical and committed scholarship can thrive in diversity with no aspiration to lay down a 'correct' theory or method. The element of cohesion is provided, in the first instance, by a shared rejection of the dominant tradition of Anglo-American legal scholarship, the expository orthodoxy or, more crudely, the 'black-letter law' tradition. But the critical movement also shares a recognition of the limitations of the socio-legal approaches which have characterised some recent attempts to escape from orthodoxy which tend to see law through the conceptual apparatus of other disciplines. There is, as well, a shared concern with the politics of law, with the stress on law as significant precisely because it is not immunised from the realm of politics and thus has definite effects and consequences for the multitude of arguments, battles and struggles which produce the human condition. The formative statement of the Critical Legal Conference put it this way:

> The central focus of the critical legal approach is to explore the manner in which legal
> doctrine and legal education and the practices of legal institutions work to buttress and

1

support a pervasive system of oppressive, inegalitarian relations. Critical theory works to develop radical alternatives, and to explore and debate the role of law in the creation of social, economic and political relations that will advance human emancipation.

But, as with any family resemblance, there are also important differences. Thus, for example, the early period of the critical legal studies movement in the U.S.A. was characterised by the key role played by one or two individuals which resulted in a certain surface uniformity in language and style of presentation, whereas in Britain there has been no such unifying individual or group of individuals. Our colleagues in the U.S.A. have been more prepared to borrow extensively from a great diversity of intellectual traditions to produce a *mélange* of influences. In Britain critical legal studies has been less eclectic: the key traditions informing debate have been Marxism, feminism and critical social theory of the Frankfurt variety.

The essays presented here bear strong evidence of a more recent intellectual engagement. A rough characterisation of this controversy is that of the issues joined between 'critique', drawing heavily on Marxism and critical social theory, and 'post-modernism', drawing on Foucault and deconstruction, for example. There is a growing following for Lyotard's post-modern clarion: "Let us wage a war on totality; let us be witness to the unpresentable; let us activate the differences . . . ."[2] It remains to be seen if the critical legal studies movement can accommodate the gulf between these two traditions. They are both well represented in our collection: Hunt, Cotterrell, Ireland *et al.* and Thompson exemplify different aspects of the tradition of critique. Hirst and Jones, Douzinas and Warrington, and Rose reject critique and, again with considerable variation, epitomise post-modernist themes. It is far too early to summarise this engagement, let alone to announce the triumph of one side or the other or to celebrate a successful synthesis.

Yet, despite the fact that engagement and controversy are at the very heart of the critical project, the essays presented here are, in a sense that is both hopeful and accurate, a 'collection'. The diversity of post-modernism and its break with critique have, somewhat paradoxically, provoked greater communication and cohesion within critical legal studies in Britain. There is a significant core of unity, even if expressed in different language, in opposition to the dominant orthodoxies in legal scholarship and in agreement around a commitment to the necessity and possibility of social transformation.

In short, critical legal studies in Britain has been able to accommodate a diversity of perspectives whilst retaining an effective identity. Not everyone within the critical legal studies movement shares the same concerns; the family resemblances result in overlapping and interlocked configurations of intellectual and political concerns which continue to ensure that the critical movement provides a friendly and supportive framework for discussion and debate within legal studies.

This collection is by no means exclusively concerned with general theoretical debate. It features the strong presence of essays concerned with the relevance and application of a critically informed approach to important fields of substantive law. One of the significant differences between critical legal studies and many 'social' approaches to law is the former's concern to take legal doctrine and judicial reasoning seriously. The essays on contract law (Collins), trusts (Cotterrell), company law (Ireland *et al.*) and labour law (Conaghan and Chudleigh) are of interest not only for their contributions to their respective fields but for their contrasting and complementary methods of interrogation of substantive law.

We would like to signal an important omission in the hope that it will be made good. These essays have little to say about the varieties of legal practice and their problems. The work presented emanates from those working in legal education. Whilst the aspiration of critical legal studies is strongly committed to developing an interchange and co-operation with radical legal practitioners and other legal activists, little progress has been achieved. This is not the occasion to explore the problems involved; we merely wish to signal this as an issue which the critical legal studies movement must address more productively.

We would like to thank all of our authors for their co-operation. We would like to thank the publishers and the editorial team of the *Journal of Law and Society* for encouraging and facilitating this project.

NOTES AND REFERENCES

1   Details about the Critical Legal Conference can be obtained from Alan Hunt, c/o Law School, Middlesex Polytechnic, The Burroughs, London NW4 4BT.
2   J.-F. Lyotard, *The Postmodern Condition: A Report on Knowledge* (1984) p. 82.

The Critique of Law:
What is 'Critical' about Critical Legal Theory?

ALAN HUNT*

INTRODUCTION

Critical legal theory is the *enfant terrible* of contemporary legal studies. It delights in shocking what it takes to be the legal establishment.[1] Its roots lie in a deep sense of dissatisfaction with the existing state of legal scholarship. These dissatisfactions and grievances are many and varied; some are more concerned with the state of legal education, others with the political conservatism of legal education, whilst others experience frustration at the failure of orthodoxy to grapple with what they see as the real problems of the role of law in the contemporary world. Advocates of critical legal studies may not all share the same rank ordering of dissatisfactions but are all reacting against features of the prevailing orthodoxies in legal scholarship, against the conservatism of the law schools and against many features of the role played by law and legal institutions in modern society. These reactive roots explain why the development of critical legal theory has taken the forms of 'movements', albeit loose and unstructured in character (Conference on Critical Legal Studies in the United States of America, *Critique du Droit* in France and Critical Legal Conference in Britain) which pre-date the emergence of any clearly formulated and generally agreed theoretical position. The situation of the critical legal studies movement is not too dangerously distorted if one puts the point polemically; it is a movement in search of a theory, but at the same time it is a movement which has not agreed that such a theory is either possible or desirable.

This paper explores the question: does critical legal studies have the potential to go beyond its reactive origins and develop a viable alternative theorisation that is capable of providing a new direction for legal scholarship? I will offer an account of the distinguishing characteristics of the critical movement and then make some suggestions about the possible direction of its development.

* *Law School, Middlesex Polytechnic, The Burroughs, London NW4 4BT, England.*

At the outset it is important to appreciate that the reactive aspect of critical legal theory signifies something more than the mere youthful debunking of orthodoxy. It fulfils two important roles. First, it insists that there is an orthodoxy that needs to be and can be challenged and that the debates and disputes which take place within legal scholarship are arguments within a more or less monolithic tradition. One important part of the critical project is the need for continuing debate about both the nature of orthodoxy and how much of it should be jettisoned. A second function of reactive scholarship is to draw attention to the very real difficulties involved in mounting a challenge to a well-established orthodoxy. A primary characteristic of critical legal theory lies in the insistence that it is both possible and necessary to think differently about law.

The aspiration to think differently about law raises a set of issues about the choices involved in seeking to specify that 'difference'. The project of critical legal studies is marked by diversity. Some of this diversity may indicate substantive intellectual and political differences between participants. But this diversity also attests to a less conflictual source of divergence, namely, the mutual recognition that the problems encountered in both imagining and then articulating an alternative require a considerable degree of experimentation in the construction of such an alternative.

The question of whether it is either possible or desirable to construct a 'general theory' is a major source of tension amongst critical scholars. One trend insists that the very project of 'general theory' should be abandoned.[2] This argument is strongly influenced by recent debates, in particular, in modern pragmatist philosophy, deconstruction and post-structuralism.[3] Others continue to see value in seeking to elaborate an 'alternative general theory'. The issues involved here are important and provide much of the general terrain of controversy within critical legal studies. I will return in the next section to take up these issues.

Another important dimension of the search for an alternative revolves around what I will call 'the problem of politics'. The relationship between politics and legal theory exhibits a number of different but related aspects. First, many proponents wish to espouse an explicit political commitment in that their work seeks to contribute towards some political goal. A typical formulation expresses commitment to overcoming 'domination' and 'hierarchy'.[4] This concern involves a rejection, on the one hand, of the prevalent apolitical stance of much legal scholarship founded on the belief in the possibility of value neutrality which portrays the lawyer as a technical expert. The concern with politics within critical legal studies involves a commitment to some conception of 'praxis', of the interaction of theory and practice. Finally, there exists a generalised commitment to activism in general, and legal activism in particular, with the objective that the committed legal academic can and should be able to contribute to the activist struggles of the day. Yet at the same time there are significant differences over the possibility and role of such activism. These dimensions lead to a general concern with 'the politics of law'.

So far I have suggested that a number of the distinctive characteristics of the critical legal studies movement flow from reactions against the prevailing orthodoxies. But the movement has now been around sufficiently long that it must soon pass beyond the stage of debunking and trashing orthodoxy; it is having to grapple with the problems of advancing a distinguishable and working alternative. Such an alternative, even if it resists the self-description of being a 'theory', must include such general features as a conceptualisation of its object(s) of inquiry and some statement of the inquiry procedures or methods which it employs. But, as I hinted above, there is a strand within the critical tradition which has considerable reservations about this attempt to give a generalising statement of the critical project. They see it as self-deception and likely only to reproduce, albeit in radical guise, the errors and mistakes of those theories which it rejects. So, before advancing an argument which outlines the elements of a critical theory of law, it is necessary to consider this tension within the movement more closely.

ON THE POSSIBILITY OF THEORY

In confronting what is perhaps the most important controversy within critical legal studies I should make clear my objectives. I want to comment on one of the big intellectual issues of our time and quickly make clear that I have no original contribution to make, but I do want to suggest a way in which critical work can continue without pushing aside or ignoring the 'big' metatheoretical issues. Much hinges on how these issues are posed since this in turn determines how the lines of battle are drawn. What follows is an attempt to sketch the issues making use of a metaphor.

As we approach the end of the century we are sitting anxiously on the edge of a glacier aware of its ultimate fate but impressed by its endurance. The seeming solidity of the main face, called the Enlightenment, continues to hold to the possibility of objective knowledge realisable through natural and social scientific procedures. Piling up behind and threatening to displace this long-standing and already factured edifice are a complex intermeshing set of newer glaciers, each having their own distinctive origins. They have many and varied names: linguistic philosophy, phenomenology, post-structuralism, decon-struction, pragmatism and relativism to name but a few. They are all expending some part of their energy pushing in roughly the same direction. They insist that the Enlightenment created a myth of science which held out an evolutionist and progressive image of accumulating knowledge giving access to reality. These newer glaciers challenge the most basic tenets of the Enlightenment beliefs. They insist, traumatic though it may be, that the glacier Enlightenment will and must collapse soon, and in turn they concede that whatever post-Enlightenment way of thought emerges will in its turn be displaced by glaciers whose shapes and names we cannot envisage.

7

How does this sketch link up with critical legal studies? The critical school is self-consciously engaged in confronting a very profound intellectual challenge to the conventional methods and preoccupations of legal scholarship which have been generated through the attempt to come to grips with contemporary developments in philosophy, sociology and literary theory. The central issue stems from pressing to their most disturbing implications the consequences of accepting the culturally constructed nature of social existence. The need to pursue this path has come about because of a deep disenchantment with all those intellectual traditions since the Englightenment which claim to offer the possibility of access to a verifiable truth. The challenge requires us to explore the implications of the fact that our very capacity to pose such issues, namely language, is the paradigm case of cultural construction. Can we sensibly claim to go beyond the socially constructed languages or discourses which we can deploy to reach a reality which is not itself constrained by language/discourse? Or does language provide not only the content but also the barriers to what we can communicate about? We are challenged to renounce the reassuring belief that our discourses stand in some relation of 'correspondence' to a reality independent of consciousness. We are not asked to surrender our working assumption that such a reality exists but rather to give up the complacent assumption that our thought and talk can arrive at some verifiable or objective access to that reality. It is this central intellectual challenge and its ramifications to which critical legal studies is currently seeking to respond in the arena of legal studies.

The challenge outlined above comes in many different forms and from different disciplinary sources. I will focus attention on the recent flurry of work which represents a newer and deeper engagement between relativism/ pragmatism and realism. I will single out just one strand which is not only the most accessible but which is also having a significant impact on critical legal studies in both the U.S.A. and Britain and is personified in the writing of Richard Rorty.[5] Rorty's critique of the Enlightenment project is directed against the pretensions of its theory of knowledge (epistemology). He declines to present an alternative epistemology because he rejects its very premise that we can find a way to make our thought and theory 'correspond' to reality. His anti-epistemology insists on the 'contingency' of language and that all we have available are different conversational strategies or language-games for talking about the things that interest us. None of these can have any privileged status by which we can claim that they provide a 'right answer' in the sense of providing a correspondence to reality. He denies that this argument involves a relativist claim that any language-game is as good as any other. We can and do make choices between alternatives and indeed our social history is significantly influenced by major shifts in the language-games that people employ such as the abandonment of the theological language that was the great achievement of the Englightenment; where that intellectual movement went wrong was in erecting reason or science as the substitute for theology. The crux of his position, as it affects my present concerns, is that when we choose

8

between alternative language-games we can make no stronger claim for our choice than that 'it works', and not that it is true.

What he does not, in my view, satisfactorily address is whether there is an important distinction, as I believe there is, between the claim that 'Language-game X works for me' (that is, relativism) and 'Language-game Y works for us'. 'Working-for-us' allows the possibility of a sociology of knowledge which can seek to explain the sequence of language-games which have played major roles for whole communities across significant periods of time and to show that these have made it possible to say and to do what was not possible before. This, I suggest, leads back to the major controversy because it requires us to confront the question: do different language-games merely allow us to say different things or can we claim that one rather than another makes it possible for us not only to say something different but to *say something more* or to *understand more*? Claims of this sort are inherently controversial because they necessarily appeal to some criteria of 'more' that is external to each language-game. The trouble with Rorty is that he rejects both of these choices while failing to elaborate any third-way account of what the claim that 'it works' might mean.

To return to the issue as to whether the critical school should pursue the project of developing a theory is to pose the choice between 'theory' and 'conversation'. To renounce theory in favour of conversation is seen as avoiding the pitfalls of unwarranted claims to truth and correspondence to reality. The counter to this objection is that the renunciation of theory can only have the result of either importing an implicit theory *via* the concepts used in the conversation since there can be no concepts that are theory-free, or by relying only upon commonsense or idiomatic language of rendering the conversation dependent on intuitive understandings between participants. We cannot evade theory since theory is nothing more than the positing of connection/interconnection between two or more concepts. There is no escape from theory; no conversations can be free of it. The best that we can do is to be as self-conscious as possible about the assumptions and connections which we bring into our conversations.

While the philosophical debate proceeds we should not let its heat obscure the extent to which there is also an important area of consensus within critical legal studies. Whilst critical theorists disagree amongst themselves about whether 'reality' is the goal of inquiry there is agreement that reality cannot be approached directly, that there is no royal route to knowledge and that there can be no claims to absolute knowledge. Similarly, there is a general agreement around the necessity of an hermeneutic approach, broadly conceived, which insists upon the social/cultural construction of social life and that enquiry must embrace the meanings of social contexts for their participants. It may be that we can embrace the hermeneutic and linguistic shift in contemporary thought without endorsing the wholesale exclusion of the extra-conversational context of the physical, environmental and technological conditions of social life. The positions adopted by individuals within the critical camp will continue to be influenced by the position which they

9

espouse on the general philosophical issues but there is no barrier to a fruitful exchange even if some feel that the use the label 'theory' may seem to claim more than they believe to be possible or desirable. The danger of purporting to abolish theory is that it implies that a troublesome problem has been avoided. But it cannot be so easily escaped; we must recognise that the best we can do is to engage with the contestable character of all theoretical enterprise. Thus, for example, we cannot abolish abstraction from our conversations, but we can debate the appropriate form and level of the abstractions which we employ.

We are still confronted by the concept of law. This remains more rather than less important as we come to recognise and explore the diversity or pluralism of the phenomena designated by the concept 'law'. Until such time as we are persuaded to renounce the very concept itself we are constrained to pursue its theorisation, that is, to explore different ways of formulating and explicating both its internal and external connections. We are required by our own conversation to accept that there can be no escape from the project of theorising law.

INTERNAL OR EXTERNAL THEORY?

If it is not only possible but, as I have argued, desirable and necessary to pursue the objective of advancing a general theory of law, it is necessary to consider what kind of theory we should be seeking to develop. Critical legal theory must first confront the problem posed by the choice between an internal and an external theory of law. The dominant tradition of contemporary legal theory is epitomised by H. L. A. Hart and Ronald Dworkin, who despite their other differences insist upon the adoption of an internal perspective. I want, first, to criticise the conventional internalism of Hart/ Dworkin legal theory. I will then consider whether this criticism leads critical legal theory to adopt an external perspective or whether we can avoid this unsatisfactory either/or choice.

Internal legal theory is 'internal' in a number of different but related senses. At the most general level it sees law through the eyes of judges and lawyers. Thus, for example, the questions which it addresses are those which concern or perplex lawyers; hence the preoccupation with how judges either do or should carry out their judicial function narrows or restricts the scope of 'legal theory' to little more than the theory of the judicial decision. This approach goes hand in hand with the adoption of the standpoint or perspective of judges or lawyers as defining the field of inquiry for legal theory. Nothing that passes as legal theory has ever, to the best of my knowledge, adopted a victim or defendant perspective.[6] Internal theories exhibit a predisposition to adopt the self-description of judges or lawyers as primary empirical material; their stated views on what they do and why they do it are treated as direct evidence about the nature of legal practices. There is thus a naive acceptance of legal ideology as legal reality.

Internal theory is simply *too close to its subject matter*. This proximity to law and its privileged participants gives rise to normative consequences, either implicit or explicit, through the adoption of the values of legal professionals. This is especially evident in Ronald Dworkin's commitment to 'law as integrity' in order to provide "the best justifications of our legal practices as a whole".[7] Given this explicit commitment and partisanship it is astounding that when he turns his fire on critical legal studies, after expressing the hope that some within the movement can be harnessed to the aim of law as integrity, he attacks an alternative partisanship:

> But others [unspecified] may have a different and converse goal. They may want to show law in its worst rather than its best light . . . to move towards a new mystification in service of undisclosed political goals.[8]

There are two important differences between the liberal and the critical project revealed by Dworkin's formulation. First, it is perfectly proper for him to take issue with the 'political goals' of others but these are no more undisclosed than his own. As I have argued, it is a characteristic of the critical school to take a stand in favour of commitment/partisanship in scholarship. There remains much that the critical movement needs to do in clarifying its objection to 'illegitimate hierarchies' or to 'alienation'. But Dworkin's imputation of "undisclosed political goals" has a very unsavoury ring about it. There is something frustrating about liberalism's smugness about its own commitments whilst being dismissive about alternative commitments. It is significant that Dworkin avoids or refuses this engagement with radical or socialist positions and engages only with conservative or neo-liberal positions.

Secondly, it is a travesty of the views of the critical school to allege that their project is to show law in its worst light. A distinctive feature of critical scholarship is *a deep perplexity about law*. We perceive law as involving *both* negative and positive characteristics. There are many ways of formulating this tension but one expression of it is that we recognise the attractiveness of the rule of law and its aspiration to rational and consensual social ordering, but at the same time we insist that in societies exhibiting systematic socio-economic inequality the espousal of the rule of law buttresses and legitimates those inequalities. I conclude that the differences between the partisanship of liberal and critical legal theory justify a claim for the superiority of the latter. Critical scholars are genuinely undecided about a whole series of major questions about law such that, without renouncing their partisanship, they can come closer to realising classical academic standards of objectivity (even whilst having well-founded doubts about the possibility and desirability of such universal standards fashioned outside of current intellectual and political engagements) than their liberal rivals.

There is one further objection to the internal perspective: the adoption of such a position seems to lead its proponents to posit a clear inside/outside distinction in a manner which erects law as an autonomous field of inquiry; law is treated as sufficient to itself. Even with the mild socialisation of legal theory during the twentieth century it has relied upon an inside/outside imagery within which law is both influenced by and influences the 'external'

11

world; this way of conceptualising law is deficient because it retains the assumption of law as an autonomous field.

If 'internal theory' is deficient does this commit the critical school to the adoption of an 'external theory? It certainly does not if 'external' is treated as involving the adoption of a detached behaviouralism which self-consciously chooses to ignore the meanings associated with the consciousness of legal actors. Behaviouralism is but a sociological variant of the most rigid legal positivism. The concern with meaning, legal language and interpretation is common ground between much modern liberal legal theory and critical theory.

There are also problems with the adoption of an external perspective which disclaims interest in 'lawyer's problems' and focuses upon the impact of law on the wider society. The history of socio-legal studies and the sociology of law has been dominated by this response which has had the practical result of establishing an intellectual division of labour between itself and legal theory which hold each other at arms length. One of the most distinctive features of critical legal studies has been that it has joined battle with liberal theory in a way in which the various trends within the sociological movement in law failed to do. Critical approaches are centrally preoccupied with legal doctrine and with judicial decision-making. Expressed as a slogan the critical movement has insisted on *taking doctrine seriously*. This leads them also to follow Dworkin in taking rights seriously even though their work reveals rights to be ambiguous and problematic. My argument appears to point towards the rejection of external theory, but I want to hold back from that conclusion because there is at least one version of externalism that deserves to be defended.

It is important to defend the necessity of critical theory distancing itself from the assumptions and taken-for-granted attitudes and prejudices of legal professionals. This does not involve, as Dworkin quoted above suggests, a choice between being 'for' or 'against' law. It simply insists that what judges and lawyers think and feel about law, how they explain and legitimise their various practices must also be subject to a scrutiny which preserves a critical distance between itself and those whose practices the theory seeks to understand. There is one important and very visible difference between liberal and critical theory: critical theory employs the concept 'ideology', a concept systematically absent from liberal theory.[9] Once we dispense with a crude version of ideology as falsity it becomes clear that what the concept 'ideology' provides is precisely a way of problematising the attitudes, beliefs and values of legal actors. It makes it possible to ask questions about the formation of the consciousness of legal actors, about the internal relations between the constituents of their beliefs and also to make the consequences that flow from these beliefs a central focus of legal theory.

There is a related but more general sense in which a critical perspective needs to defend a more complex version of external theory. Critical theory must be external in the sense that it seeks to overcome the closures or silences generated by internal theory. The drawing of the conceptual boundary of law

12

and the hoisting of the flag of legal theory over that terrain is not an innocent act. The manner in which the boundaries are stipulated determines both the set of questions with which the inquiry is concerned and, at the same time, it excludes or silences other issues. Given the long predominance of liberal legal theory, it is difficult to make the first steps in marking out an alternative theory for each of us is deeply imbued with the influence of that tradition. It is, therefore, necessary to self-consciously explore the closures or exclusions effected by the dominant tradition since the effect of closure is not merely that of absence but rather is to render other issues invisible.[10] Perhaps the most important closure produced by liberal theory is the result of its theoretical and ideological adherence to the doctrine of the separation of powers. The closure that results is the radical separation of state and law which takes the form of the absence of the concept of the state entirely or the employment of a naive theory of the state exemplified by Dworkin's equation of state and community in which officials are merely servants of the community carrying out public duties.[11]

These considerations enable me to offer a solution to the question of whether critical legal theory favours an internal or external perspective. My answer is, first, that the style of theory must be external in the sense discussed above of maintaining a critical distance from the self-conceptions of legal professionals. But, secondly, it is able to refuse the choice between internal and external perspectives because through its reconceptualisation of the field of inquiry, illustrated for present purposes by the aspiration to embrace the law-state complex, it has so redrawn its boundaries that the problem is no longer relevant.[12] This boundary changing aspect of critical legal theory accounts for some of the hostile reactions it has encountered since it does involve a challenge to the form in which law is currently constituted as an academic discipline.

FROM CRITICISM TO CRITIQUE

The account of critical legal theory offered thus far has portrayed it, in the first instance, as reactive against orthodoxy and, subsequently, as being engaged in exploring the creation of an alternative theory, the first stage of which is the search for alternative starting points, different boundaries and conceptualisations of the object(s) of inquiry. At this stage the project advances more ambitious and controversial claims which involve going beyond 'criticism' to the pursuit of 'critique' as the approach or methodology of a critical theory of law. I will consider the nature of 'critique' and then examine some of the controversies and difficulties which surround such a project. It should be noted that I will employ the idea of 'approach' rather than 'method' because the latter carries with it the implication that it is both possible and desirable to stipulate general procedural rules for the conduct of inquiries. The search for an 'approach' is intentionally agnostic concerning the possibility and desirability of prescriptive methodologies.

By 'critique' I understand an approach which starts with internal criticism of existing theories in terms of their own criteria and then proceeds to generate the conceptual equipment necessary to overcome the deficiencies and closures discovered in the theories examined, and at the same time to understand the social origins of the influence wielded by the theories criticised. It is thus concerned to understand the historical nature of these theories and the conditions which affect the possibility of the emergence of an alternative theory. This concern to locate the historical context makes it possible to advance claims about the development of 'better' theory in the sense of serving to address historically generated questions which a prior theory either failed to address or was unable to address satisfactorily. Whilst we cannot ignore the linguistic and cultural constraints on the production of our ideas we can, through critique, aspire to push our language and our theory beyond the substantive and historical limits of the theories with which we engage.

Consistent with my stated intention of avoiding the temptation to erect a stipulative methodology I will avoid suggesting that critique involves any sequential stages of inquiry; instead I will examine in more detail the different elements which together make up the critique approach. It is an important characteristic of critique that it does not seek to engage immediately with the 'reality' of its object of inquiry.[13] Rather criticism is directed, in the first instance, at *theories* of law. This internal criticism or immanent critique of theory in its own terms permits debate about the appropriate style of criticism. One of the most common forms practised by critical legal studies is to examine the internal consistency of the theory; a characteristic conclusion being one which concludes that liberal legal theory is contradictory.[14] It should be stressed that in itself this form of criticism is practised in most forms of scholarly debate. Another style focuses attention upon extracting the assumptions which underly the theory in question. In critical legal studies this has often taken the form of identifying the assumptions that liberal theory makes about the notion of the legal subject, or about the forms of human association. Associated with one or both of these styles of criticism and beginning to mark out a distinction between criticism and critique is the search for what may be called the social origins of the theory and thus to locate it in its historical context. In general the concern is to understand why it was in the specific historical context that some particular theory was proposed and to account for its influence.

An additional characteristic style of criticism is that of ideological critique. Closely connected with the explorations of the social origins of theories, it explores the ideological presuppositions, the taken-for-granted and commonsense knowledge on which the theory relies. There is another variant of ideological critique which is often confused with the search for the ideological content of the theoretical text. In order to make this distinction we may talk about the ideological practices of a social group such as lawyers and judges; such an investigation explores the ideological content of the beliefs and justifications of the non-theorist. While textual ideology and ideological practices are distinct, the examination of their interrelationship can contribute

14

significantly to the quest for the social origins and role of the theory under consideration.

Another element of critique again starts with the examination of particular theories but this time focuses attention on that which the theory excludes and on how conceptual barriers are created which divide the object of inquiry internally, for example, by deploying a classification scheme. Critical legal studies has thus paid much attention to the pervasive effects of the public/private distinction in legal theory and doctrine.[15] The quest for silences, barriers or closures has an important constructive significance because it begins to point the direction towards a reconceptualisation which removes these impediments so as to allow what was previously invisible to become part of the reconstructed theory. For example, the critical project has identified the fact that the concept and reality of 'power' is invisible to liberal jurisprudence and is thus led to explore how power is to be inserted as a major focus within its alternative perspective. The project of developing an alternative or reconstructed theory thus flows directly from the internal or immanent critique. Reconstruction flows from criticism in the sense that the latter points towards the new or additional concepts, or more generally to new ways of thinking and talking about the object of inquiry which hold out the prospect of transcending the deficiencies and closures of the existing theories. The final selection of concepts and their elaboration into an alternative theory involves the selection of some explicit normative criteria which express the goals of social transformation through which critique seeks to link theory and practice. The elaboration of these criteria also provides a further dimension to the criticism of existing social conditions as well as providing objectives for the social transformations which it aspires to participate in. It is in this context that critical legal theory must be concerned to clarify its normative commitments. The internal pluralism of critical legal studies is revealed by its widely varied normative projects which range through varieties of libertarianism, radical liberalism and humanist socialism. There are, for example, wide differences over what role should be envisaged in a future society for law as a principle of social organisation. It is an open question as to whether critical legal studies can and will sustain its cohesion, given the considerable variation in the objectives of its tranformatory project.

The view developed above is one which holds that critique does not involve a single prescriptive methodology but rather involves a combination of some (but not necessarily all) of the elements which have been identified and distinguished. The treatment is by no means exhaustive but I do want to comment upon one important and neglected problem: what part, if any, does prescriptive or empirical evidence play in critique? The work produced to date by the critical school has been light on and even dismissive of the deployment of empirical evidence.[16] But empirical study is already inescapably present within the critical project; for example, the ideological critique which seeks to establish the link between the content of legal theory and the ideology of legal professions is an empirical question, and a complex one at that.

15

Empirical evidence has another and more general role within the critical project. It facilitates the identification of deficiencies within legal theory because it brings to the surface features that are ignored or unsatisfactorily explained by the prevailing theories. For example, liberal legal theory offers little or no account of the widespread ambivalence towards law of the great bulk of the population. I suggest that social ambivalence towards law reveals deep tensions that exist between the different principles of social ordering that co-exist within contemporary societies. My present concern is not to substantiate this argument but to use it to illustrate the contention that empirical evidence has an important role in the critical project through its ability not only to alert us to deficiencies in existing theories but also to open up constructive lines of enquiry and conceptualisation which may contribute to a more satisfactory understanding of those elements of our experience of law.

TOWARDS A RELATIONAL THEORY OF LAW

A relational theory of law sets out to generate a reconceptualisation of the field of inquiry of legal studies. It proposes an analysis which posits the existence of a number of different forms of legal relations which interact in varying ways with other forms of social relations. Its project is one which takes 'law' as its object of inquiry but which pursues it by means of the exploration of the interaction between legal relations and other forms of social relations rather than treating law as an autonomous field of inquiry linked only by external relations to the rest of society. Relational theory proposes an approach which is both functional and critical. It poses the question: what part, if any, do legal relations play within any selected area of social relations and under what conditions can that role be transformed? The approach thus draws upon a sociological model of analysis but it differs from the conventional approach epitomised by the sociology of law since its emphasis upon the variety of forms of legal relations captures the significance of the diversity of legal phenomena (legal pluralism) by insisting that the exploration of the internal interconnections between different forms of legal relations will provide important insights into the role of law. The approach outlined can be described as an holistic approach without importing any Hegelian inferences of a metaphysical unity of social phenomena. Rather it is holistic in the sense that it insists that law as an object of enquiry can be be approached by focusing upon the interaction betwen legal and other forms of social relations.

Considered as an abstract model relational theory starts from 'social relations' as the general form of sociality. Different types of social relations may next be identified; for illustrative purposes these can be limited to economic, political and legal relations.[17] Any concrete social relation will be likely to involve a specific combination of these abstract categories. For example, employment relations involve economic, legal and other forms of relations. When we focus our attention on legal relations, relational theory makes the important claim that the forms of legal relations can and should be

16

linked back to the primary types of social relations. Schematically we may identify economic-legal relations (concerned with access to and control over economic resources), politico-legal relations (concerned with the distribution of authority), etc.; thus all legal relations involve the presence of other forms of primary or abstract social relations. To take an obvious but important illustration: the social institution of marriage involves a number of different forms of social relations (legal, economic, gender, sexual relations, etc.); such a conceptualisation makes it possible to explore questions about the role which law plays in the development and change of this and other social institutions and practices.

It would be possible but not very helpful to elaborate a much fuller classificatory model; relational theory should not, I suggest, seek to develop a grand classificatory scheme. A better approach will be to gain experience through engaging with more concrete analysis of specific forms of legal relations by employing classifications that appear pertinent. On the basis of such an approach issues and controversies will inevitably arise about the most fruitful classifications to be employed and how they are to be conceptualised. I have in mind that it is very much easier to identify classificatory types which stand in a direct connection with institutions; more difficulties are involved in the classification and characterisation of affectual and interpersonal relations.

The merits of relational theory can only be established through their application; other than the general claim to provide a holistic capacity which does not artificially separate legal from other forms of social relations, relational theory facilitates the recognition and exploration of the degree and forms in which legal relations penetrate other forms of social relations. This point does not just involve the well-known thesis that modern law increasingly reaches its regulatory arm into more and more social relations. It also embraces the idea that the 'presence of law' within social relations is not just to be gauged by institutional intervention but also by the presence of legal concepts and ideas within types of social relations that appear to be free of law. For example, ideas of possession and of contract penetrate many forms of interpersonal relations. Another line of thought stimulated by relational theory draws attention to the differential combination of legal and non-legal relations present within particular types of relations which leads to the suggestion that this affects and possibly determines different *forms* of legal relations depending on the social practices and institutions to which they relate. Employing an approach similar to that outlined above, Boaventura de Sousa Santos has distinguished between four distinct forms of law (domestic, production, territorial and systemic law) which are in turn associated with corresponding mechanisms of power and forms of rationality.[18]

It follows that if we direct our attention to the forms and mechanisms whereby legal relations penetrate social relations we must also focus attention on the reverse process. The field of legal relations is not autonomous and is marked by the penetration of extra-legal relations. For too long the study of judicial decision-making has been preoccupied by the quest for distinctive and exclusive forms of legal reasoning. A relational approach should examine

17

both the presence and the source of other discursive and rhetorical forms which are not simply variant forms of legal reasoning but derive their significance and their legitimating capacity from the forms of social relations from which they originate. Thus the controversy over the place of policy analysis in legal thinking can be pursued by drawing attention to the interaction between legal and bureaucratic decision-making characteristic of the administrative state.

This essay has explored what is involved in the critical legal studies movement realising its critical objectives. I have urged that the critical school cannot avoid the challenge of elaborating a distinctive theory of law. I have argued in favour of a distinctive approach of critique. I have also argued that it must be transformative in that it should strive to contribute to some specified goal(s) of social change. Finally, I have suggested that a relational theory of law has potentially the greatest capacity to fulfil these aims. The major claim that can be made for a relational theory of law is that it overcomes the divide, discussed above, between internal and external theories of law or to put the same point a different way, to overcome the divide between jurisprudence and the sociology of law. It gives an important place to the traditional concerns of liberal legal theory but, at the same time, makes it possible to pursue the critical objectives which mark the distinction between critical legal theory and liberal legal theory.

NOTES AND REFERENCES

[1] In the U.S.A. some exponents have explicitly celebrated the joys of 'trashing'; see Kelman, "Trashing" (1984) 36 *Stanford Law Rev.* p. 293.
[2] This position is represented in this volume by the papers of Paul Hirst and Phil Jones and of Nik Rose.
[3] This resistance to the very possibility of 'general theory' is in evidence in the conversational exchange between Duncan Kennedy and Peter Gabel, "Roll Over Beethoven" (1984) 36 *Stanford Law Rev.* p. 1.
[4] There exists a continuing hesitancy about the relationship between critical legal theory and socialism. In the U.S.A. this is part of the deeper consequences of the absence of a strong socialist tradition. In Britain the hesitancy is a manifestation of the wide-ranging debate on the Left about both the characteristics and possibility of a viable socialism.
[5] R. Rorty, *Philosophy and the Mirror of Nature* (1979), *Consequences of Pragmatism* (1982); for a very readable presentation of Rorty's views see the set of three articles in *London Review of Books* (Spring-Summer 1986). On realism see the very spirited defence in S. Sayer, *Reason and Reality* (1985).
[6] In contrast, sociology of law has generated interesting accounts of the criminal process by adopting a defendant perspective; a classic illustration is Blumberg's "The Practice of Law as Confidence Game" (1967) 1 *Law and Society Rev.* p. 15. The adoption of a 'victim' perspective has been urged by at least one critical legal theorist; see Freeman, "Antidiscrimination Law: A Critical Review" in *The Politics of Law* (1982; ed. D. Kairys) p. 96.
[7] R. Dworkin, *Law's Empire* (1986) p.vii.
[8] *Id.*, p. 275.
[9] For an extended discussion of the application of the concept of ideology to legal studies see Hunt, "The Ideology of Law" (1985) 19 *Law and Society Rev.* p. 101.
[10] Both Althusser and Foucault stress that theoretical closures render alternatives invisible. Althusser makes the important additional qualification that alternatives are rendered invisible to theory in *Reading Capital* p. 27.

11   The absence of anything beyond a naive theory of the state gives rise to a paradox in Dworkin's theory. On the one hand, the state is nothing other than the organised expression of the community but, on the other, it is against this state that citizens are empowered with rights as trumps against the state. Beyond a commonsense suspicion of the state he offers no account of why the state so conceived might be the enemy of citizen's rights.

12   It must be stressed that the conceptualisation of the terrain of legal theory is not completed by the formula 'law-state complex'. Though important, this is only the most immediate illustration of that process. The remaining questions are more difficult and are (fortunately) outside the scope of my immediate concerns although some of these issues are taken up again in the final section.

13   I bracket 'reality' out of deference to the philosophical problems considered in the third section above. However, I do want to insist that even the most committed pragmatist/relativist accepts the self-evidence of our common and shared experience; their reservations are primarily concerned with absolutist claims, which Rorty demarcates with capitalisation: 'Truth', 'Reality', etc. Just as Rorty is correct in contending that there is nobody who defends full-blooded relativism so it is true that there are no defenders of 'Truth', 'Reality', etc. in the form that Rorty objects to them.

14   See, for example, Kennedy, "The Structure of Blackstone's Commentaries" (1979) 28 *Buffalo Law Rev.* p. 205.

15   On the public/private distinction see Hugh Collins' paper in this volume; see also Horwitz, "The History of the Public/Private Distinction" (1982) 130 *University of Pennsylvania Law Rev.* p. 1423; Olsen, "The Family and the Market" (1983) 96 *Harvard Law Rev.* p. 1497.

16   A powerful plea for the importance of empirical material within critical legal studies is made in Trubek, "Where the Action Is: Critical Legal Studies and Empiricism" (1984) 36 *Stanford Law Rev.* p. 575.

17   A working model of relational theory would, of course, require a more elaborate typology of social relations.

18   Boaventura de Sousa Santos, "On Modes of Production of Law and Social Power" (1985) 13 *Int. J. Sociology of Law* p. 299.

The Critical Resources of Established Jurisprudence

PAUL HIRST* and PHIL JONES**

Critical legal studies must reject the notion of 'critique' as its dominant intellectual principle. 'Critique' implies a double rejection of the criticised – a new critical theory uncontaminated by established jurisprudence which will facilitate a new practice in relation to law and, ultimately, the emergence of an alternative which has shed all the undesirable features of existing laws and legal forms. Attachment to the notion of critique arises in part from the desire for distinctiveness, to show the critical legal studies movement to be decisively different from the *ad hoc* radical criticisms of law and from giving established modes of legal theorising and approaches to the study of law a radical twist. It implies a challenge to practitioners and academics who adopt a 'pink but expert' stance. All well and good, but the notion of 'critique' involves a real danger, the rejection in the name of radicalism of the genuine benefits entailed in western liberal legal systems and the forms of knowledge developed by legal theorists in the critical elaboration and defence of western liberalism. By liberalism we mean a primary concern with the freedom of the citizen and of associations freely formed by citizens.

'Critique' is a concept with a solid Marxist-Hegelian pedigree, but to adopt the stance of 'critique' one need subscribe neither to dialectical-materialist metaphysics nor to Frankfurt School critical theory. Aside from specific theorisations, the notion involves the supposition that contemporary reality contains within it an alternative, an emerging possibility that will supplant existing forms of organisation and which is superior to them. The task of theory or critical knowledge is to discern that alternative and to do so it must cast aside the forms which are tied to the existing conditions and the ideas implicated in them. This rejection need not imply a Marxist politics any more than a Marxist theory; anarchists, radical feminists and radical ecologists all advance versions of the notion of 'critique'.

'Critique' would be a harmless game played by intellectuals if it did not include one essential feature: it is a challenge to existing institutions and ideas

* *Professor of Social Theory, Birkbeck College, London WC1E 7HX, England.*
** *Senior Lecturer in Law, The Polytechnic of Central London, London WC1, England.*

which rejects them wholesale. The essence of critical theory, a theory which penetrates behind appearances and given forms, is the existence of an 'alternative' - a concrete possibility radically different from the forms dominant in the present and contained as a successor to them within contemporary reality. Without the 'alternative' critique disintegrates and turns into criticism, change becomes definite projects of reform rather than being the revolutionary essence in reality itself, anticipating a future to be. The notion of an 'alternative' implies that what is supplanted has a characteristic form and a distinctive governing principle, that it can be replaced without admixture with that which supplants it and without loss. In the case of law the notion of an 'alternative' supposes that what is to be supplanted has an institutional form tied to the existing social arrangements and has a function only within such arrangements. Thus Marxism traditionally supposed that law was definitely tied to capitalist commodity production and to the class state and that in the course of creating a communist society distinctively legal forms of organisation and regulation would wither away along with the state itself.

Few now support the crasser forms of the revolutionary Marxist approach to law and only a small number of people of whatever persuasion imagine that a radical alternative to law as we know it is a feasible objective for political struggle today. The danger in retaining the concept of 'critique' is not so much the conscious striving for an unattainable alternative, a utopia, but the unconscious retention of the habit of thinking in antinomian terms, as if the present legal forms and institutions were an entity which can be challenged in essence. The danger of 'critique', rather than criticism, is that it will unify law as the object of critique and ascribe to it a single social function. If absurd revolutionary optimism is avoided, the result of retaining the form of 'critique' is a pessimism that denies all aspects of the present any legitimacy, but cannot in practice supplant it. The revolutionary is replaced by the cultural critic.

As we have said, Marxism is not the only form of 'critique'. But its failure is instructive and ought to sober those who seek some other 'alternative'. As a political theory Marxism claimed to supplant and render obsolete over two thousand years of political and jurisprudential thinking about the state and law. Marxism rejected detailed thought about the contemporary institutional forms of either the state or law because both were forms destined to become obsolete and to be replaced without loss. Marxism is a failure as a political theory because it stakes all on an impossible alternative, an advanced society with modern industry but without either a separate public power or a formal legal framework. No one seriously believes that the state will 'wither away'. Once the full extent of Marxism's failure in this matter of political theory is clear we should begin to undo its demolition job, its critique of existing forms of political and legal theory. We cannot remain in that special variety of post-Marxist prison where Marxism offers no distinctive potential future and yet existing forms of thought and institutions are half unconsciously rejected as 'liberal' or 'bourgeois'. Marx certainly would not have done so, the great objectivist would have faced circumstances and set to work repairing the damage. Two thousand years of theorising and intellectual work have to be taken off the garbage heap and carefully sifted.

In particular we need to be specially careful about the last two hundred years, the period when Marx and Marxists faced their contemporaries and near-contemporaries as political competitors and were ruthless in their usage of them for being such. It is in that period that liberal political theory elaborated its doctrine and stated the social, political and legal conditions for the irreducible minimum of freedom of the citizen and of associations freely formed of citizens. In particular, it is necessary to re-evaluate attempts to refine and defend liberalism in the conjuncture of the death of Marxism in Stalinism and the challenge of fascism. The most sophisticated legal theorists of Marxism, those who enjoyed the freedom to think, Karl Renner, Otto Kirchheimer and Franz Neumann all adopted variants of liberalism and political democracy. To borrow a phrase from another and more sinister discourse, this is no accident.

We shall claim that at least four traditions in modern western jurisprudence together provide elements of an account of an advanced liberal-pluralist political and legal order. We shall claim that such an account is essential for the criticism and reform of the dominant forms of politics, that it is no *apologia* for existing conditions and a simple ideology which flings the 'freedom' of the West against the 'totalitarianism' of the East. On the contrary, we face a conjuncture where the advanced-industrial societies of East and West both desperately need reform, a need recognised even by the leaders in the East and a need barely recognised by either leaders or populace in the West. If the U.S.S.R. desperately needs liberal-pluralist reforms to drag it out of its post-Stalinist bureaucratic-sclerotic coma, the U.S.A. needs liberal-pluralist reforms to prevent it sinking into a state not far removed from a capitalist plutocracy.

The four traditions are: (i) the defence of the political autonomy of law as essential to democratic pluralism advanced by Otto Kirchheimer and Franz Neumann;[1] (ii) the defence of the primacy of freedom of citizens and of the freedom of associations formed by citizens against the state by English 'pluralists' like F. W. Maitland and J. N. Figgis, using critically Otto von Gierke's theory of associations;[2] (iii) H. L. A. Hart's defence of the 'internal view' in relation to the citizens of a legal order, an order which they accept and comprehend as legitimate;[3] (iv) Carl Schmitt's authoritarian conservative exposure of the blindness and limits of clasical liberalism, the need to recognise friend-enemy relations and the state of exception when formulating the rule of law.[4]

Others less directly jurisprudential could be added, such as the pluralist theory of political competition of R. A. Dahl, but space forbids excursion outside the arena of legal theory here.[5]

Western pluralism and liberalism (in the senses used above and *not* in the sense of the essentially economic liberalism of F. A. von Hayek) are a heritage we renounce at our peril. This is not to say there is nothing to criticise in the contemporary western democracies which formally claim to be liberal and

23

pluralistic – on the contrary our theoretical heritage suitably exploited provides both the intellectual tools for criticism and value standards for justifying criticism. What it does not sustain is the notion of 'critique'. On the contrary, within any intelligible future short of the complete ruin of western societies and polities, liberal-pluralism demonstrates certain forms of organisation and certain value standards which are unsurpassable, to which there is no 'alternative'.

LEGAL ORDER AND PLURALISM

Liberal pluralism makes the freedom of the citizens and associations freely chosen by citizens its primary value and theoretical concern. But the very notion of a legal order implies a 'pluralism' of another sort: it is difficult to conceive of a legal order in a society without institutional differentiation and with a single and binding code of conduct. 'Law', yes, but not a legal order. A legal order is not primarily a code of sanctioned norms applied to the conduct of individuals. The Decalogue is 'law' in the sense of a set of rules governing conduct applied by authorities whose powers have become customary but it does not give rise to a legal order as such. In this sense John Austin's distinction between 'law' and 'positive morality' had value, even if it is unsustainable in his own theoretical terms. For Austin the difference turned on a determinate superior whose commands were habitually obeyed, but the essence of a legal order consists less in the determinateness of the superior than in the character of the agents regulated. A tribal chieftain is a 'sovereign' for Austin, if his status is that of an uncommanded commander. But a chief is not a separate public power; to twist Austin's term, he is an expression and executor of customary positive morality. A separate public power, regulating through a legal order, exists when its task of regulation is open-ended and its role is independent of given customs or the opinions of a singular body of subordinates. The separate public power and independent legal order exist because they regulate a public sphere of institutional complexity: individuals who occupy multiple and distinct roles, institutions and associations with a distinct function and corporate life. Then, given this complex 'civil society', separation determinateness and primacy belong of necessity to the public power; it begins to resemble a 'sovereign' in Austin's sense, claiming to be the dominant source of binding rules and the society of societies, above the associations and roles of is citizens. A legal order implies a differentiated public sphere, society must be composed of associations and differentiated roles to require a 'sovereign'.

Law in the developed sense of a legal order implies three major elements. The first is a realm of differentiated agencies of decision, a complex of independent decision-making agencies interacting in some definite area of activity and where conduct is not given or exhaustively prescribed. Such a realm requires regulation, and static custom alone will not suffice, but that regulation does not, as such, presuppose a single separate public power. It presupposes some arrangements acceptable to the agents – such as a representative council elected by them or an agreed arbitrator. Trade associations or cartels are examples of such regulation.[6]

Secondly, as we have seen, one realm of differentiated agencies of decision does not imply a legal order, merely some regulatory arrangements. It is the interaction of a number of distinct realms of such agencies which changes the picture. Such an interaction requires one overall instance of regulation, separate from and not reducible to any one area of activity or agent. The complex interactions of realms and agents prohibit *ad hoc* negotiation and co-ordination, such an instance of regulation must be both separate and compelling – a single public power. But it cannot be the *ad hoc* rule of Austin's 'sovereign' - its power to make rules may or may not be unlimited in content but cannot be so in form. 'Commands', however determinate their source, have an indeterminacy of form that threatens regulation and co-ordination. Command is acceptable if law is to be like the Decalogue with a determinate superior added, but not if its task is to facilitate the interaction of numerous and complexly related spheres of activity and agents within them. It follows that the public power must itself take a rule-governed and relatively predictable form, the question is not merely identifying the 'sovereign' by rules of recognition but of ensuring that its legislation is of some social utility, that is, because its action is itself codified its enactments are not merely knowable as such but sufficiently non-capricious.

The Roman Empire was the first fully recognisable legal order. Its later rulers claimed a 'sovereignty' sufficient to please the most hardened Austinian. Its legislation was dominated by the principle that the ruler's will has the force of law, an absolutism sufficient for the most desperate Hobbist. But what is regulated by such laws is a complex multi-national assemblage of citizens, cities, corporations and associations. The Emperor's will is the source of law, but if the Emperor's word is law it is only so in a meaningful sense, possessing social utility, if that word takes the form of law, not whims or merely particular commands. The elaboration and codification of Roman Law represented a continued effort to meet this standard despite considerable instability and periods of arbitrary rule.

Thirdly, such an interacting set of realms of differentiated agencies of decision needs to be regulated, but it can never be reduced to the equivalent of a group of persons bound by exhaustive repertoires of prescribed conduct. The interaction of distinct realms and the differentiation of independent agents necessarily give rise to conflicting interests between and within realms. A society with a legal order necesarily exhibits the conflict of interests; such systematic conflict and its regulation are simply different aspects of the same phenomenon. Therefore, even in a society with a supreme and all powerful ruler like the Roman Emperor there will be conflict and its intellectual reflection. A legal order has always implied alternatives within itself – different conceptions of the political form and function of that order. Law is about public issues in a legal order, not merely a set of closed rules for private conduct. In this sense since the very beginning of jurisprudence there have been options and arguments as to the form and content of law. Legal reasoning has existed to debate the public issues that arise from conflicting interests. Since at least the days of Bartolus of Sassaferrato western jurisprudence has been characterised by open critical debate. The critical legal studies movement is thus the latest in a long line of disputes and conflicts within the reasoning which is a necesary part of a legal order. Even when jurists were faced with debating the claims to absolute and illimitable authority on the part of the Empire and the Papacy, there were arguments between these powers and on behalf of lesser powers, such as the free Italian cities.

We can see, therefore, that the single public power may not be liberal pluralist in the modern sense but that it exists because of a complex plurality of activities, associations and agents. A legal order is necessarily bound up with a certain degree of social pluralism. Absolutist jurisprudence from Bodin and Hobbes to Austin succeeded in clearly formulating the claims of that single public power in the form of the modern state. In conceiving of 'sovereignty' it accomplished this task exceedingly well but at the expense of neglecting to conceptualise the social pluralism which is the very *raison d'être* of a legal order. It would be a pity if we were to make exactly the opposite error, that in our hostility to political power used unjustly, excessively and oppressively we rejected the concept of legal order and in so doing were driven to deny the social pluralism on which it is based. Modern societies are unlikely to become less institutionally complex, less socially differentiated and more morally homogenous than the Roman Empire. If that is so then such societies cannot dispense with a legal order; only simple communalistic society without complex social division of labour and with a single and tyrannically prescriptive moral code can do that. If anyone wants such a society in the name of socialism, anarchism, feminism or ecologism then they must set an absolute zero value on human freedom. Freedom only exists because of the messy conflict of independent agencies and their distinct interests. It is sustainable and tolerable, as *freedom*, only when contained – at some minimal degree of effectiveness – by legal regulation.

We have a choice between building on the conceptual achievements of liberalism and pluralism or talking nonsense – in other words no choice at all. Liberal pluralism tries to express the forms of political/legal organisation consistent with that plurality of agencies and associations which makes regulation necessary. It challenges absolutist jurisprudence. The public power must not only regulate but answer to society, and it also demands from the agents and associations some minimum level of commitment to the norms necessary to a pluralist society and polity. It is a critical challenge to a certain conception of the state and to a certain conception of social agents, to absolutism (whether legitimated by democracy or not), and also to economic liberalism which puts the freedom to buy and sell above a morally sustainable and politically democratic social order. Liberal political jurisprudence is far from an uncritical justification of the *status quo*; it is a body of thought which can be challenged and build on the political and legal world we inhabit and does not need to deny it in the service of some supposed 'alternative'.

Liberal pluralism advances a number of propositions which it is difficult to challenge and they point to the gains and advantages of a liberal democratic political-legal order which cannot be supplanted, only destroyed or replaced by second-best substitutes. We will summarise these in a set of claims:

(a) A legal order depends on the existence of the state: therefore to supplant law is to abolish the state as a separate public power. This is in effect to raise the question of the withering away of the state. We have seen that a complex society with social differentiation and division of labour requires a separate public power as a condition of the interaction of the components of its 'civil society'. We have a choice between anything approaching civilisation and a stateless society. The issue is the *form* of state and law and not the existence of the state. A legal order is not co-extensive with and definitive of the state. States arise from and to further political struggle. No theory of the legal order, no liberal vision of political organisation can survive as a serious challenge to political realism if it ignores the challenge of friend-enemy relations and unless it makes an effort to explain how such political struggle can be minimised and contained. This cannot be done by liberal-constitutionalist dogmas alone but by specific *political* provision. This is the challenge of Carl Schmitt's authoritarian conservative jurisprudence. *The Concept of the Political* needs to be dealt with by liberal-pluralist jurisprudence, not ignored as illiberal and reactionary.

(b) A pluralistic 'civil society' requires at minimum a *Rechtstaat* and some elaborated rule of recognition, which not merely identified the source of law but also requires that legislation and legal norms take the form of being a 'law'. Such an ordered society is perfectly compatible with authoritarian rather than democratic political rule. A 'pluralistic' civil society is matched by a pluralistic political system only when the following conditions are met:

(i) A number of distinct and legitimate political forces compete to influence the public power and continue to enjoy such a measure of influence that they remain in the competition. Distinctive political parties competing in democratic elections are merely one crucial sub-set of such relatively open political competition.

(ii) The pluralism of political-organisational competition is based on and derives its support from a broader associational pluralism. Social activities are organised by bodies formed by freely associated citizens and whilst these are regulated by the public power they act as independent agents and are not directed in the actions by it.

(iii) No large body of adult citizens exclusively defined by certain attributes is denied by the public power the capacity to engage in political competition and the freedom to form associations.

(iv) No body of citizens is so subordinated to any other citizen or association as a condition of earning their livelihood that they lack the capacity to enter political competition or form associations as agents in their own right. It follows that a pluralistic polity is one where laws need to meet a double substantive test: they must command assent from diverse active and influential agents and associations, and they must not only have utility in furthering the effective interaction of agents and associations but must not systematically subordinate without good cause any group of agents and associations in doing so. It should be evident to anybody who reads this that much legislation simply fails this double test in the West today. To meet this test laws and legal norms must be relatively elaborated rules and provisions, assessed and debated before being put into effect, and overseen in their application by competent specialists. Only on the basis of a degree of certainty of content and consistency of application can they be known to be equitable enough in their actions to command consent.

(c) This requirement explains why the legal order of a pluralistic society cannot tolerate a large amount of informal justice and *ad hoc* adjudication and arbitration. The framework of interaction of groups, associations and agents must be sufficiently predictable that agents can rely on the public power and on others. Trust of others and assent to authority require a measure of certainty. Kadi justice is intolerable in defining central aspects of the legal order of liberal-pluralist society. Some pluralists and critics of the centralised and hierarchical state in attacking 'sovereignty' challenge the idea of a legal order with formal rules and functionally competent specialists as well. G. D. H. Cole in his guild socialist phase is a good example of a social theorist who sought to retain the benefits of modern industry, division of labour and social pluralism without a separate public power.[7] His answer to problems of regulation and the determination of the limits of competence was a 'court of functional equity' which would sort out by *ad hoc* decisions all the conflicts that would inevitably arise between the different functionally specific associations. Recently Burnheim has virtually re-invented Cole's functional democracy and with it *ad hoc* arbitration by courts presided over by non-specialists.[8] Far from supplanting the sovereign state and formal law these 'alternatives' need the supplement of aspects of the thing rejected, except that law and legal regulation re-appear in forms less adequate and appropriate. Figgis was never so naive nor was Maitland; they envisaged sovereignty in a pluralist state, not the virtual abolition of a separate public power.

(d) Law is not merely a constraint externally imposed on associations and agents, it provides an intelligible guide to action for those agents. Law provides not merely the conditions of compliance, but the intellectual means to anticipate and predict, to extend conduct to analogous situations. Modern social pluralism has been accompanied by and in a considerable measure produced by advanced individuation. Initially such individuation developed in Christian congregations, particularly in the seventeenth century, on the

28

basis on a personal relation to God, and the control of conduct through introspection and 'conscience'. From God's Law it has been extended to civil laws and social conduct in general. H. L. A. Hart is correct to stress the real gains that emerge when subjects of the law adopt an 'internal point of view' and become citizens and agents who internalise the law as valid rules for their own conduct. In this circumstance law largely becomes an automatic technology of the agent's calculation; it permits sophisticated associations both to function internally and to interact with others with a minimum of friction and a minimum of constraint on the part of the public power. Hart's concept is a valuable tool of criticism in that so much of our legislation and regulation spurns the internal point of view, it regards the subjects of law with suspicion and contempt. The concept also serves as a devastating critique of any form of legally sustained social discrimination. The 'internal point of view' is often less a description of many individuals' relations to the law than something to be constructed in a liberal-pluralist citizenry by economic, social and legal reform. It implies a well-educated, economically secure and politically influential populace who can identify with political authority and can accept and use the law as a technology for action. This is self-evidently not the case for many people in Britain or the U.S.A. today.

(e) In this highly abstract and ideal-typical analysis of pluralist legal order the state as a separate public power has a limited set of functions. Its task is to regulate the interaction of agents and associations. No reference has been made to the state as an omnicompetent administrative machine organising and providing for diverse social needs and activities. The liberal-pluralist legal order does not have an easy place for what Carl Schmitt called the 'total state'. The 'pluralist' theory of the state and associations advanced by such thinkers as Gierke, Figgis and Maitland did not do this because of some oversight but because they placed a primary value on the freedom of agents and associations. The 'total state' has emerged from the dual pressures of mass industrial warfare and the consequent mobilisation of all social and economic resources for 'total war', and from democratic demands for social welfare and greater equality in access to health, education, housing, etc.

Ultimately such a 'total state' is incompatible with a liberal-pluralist order. It is virtually incapable of political supervision and it confronts citizens and free associations of citizens as a power they can barely challenge, and uses its continued adoption of a formally *rechtsstaatlich* character as one more device to subordinate. This fact implies taking the pluralist theory of associations and of the role of the public power in a society of associations seriously. For the pluralists 'civil society' is a society of associations, not of atomised individuals. Associations freely formed of citizens should perform all major tasks – production, distribution, education, etc. That implies limits to the purely private accumulation and ownership of economically productive wealth – firms should be co-operative or associative. Such a system implies genuine options for members of society and a definite but containable public power. That power permits the interaction of associations and does not supplant them. As a theory it is the only realistic answer to the 'total state'; 'big government' cannot be contained by the measures proposed by the liberal constitutionalist theory of representative government, it can only be replaced. If we are to enjoy the benefits of modern industry, division of labour and freedom of association we cannot 'smash' the state. If we expect it to perform every social function and administer every activity we cannot expect genuine democratic control but only a plebiscitarian formal legitimation of administration. The only answer is to limit the state to tasks which it can perform and which 'civil society' can accept and give assent to without being crushed.

To create the state of the pluralist theory of associations three conditions need to be satisfied:

(i) The reduction of international tensions to a level where external defence ceases to be a primary call on the organisational skills and economic resources of society, where political authority need not be ever more centralised in the ruthless pursuit of military success.

(ii) Either major sources of inter-group and inter-associational conflict are eliminated, or a strong consensus is built to sustain those norms of political life which effectively contain those groups which reject and seek to overthrow the pluralist framework. Carl Schmitt pointed to this dilemma, a dilemma in the liberal concept of basic freedoms of political action, that is, there needs must be a constitutional defence of those freedoms against agents and groups who use them in order to establish a non-pluralist regime. The public power must, therefore, be able to contain and deny an 'equal chance' to those forces which seek to overthrow the existing order. This dilemma is most acute in a 'total state' within a parliamentary-democratic framework. The stakes of winning are immense – a group can use political freedoms in order to deny others an equal chance and also by using virtually unlimited state power once it has won an election. In a pluralist state, as advocated by Figgis, the stakes of victory are much less; the state has essentially a regulatory function and it faces a highly organised civil society of active and powerful associations.

(iii) Strict limits are placed on the forms of ownership permitted for economically productive wealth and on the extent to which any co-operative or association may control its sphere of economic activity.

These conditions are difficult to satisfy but they are not impossible in the way Marxism's communist utopia is. Furthermore, failure to satisfy them does not invalidate other aspects of pluralist theory or reduce its critical power.

(f) The political pluralism of Figgis clearly implies a minimum social morality necessary to support the legal regulation of group interaction, groups accept the validity of other associations freely formed of citizens doing things as they wish. This minimum is actually rather a lot. It implies acceptance of ethical

30

pluralism and the acceptance of parallel associations and groups doing things their own way. It therefore excludes 'totalising' ethical projects which seek to subordinate the conduct of others to their rule. Outside of an irreducible minimum of criminal laws agents' and associations' conduct would have to be tolerated and at best preached against. Some religious groups and some forms of 'lifestyle politics' would find this ethical pluralism hard to accept and might well fall under a version of the constitutional defence of the 'equal chance' we outlined above. No society can exist without some measure of force and the suppression of some of the options for conduct some of its members may envisage. The defence of ethical pluralism against moral totalitarianism seems to us no great loss. Ethical pluralism is another of the unsupplantable gains of the liberal pluralist tradition in jurisprudence.

The pluralist theory implies radical changes in political and social institutions but it is not utopian in the way that the ultimate post-political goals of Marxism are. In a society with widespread inequality in political, economic and educational resources pluralism would actually be pernicious, for it would cement and enhance the autonomy of the well-endowed. In a society falling far short of substantial equality on the part of its citizens, public provision to meet needs and counteract unequal distribution will remain essential. The great advantage of pluralist theory, however, is that it does not depend on all-or-nothing revolution in social organisation. The pluralisation of political authority, the creation of a multi-centred state with distinct functionally specific dimensions of authority, and the pluralisation of social relations, the transfer of functions to co-operative and associational institutions could proceed in a relatively piecemeal manner.

Pluralism is not trapped in a contradiction of political action which has bedevilled Marxist states and which has been ably delineated by Chen Erjin.[9] Erjin demonstrates that the Marxist theory of class struggle and the dictatorship of the proletariat requires the ruthless concentration of state power to crush 'class enemies'. That concentration, however, inhibits the Marxist goal of a freer society based on the self-action of the people which would be necessary for the construction of non-authoritarian socialism. The socialist state, if it ruthlessly pursues the 'dictatorship of the proletariat', pulverises and disables civil society and tends to convert all those who challenge it in the name of freedom into enemies. Pluralism, on the contrary, moves in an opposite direction and enables diverse political and social forces. It permits diverse forms of economic and social organisation, diverse aims and ideals. Pluralism's foes are threefold: centralised state power ruthlessly pursuing international conflicts and the internal 'pacification' necessary to further them; unequal concentrations of the productive wealth of society directed in an authoritarian manner; and religious/ethical movements which seek to impose one prescriptive moral code of conduct on all. As such it can appeal widely and to all who, whatever their other disagreements, put the freedom of citizens and freely formed associations first in their order of social values. The project of a pluralist politics and the creation of a pluralist legal order in an advanced liberal society provide a valid basis for a jurisprudence

31

that can challenge authoritarian socialism and (barely) liberal capitalism. It draws on central aspects of established western jurisprudence for its tools of criticism and its proposals for change.

NOTES AND REFERENCES

[1]   Kirchheimer's views from the Weimar period on into the 1950s are to be found in his collected essays entitled *Politics, Law and Social Change* (1969; eds. F. S. Burin and K. L. Shell). Neumann's views on the necessity of a liberal-democratic political and legal order are likewise to be found in his collected essays entitled *The Democratic and the Authoritarian State* (1957).

[2]   There is a massive literature on the varieties of pluralist theories of the state. For a thorough early survey of English and Continental trends see K. C. Hsiao, *Political Pluralism* (1927) and for a more up to date survey of one aspect of the literature see A. Black, *Guilds and Civil Society in European Political Thought from the Twelfth Century to the Present* (1984). D. Nicholls, *The Pluralist State* (1975) offers an able exposition of English pluralism, centred on J. N. Figgis. Figgis' most impressive and relevant work is *Churches in the Modern State* (1913). For Maitland see his "Introduction" to Otto von Gierke *Political Theories of the Middle Age* (1900) and for a thorough account of Gierke himself see J. D. Lewis, *The Genossenschaft Theory of Otto von Gierke* (1935).

[3]   The classic statement of H. L. A. Hart's position is to be found in *The Concept of Law* (1961).

[4]   The key starting point for Carl Schmitt is his seminal *The Concept of the Political* (1976) but see also his *Political Theology* (1985) and *The Crisis of Parliamentary Democracy* (1985). G. Schwab's critical introduction *The Challenge of the Exception* (1970) is valuable. Schmitt was, it must be noted, a critic of the pluralist theory of the state; his strictures are telling against G. D. H. Cole and H. J. Laski but are less so against Figgis, see "Staatsethik und Pluralisticher Staat" (1930) in Schmitt's *Positionen und Begriffe im Kampf mit Weimar-Genf-Versailles* (1939). We are grateful to G. L. Ulmen for this reference.

[5]   Paul Hirst has attempted to argue that R. A. Dahl's theory of pluralistic political competition (in the American political science sense of 'pluralism') is by no means an apologetic description of western liberal-democratic regimes but, on the contrary, the basis for a critical standard of measure of their democraticness. Dahl's pluralism has much to teach the left about the analysis of capitalist politics. See Paul Hirst, "Retrieving Pluralism" in *Social Theory and Social Criticism – Essays in Honour of T. B. Bottomore* (forthcoming; eds. W. Outhwaite *et al.*).

[6]   For a fuller discussion of this point see Paul Hirst, *Law, Socialism and Democracy* (1986) chap. 2, pp. 16-27.

[7]   See G. D. H. Cole, *Guild Socialism Re-Stated* (1920) and *The Social Theory* (1920).

[8]   See John Burnheim, *Is Democracy Possible* (1985).

[9]   See Chen Erjin, *China, Crossroads Socialism* (1984).

On the Deconstruction of Jurisprudence: Fin(n)is Philosophiae

COSTAS DOUZINAS* and RONNIE WARRINGTON*

DECONSTRUCTION

Deconstruction[1] proposes a reading of texts, especially philosophical texts, drawing on literary criticism. It claims that the old distinction between philosophy and literature, that the former gives a scientific insight into truth which the latter obscures in the play of language, is simply untenable. Philosophical texts are linguistic constructs, inevitably subject to the figurality of language. The fully transparent logical language that philosophers, such as Locke or the early Wittgenstein, have tried to create in order to free their discourse from the dangerous 'irrationality' of the always present rhetoric of language,[2] is simply a rhetorical game. Thus, deconstruction brings to the surface in its analysis of texts, the revenge of language (of literature with its rhetoric) on philosophical claims (of science with its systematicity). As the buried figures of the most austere logical languages are brought into the open, philosophy turns out to be an "endless reflection on its own destruction at the hands of literature".[3] The argument then is that all philosophical texts involve linguistic play. Further, the rhetorical analysis shows the 'unconscious' text undermining the 'conscious' pretensions. Even those texts that appear stubbornly to resist deconstruction are exposed by fastening on their figures "to the point where their effects are all the more striking for having taken hold of their text".[4] Texts which actively deny deconstruction are those which claim to be a privileged site of merger between truth, authentic meaning and language. Deconstruction shows how figurality never permits such an assured correspondence, how indeed it dissolves any prioritisation between 'proper' and 'figurative' senses. In particular, the metaphors of texts are scrutinised to reveal the impossibility of closing down meaning, and to show how the means claimed to contain meaning are, at the same time, those that ground the opposites of the apparent claims.

In this paper we propose a rhetorical and deconstructive reading of a text of modern jurisprudence. In doing so we use the very figural language that we

* *School of Law, Middlesex Polytechnic, The Burroughs, London NW4 4BT, England.*

Our particular thanks to Shaun McVeigh; also thanks to Iri Jameson and Alan Hunt. An extended version of this paper is available from the authors.

33

claim is also the source of delusion. We claim no choice – for this same figural language is also the source of all meaning and it is all we have available for dismantling the ruses of our text. And, as such, we open ourselves to our own text's deconstruction.

A TEXT

We take as our text *Natural Law and Natural Rights*[5] by John Finnis. This work attempts to restore a lost dignity to natural law theorising. It claims that arguments for natural law do not have to be based on theology. The usual presentation is, therefore, reversed. It is not that the existence of God posits natural law, rather the existence of natural law leads to a quest for God. God is merely a desirable, though not essential, supplement. Natural law itself begins with reason. The text sets up its own claims to a rigorous epistemology in order to establish the universal form of reason which demands natural law as the result of its investigations. It therefore deals with the requirements of a timeless logic. The claim to deal in universals enables the text to dismiss rival theories when they fail to meet the never-changing standards of logic that the text requires of all arguments. It is in its claims to its own consistency, rationality and logic that the text's contribution to natural law and legal theory lies. And it is here, in these grand and self-consciously rigorous claims to truth telling, that we centre our own claim to a deconstructive reading. It is here that the text deconstructs itself, for these same elements that give it such strength and provide its most interesting and important contributions are also the focal points for an unpicking of the metaphorical ruses that enable a deconstructive account to proceed.

The text argues that certain values, such as the preservation of life and the concern for truth, have been common to all societies. These values can be derived from the principles of "Practical Reasonableness". Practical reasonableness means that each individual is capable of understanding that certain basic values are fundamental and incontrovertible by an intelligent grasp of the undemonstrable (because self-evident) principles which are first principles. The crucial link is "self-evidence". Through the use of intelligence, in an unmediated flash seven basic values are recognised from which all other forms of good can be derived.

The text uses the value of knowledge as an example of how a basic value can be derived from self-evident principles of practical reasonableness. Let us, briefly, follow the way this is done. It starts with an arresting question and assertion: "Is it not the case that knowledge is really a good, an aspect of authentic human flourishing . . . and that there are no sufficient reasons for doubting it to be so?"(p.64). It continues: "The good of knowledge is self-evident, obvious. It cannot be demonstrated, but equally it needs no demonstration"(pp.64-65). It is obvious to anyone who has experienced the "urge" to question and followed through that urge. This appeal to the obvious is "not something fishy"(p.67). Just as the rules of formal logic cannot be demonstrated as being valid, because any demonstration would require the

34

use of such rules and hence be circular, and yet these rules, nevertheless, are obviously valid, so too with the self-evident good of knowledge. Like formal logic, knowledge is derived from principles that "are obvious – obviously valid – to anyone who has experience of inquiry into matters of fact or of theoretical (including historical and philosophical) judgment they do not stand in need of demonstration . . . the principles of *theoretical* rationality are self-evident. And it is in these respects that we are asserting that the basic *practical* principle that knowledge is a good to be pursued is self-evident"(p. 69). The claim, then, is that the good of knowledge, an essential aspect of human flourishing, is an underived principle.

Knowledge, as a good, is linked directly to truth. Truth itself, which the whole text wishes to lay clearly before us, is a simple matter: " . . . we want the truth when we want the judgments in which we affirm or deny propositions to be true judgments . . ."(p. 59) Truth-knowledge, then, is something which comes from principles which are first principles, and as such underivable. The operations of the text are clear: from self-evidence, to knowledge, to truth, an obvious and unquestionable progression.

The other forms of the basic values could be derived by a similar process. But as the seven basic goods cannot be pursued equally at all times, choices must be made. The method of practical reasonableness, one of the basic goods, tells us both how to make choices and what is a morally reasonable choice to make. It consists of certain methodological requirements that any reasonable person must follow in life, like the need to establish a coherent plan of life, not to choose arbitrarily between values or persons, to promote the good of the community.

This last requirement, the common good, is a central feature of the text; it allows for the relations between human beings to exist and develop, that is, the relation between individuals and others is mediated via community. The community is developed by an upward progression, passing from friendship between two people, through the family, until we reach the "complete community" and "the international community". The family is not able to provide all the aesthetic and material resources necessary to enable the individual to participate in the basic values.

Thus, the community will provide the setting in which the individual, guided by the requirements of practical reasonableness, can achieve or strive to achieve the basic values. Morality is the product of this method of analysis, and natural law itself is the set of principles that order, or ought to order, the life of the individual within the community. This analysis enables the text to confront the central problems of jurisprudence from a set of self-evidently valid principles which are always already given. A large part of the text is, then, a detailed working out of the implications of these principles, for example, in terms of justice, rights and obligations for the system as a whole.

Well-being is often expressed as human "flourishing". The notion is "multi-faceted": "Only an inhumane fanatic thinks that man is made to flourish in only one way or for only one purpose"(p. 113). The requirements of justice, for example, "are the concrete implications of the basic requirement of

35

practical reasonableness that one is to favour and foster the common good of one's communities"(p. 164). Justice is not synonymous with equal treatment. Similarly with rights; despite abuses (by "fanatics") rights talk correctly emphasises "the truth that every human being is a locus of human flourishing"(p. 221). The basic forms of human flourishing can be grasped by any person prepared to undertake the necessary labour of thought to understand her or his own natural inclinations and realise that what is good for the self is good for others too. "After all, the basic forms of human flourishing are obvious to anyone acquainted, whether through his own inclinations or vicariously through the character and work of others, with the range of human opportunities"(p. 371). "[T]he basic forms of human flourishing are obvious." Obvious, self-evident, flourishing; the key ideas which allow the text to make its claims.

LITERARY REFRESHMENT

Let us pause here. We have a jurisprudential essay on the proper basis of natural law theorising. The next stage would then involve an assessment of the work's importance and quality in relation to that tradition. Usually, that is. Instead, we suggest the commencement of a process of reversal. Instead of seeing the production of written texts as merely the vehicle through which the philosopher reaches towards truth, we start to see jurisprudence or law as merely just another form of text to be read with whatever critical insights our theories of reading can bring us. Post modernists claim that all forms of enquiry that concern themselves with texts are simply exercises in literary criticism. As Rorty[6] puts it: " . . . twentieth-century textualism wants to place literature in the centre, and to treat both science and philosophy as, at best, literary genres". Similarly: "The study of law is a very specialised form of literary pursuit".[7] We therefore briefly turn to a text which is paradigmatically literary to see how a textualist approach can show it deconstructing itself.

In *Endymion* Keats embellished his text with the imagery of flowers:

> Our feet were soft in flowers. There was store
> Of newest joys upon that alp. Sometimes
> A scent of violets, and blossoming limes,
> Loiter'd around us; then of honey cells,
> Made delicate from all white-flower bells[8]

But the embellishment is not neutral – it turns into a displacment of the text itself. The symbolic and all pervasive use of flowers helps to decentre the text in an almost literal manner. In the very flourishing of the fleuristic imagery towards which Keats is continually drawn, the sense of narrative of *Endymion* is lost.

According to Aske,[9] Keats starts *Endymion* with the hope of control over his story, and the language he will use. His aim is simply to return to the primitive and natural beauty of mythical Greece. This aim is always unreachable. Keats' parergonal style decentres "the one bare circumstance" of the story. "There is in other words, no text beyond the flowers of speech."[10]

Keats seeks to represent an origin of antique beauty and innocence, a perfect repetition of the unrepeatable:

> To write in this way would be for Keats, as it is for Derrida's Rousseau, to aim at "the greatest symbolic reappropriation of presence" - specifically the 'presence' of antiquity in all its glory and loveliness. And yet, as de Man reminds us, this nostalgia for presence can never be satisfied, since it is impossible for poetic work and natural object (signifier and signified) adequately to coincide . . . .All this language [of flowers] can do is to cover over the origin's absence, to 'dress' wilderness with flowers of speech, in its errant and endless search for pure representation of that beautiful Greece with its beautiful tales.[11]

There are three crucial ideas in this deconstruction of *Endymion*. First, the attempt at reappropriation of an origin, the quest for the classical natural beauty of an innocence which is unrepeatable yet continually to be sought. Second, this failure to recuperate the unobtainable results in a parergonal excess, which destroys or decentres the attempt to recapture the beauty and simplicity of the innocence. The superabundance of the images, especially of flowers, is a negation of the very simplicity that the text can never reach. Third, this results in Keats ending not with a return to antiquity, but with nothing beyond the text. In summary, "the Romantics actually deconstruct their own writing by showing that the presence they desire is always absent, always in the past or future".[12]

PHILOSOPHICAL FLOURISH

The literary interlude now over, we return to our own literature with Aske's Keats interwoven into our own reading.

1. Classical Unity

The philosophical text is searching for a classical unity, a lost world of harmony between individual and community. As we have seen, the community is the necessary setting for individual flourishing. Keats looked back to classical Greece and her poets to find a pure unity. Likewise, the philosopher frequently turns to classical Greece and her philosophers (Plato and Aristotle) for a conception of the classical *polis* that the contemporary community should try to recapture. The quest for unity is projected back into an imaginary origin, where the self/other divide is seen not as a problem, but as a potential aid to the flourishing of everyone. Of course, rights, law and authority are absolutely necessary in the contemporary *megapolis*. In other words, the flourishing which the individual seeks is met by order, law, power. But the modern bureaucratic state also threatens individual flourishing.[13] The dilemma of the poet who can never recapture the supposed aesthetic purity of classical Greece also bedevils the philosophical attempt to construct political unity.

2. Parergonality

Keat's failure to recuperate the unattainable resulted in the smothering of the text in a superfluity of flowers. Something similar happens in the philosophical text. We saw that the good of knowledge was treated as a characteristic example of how the reader could be expected, in an instantaneous flash of intuition, to recognise a form of good, a form that is self-evidently good. But at this crucial turn the text buries the absence of any analytical argument around self-evidence by a luxurious parergonality. The strategy the text adopts is to introduce a peculiar character, the sceptic, whose misadventures occlude or smother the lack of any surface argument. The sceptic is the text's little monster, continually put to flight, only to reappear undefeated, an irreverent laughing ghost.

The text performs a three-part contest with the sceptic, which tests sight (archery), physical ability (weight lifting) and gracefulness (a gavotte). Archery: in denying that knowledge really is a good, the sceptic is refusing to fix his eyes on the target; inevitably the arrows go astray. The text tells the sceptic that the value of knowledge is not the outcome of desire; on the contrary, the desire to know is the result of the status of knowledge as a universal value. If the sceptic "fixes his attention on the possibilities of attaining knowledge, and on the character of the open-minded, clear-headed, and wise man, the value of knowledge is obvious"(p. 71). Like formal logic, knowledge is "obvious-obviously valid"(p. 69).

But the sceptic continues the contest in the weight lifting section, the weight lifted being "obviousness" itself. For the philosopher can lift "obviousness" every time the sceptic objects to the argument, so that the sceptic must eventually retire. Faced with the argument that self-evidence begins where "there is an end to derivation" (p. 70), the sceptic tries two arguments: first, the philosopher is really arguing a subjectivist position, and second, the evaluation process that is taking place in judging that someone is wise, and therefore well-off, is not like judging that someone is a bearer of infection because he has tuberculosis(pp. 71-72). The philosopher's answer is to lift once again the weight of obviousness. "But we should not be deflected. It is obvious that a man who is well informed, etc. simply *is* better off . . . .Knowledge is better than ignorance. Am I not compelled to admit it, willy nilly?"(p. 72).

Having failed to match the obvious-lifting of the philosopher the sceptic still refuses to admit defeat. Here the text challenges the sceptic to a gavotte, and gracefully dances round the argument. The philosopher claims that any attempt to argue against knowledge (based on formal logic) is a contribution to knowledge, and hence self-defeating (pp. 73-75). The sceptic is danced off the floor.

What is the basis of the sceptic's stance? It is to put forward arguments in just those circumstances where statements can be claimed as obvious only because the banal use that our culture makes of them causes them to appear so. Mere repeated flourishing of the term 'obvious' increases the sceptic's genuine inability to see the point at issue as obvious at all. Obviousness is pursued to excess in the attempt to make plausible the sheer absence of any demonstration of the fundamental point of the argument. The sceptic is continually banished to the margins of obviousness, only to reappear a little later and haunt the centre.

38

Finnis' text argues, as we saw, that any challenge raised by the sceptic to the value of knowledge would be self-defeating and claims its truth, by 'disproving', indeed ridiculing, the counter argument of the sceptic. Let us anticipate our claim: the main transgression of the sceptic is that he is an inexcusable perpetrator of tropological deceits. He has abandoned himself to the deviations of figurality. He mistakenly claims that philosophers are guilty of the figure of *reification*: they project their desires on to objects, and objectify their feelings about objects. But the sceptic is guilty of *metalepsis* (the reversal of cause and effect): he mistakenly believes that judgments of value are results of desires while in reality desires are the effects of values. He invites us to shift our attention from the 'relevant subject matter' (the self-evidence of good) to other contingent features of the world (*metonymy*: the use of a word or sentence to designate an object or property which is in some existential relationship – for example, cause-effect, part-whole (*synecdoche*) – with the habitual referent of that word or sentence). He denies that knowledge is like opening one's eyes and perceiving the black marks on a page (*simile*: the establishment of a parallellism between two meanings through the use of 'like' or 'as'). He claims that judging that a man is well off because he is wise is not like judging that he is a bearer of infection because he has tuberculosis (*chiasmus*: the cross shaped reversal of properties). In brief, the sceptic hopes to raise philosophical doubt about what is beyond doubt when one is considering the relevant subject matter (he is guilty of the central figure of *metonymy* or *synecdoche*) (pp. 71-72).

The violence of the passages indicates that the stakes are high; the sceptic has to be chased, to be banned conclusively from the text, and we the readers are asked to act as judge and jury of this ritual expulsion. What has philosophy to fear from such an inconsequential, self-defeating fool who has, apparently, abandoned the luminous, transparent, sanitised language of philosophy, science and mathematics, the language of self-evidence and the evidence of self? What the philosopher wants, then, is to exorcise the deviousness of figurality, to reclaim the clarity of the scientific language of Wittgenstein's *Tractatus*. Is it not the case, then, that the philosopher acts out once more the age-old vendetta between philosophy and literature? The philosopher tells the sceptic either to abandon the ruses of figurality, or to give up any claim to cognitive rigour. Knowledge is self-evidently a basic good. Denying that amounts to an "operationally self-refuting statement". Such statements are not logically incoherent or meaningless. But like the proposition 'I do not exist' they are inevitably falsified by any assertion of them. "They have a type of performative inconsistency"(p. 74). They suffer, in other words, from an inherent undecidability between their constative and performative modes.[14] A sceptic who denies the value of knowledge cannot asert what he means and cannot state what he asserts. Indeed, such a sceptic cannot assert anything. (p. 75) He is condemned to a permanent epistemological and practical purgatory. Rhetoric, reduced to a system of tropes, has lost both its constative ability and its illocutionary force. Considered as a system of tropes, then, rhetoric deconstructs its own performance.

This is, then, the philosophical abyss from which the text aspires to save us. To achieve this, it must either purge its language of all figurality or return to some longed for state of non-linguistic Eden, where self becomes fully transparent and needs no more wrestle with the Sisyphian task of creating a non-figural language. Self-evidence is exactly this precarious road between the Scylla of a non-linguistic congnition and the Charybdis of a non-figural language. Self-evidence is evidence of self. Evidence, *videre*, to see, to see self fully, lucidly, intuitively, without mediation, without reference to sense or sensation, desire or deviation. The evidence of self is (in a linguistically unmediated way) self evident.[15]

Self, evidence, (lucidity, transparence, presence), the good (agathon); are not these the central concepts of western metaphysics? Let us attend closely once more to the ways in which they are grounded textually. In the chapter on knowledge two different figures are used to align the reader with the philosopher against the sceptic; seduction and destruction. Seduction: the gentle(man) pedagogue, the father of light. The text knows truth and can seduce the willing (though as yet ignorant) reader into the garden of knowledge, provided foolish objections are abandoned. The unknown is to be feared, for the questions are complex, but some examples of the principles of "sound judgment" can be presented.(p. 68) And there before the unknowing reader stands the father figure or pedagogue: "the clear-headed and wise man" (p. 71). By promising fragments of "his" wisdom the writer/text can woo the reader/sceptic towards the tree of knowledge.

But within the same passage: threats, bullying, the executioner. The reader is threatened by the enormity of the speculation undertaken, and is told that she or he cannot possibly understand it all: "A proper discussion of self-evidence would have to be embarrassingly complex" (p. 67). Nevertheless, despite the refusal to have "a proper discussion", the text commands unhesitating loyalty. One is disqualified "from the pursuit of knowledge" (p. 69) if objections persist. Ultimately, the text does to objectors what Caesar's henchmen do to Marullus and Flavius; they "are put to silence". "[A]ny argument raised by the sceptic is going to be self-defeating"(p. 73). The text's truths are truths "willy nilly" (p. 72). Self-defeating positions should be abandoned. "The sceptic, on this as on other matters, can maintain coherence by *asserting* nothing" (p. 75). The volubility of the text is counterposed to the silence of the objector. Since the sceptic can only object through speech, and since speech is denied her or him, the sceptic is handed over to the executioner and put to death.

The central concepts towards which the text cajoles or compels are grounded, then, on certain value-oppositions: wise person/sceptic, author/reader, pertinacious intelligence/sophistries of intelligence,[16] toying with ideas/asserting – speaking them (p. 75). They are combined with threats and moral blackmail. Value-seductions are usually related to the so-called literary texts, they are actually admired in poetry. Threats, orders, commands, blackmail are the benchmark of legal decrees. Neither of these two modes, wooing and threatening, seduction and destruction, is usually connected with

40

so-called philosophical texts. That is the great peculiarity of our text, its patent literariness as well as its bullying. The text denies that philosophy can be built on literary devices, but at the same time it has to use such conceits to establish its truth. Is it, then, the case that the value of these values and the effectiveness of these threats depends on the possibility of distinguishing the philosophical from the legal, and both from the literary, a possibility permanently denied by the text itself?

If, then, the rhetoric of tropes was condemned as epistemologically unsound and practically immobilising, here we are faced with the other centuries old conception of rhetoric as persuasion and eloquence, a technique and art used by the speaker to convince the interlocutor about the righteousness of a cause; rhetoric as performative, assertive speech acts.[17]

We were assured earlier that figural speech cannot assert anything. Literature – the prototype of figurality – was always perceived as a self-consuming and narcissistic esoteric exercise on the deviousness of language. The philosophical purging of figurality then must pay the price of abandoning the constative mode. The epistemologically pure mode has to be the performative, a mode which does not argue, just asserts, commands, flatters, forces, rewards. Is it then the case that in order for philosophy to be freed from literature it must become an order of law? Can the performative ever attain its pure status at the expense of the constative? Has the philosopher finally purged the figures of speech and chased the sceptic intruder beyond the walls of the city to re-cover the austere, transparent language in an imperative self-revelation? Would it then be the case that if figural speech can play but cannot assert, performative speech can force – cajole and threaten – but can never state and explain its own meaning, thus denying its self-proclaimed status as truth-telling philosophy? The non-conclusive encounter between the philosopher and the sceptic is but the acting out of the aporia between constative and performative, tropes and persuasion, which stand to each other in a polemical alliance of mutually subverting support. When the text knows what it says – the job of philosophical texts – it has to act deceptively and threateningly. But when it does not act it cannot state what it knows.[18]

3. Death: of Flourishing, of Philosophy

It follows then that, as in Aske's third point, the philosopher, like Keats, ends not with the longed-for return to truth-antiquity, but with nothing beyond the textuality of his text. Let us, then, examine those basic human goods or flourishings more carefully. Flourishing in one sense expresses notions of vigorous luxuriant growth, of meaningful and successful activity. But flourishing also indicates an ornamentation, an adorning, especially with flowers, and in writing, an embellishment with flowers of speech. If, then, the self-evidence of human flourishing was presented as an espitemological haven from which devious figurality had been permanently banned, the meanings of these very flourishings are continuously suspended in the vengeful return of their congenital figurality. It is here, then, that we find the text's flourishing

41

actually destroying the possibility of human flourishing. The text is still to bloom; its flourishing is continually and critically deferred. It is essential to its argument that flourishing can be gained by individuals. Yet the text denies this possibility.

It is again a crucial metaphor that grounds this paradox. The text argues that the basic values are not goals that can ever be achieved fully. The pursuance of a human good can never be "completely realized and exhausted by any one action, or lifetime, or institution, or culture"(p. 84). The basic values are always to be struggled towards, but never achieved. They are ongoing. "Knowledge" is not a state to be achieved, but one to be worked towards. The basic values begin to appear like mirages that retreat as one gets nearer to them.

Of course, such a conclusion was not unexpected. These flourishings can never be fully grasped because, like the flowers on which they are based, they can never acquire a fixed and settled meaning. Is metaphor not a semantic deviation of a definite type, an instance of polysemia? As Nietzsche taught us, metaphor is both a source of great philosophical illusion and a means for dismantling the ruses of philosophy. Such, then, are the flowers of human flourishing. Fragile flowers, mythical flowers, flowers of speech, attempting to enchant us with their beauty, but unable to state their essence. These flowers are both philosophical deceits of the first order and useful tools to explode the myth of "naturalism" or "expressive realism": the belief in language as the privileged site where meaning and thought merge in the lucidity of intuitive self-scrutiny.[19] One of the tasks of deconstruction is to attend to the operations of metaphor, take it seriously, 'at its word', and show its operations despite authorial intention. Self, then, seems to emerge as the outcome of the difference and deferral of metaphorical configuration. The philosopher claimed a primordial sovereignty of self, only to see the text dissolve it into the undecidable polysemy of flowery figurality. We can then say, with Nietzsche, that human flourishings "are illusions about which one has forgotten that this is what they are; metaphors which are worn out and without sensuous power, coins which have lost their pictures and now matter only as metal, no longer as coins".[20]

The end, the achievement, the telos of those human flowers can only come about in the literal end, the end of life. And it does. For the text has a related figure, the death bed hour. This is claimed as an heuristic device to help make choices within and between the basic values. Let us begin where there will be little disagreement: death ends the possibility of participating in any values at all. "[D]eath appears to end our opportunities for authenticity, integrity, practical reasonableness" (p. 372). "Appears"? For the text, death suggests possibilities within speculative thought, for ruminating on the meaning of life beyond the meaning we know. Death for the text is the traditional Christian vantage point from which to view one's life as a whole. It is a device that teaches us how to make valid decisions. It is unreasonable to live from moment to moment – hence the need for a "coherent plan of life".

This death bed perspective makes practically reasonable decisions easier to make and thus enables flourishing to take place. It is not until the death hour that one can know whether or not flourishing is achieved. The deferment of any substantive flourishing for "flesh-and-blood individuals" (pp. 371-72) is thus complete and indefinite. Death becomes the end state at which we must arrive in order for human flourishing actually to be achieved. The harmony that the text craves demands its own deconstruction in its own death. Self-presence, authenticity, control of speech and writing (logocentrism in a word)[21] arrive only when the point of extinction is achieved, and when our ultimate delusions, our failures to be practically reasonable are extinguished. Flourishing can only occur at the point of ultimate denial of flourishing. Its intimate connection with death is the death of the flourishing, the extinction of the centre the text strives to achieve. Human flourishing becomes a black joke, an ultimate deferral. Our Fin(n)is becomes our aim. Our desire or need to flourish is, indeed, the ultimate consummation of the impossibility of achieving that real flourishing to which the text continually points. There is nothing beyond the text because flourishing turns out not to be a possibility until the possibility of all human action is to be extinguished. All that is left is the deconstructive text. As Selden[22] puts it: "Deconstruction can begin when we locate the moment when a text *transgresses the laws it appears to set up for itself.* At this point texts go to pieces, so to speak."

This 'going to pieces' is the result of the place of metaphor within philosophy, within language and within our text. For the death that the text announces is merely symptomatic.[23] In philosophical writing metaphor is seen as the servant of the philosopher who is in control of language; metaphor is merely supplementary. Derrida reverses this familiar claim, and with it announces a death greater than that carried in our text. Metaphor is essential for philosophy, indeed for all language.[24] At the same time it is only acceptable as truly fulfilling the function of metaphor if it is confined. Metaphor must not, for philosophy, transgress its place, it must not threaten meaning: "metaphor, therefore, is determined by philosophy as a provisional loss of meaning, an economy of the proper without irreparable damage, a certainly inevitable detour . . . .This is why the philosophical evaluation of metaphor always has been ambiguous: metaphor is dangerous and foreign as concerns *intuition* (vision or contact), *concept* (the grasping or proper presence of the signified), and *consciousness* (proximity or self-presence); but it is in complicity with what it endangers, is necessary to it in the extent to which the de-tour is a re-turn guided by the function of resemblance . . . under the law of the same."[25]

This hoped-for return, this "provisional" loss of meaning is the struggle from which philosophy emerges, but never leaves. Philosophy is engaged in an endless search for univocity. "Univocity is the essence, or better, the *telos* of language. No philosophy, as such, has ever renounced this Aristotelean ideal.

This ideal is philosophy."[26] But within this ideal, metaphor plays the role of good and evil. The good allows philosophy to reach towards meaning; the evil prevents it ever achieving it.

And in the inevitable production of polysemia metaphor goes further. In Derrida's Aristotle, being human means having control over language.

> Each time that polysemia is irreducible, when no unity of meaning is even promised to it, one is outside language. And consequently, outside humanity. What is proper to man is doubtless the capacity to make metaphors, but in order to mean some thing and only one. In this sense, the philosopher, who has ever but one thing to say, is the man of man.[27]

Metaphor, the supposed servant of the logocentric philosopher, has taken over. In its inevitable presence it destroys by ensuring that the meaning that is desired is always deferred. The conclusion is inevitable: "Metaphor, then, always carries its death within itself. And this death, surely, is also the death *of* philosophy."[28]

Finnis' text is full of metaphor. This ability to pass from signifier to signifier sets up the possibility of the philosophical text and destroys the univocity to which it points. Metaphor damns philosophy before it begins to philosophise. The text's philosophical metaphor of death is already destroyed by the metaphorical death of philosophy. The philosophical text announces the value of death but results in the death of the values towards which it strives. And in this sense *Natural Law and Natural Rights* is an exemplary deconstructive text. It sets out to rescue philosophy from rhetoric only to become an endless reflection on the end of philosophy at the hands of rhetoric.

NOMOPOIETICON LOGOPAIGNION

The text we have been examining ostensibly concerns natural law. It is a treatise on the natural law of logos (reason), yet it speaks the nomos (law) of positivism. All the elements of classical positivism have emerged through the analysis. A (knowing) sovereign (the author) commands (or bullies, cajoles or rewards) the subject (reader) who is forced to submit by the threat of sanctions (putting to silence).[29] But, we argue, this polemical symbiosis is itself an allegory for writing; linguistic and figurative play undermine the logocentric ambition to arrest meaning, and the claim that meaning and truth coincide, in an autarchic and luminous linguistic Eden. In the beginning was the Word (logos). The word created the world in its own image. But the word is written, not spoken. The logos-word cannot be tamed by the logos-reason.

Our text, then, fully anticipates its own deconstruction, and becomes the most accessible text of modern jurisprudence. And it is the old joker, Plato, for whom metaphor has become "the ground for the furthest-reaching dialectical speculation conceivable to mind"[30] who is invited at the end of our text (pp. 407-10) to narrate, self-consciously, the riddle of which the whole text is a tortured parable.

In Plato's Second Book of Nomoi (Laws), the text reminds us, the Athenian Stranger argues that everyone is a puppet and paignion (plaything) of God, who has put in all of us many conflicting strings (pleasure and pain, aversion and audacity, etc.) that pull in opposing directions. But there is one soft and gentle string, logos, insight and reason with which we should co-operate in order to resist the hard pull of all these other iron strings. The individual who understands that has achieved logos alethes (true reason). The polis which does has raised logos into nomos – the common law. Logos-nomos: this is the name of the reason of the individual and of the common reason of the state, the name of the reconciliation of self and others. A perfect harmony is thus attained in the realisation that we are puppets of a good puppeteer in whose game we participate (life is a patterned nomological play) and when we do so consciously and in reason (logonomically) we become free. Here, then, the text has arrived at the central metaphor of western metaphysics, the game that Plato has played with all of us: Logonomocentrism, the claim of the unity between self and others in the absolute reason of the law.

It is as if the text, like some Borgesian character, has finally found the ultimate word-logos[31] but cannot utter it literally, lest it be struck down like the infidel who takes the name of Jehovah in vain. And, as the final piece of the jigsaw is put into place, the text momentarily forgets its defences and disintegrates. The truth of reason and reason of the law, the two bases of logonomocentrism, are just games, the text admits, on the "meanings and references of *nomos* and *logos*" (p. 408). The text has finally come to accept that it is dealing after all in figures of speech. The ultimate Platonic truth can only be expressed as a "symbolism" (an allegory). The Athenian Stranger is a metaphor and personification of God, and God is an aimless, pointless game. Indeed, while God is the goal, the end of all serious endeavours, the individual is presented as both the creation and fellow player of "God become man" (*metalepsis*). Human participation in the divine play can be understood "by analogy with human friendship" (p. 409). Logonomocentrism, as soon as it names itself, disintegrates into the playful games of figurality. The ultimate truth promised, then, is the delusion of rhetoricity. The play of language (logopaignion)[32] creates the law of reason (nomopoieticon).[33] The nomos of logos turns out to be a nomadic nomination – a naming which differentiates and never lets meaning close. The text has finally achieved self-consciousness and has fully deconstructed itself. Instead of being about the language of law, it recognises itself as a self-referential treatise on the law of language, on differentiation, deferral and dissemination of meaning and self. The naming of the nomos of logos as the central metaphor of philosophy brings the text to its end. In Keats the philosophy of absence undermines the poetry. In Finnis, the poetry of figurality undermines the philosophy; the finish of philosophy at the hands of literature.

This, then, we claim, is the task of legal philosophy: to deconstruct logonomocentrism in the texts of the law.

NOTES AND REFERENCES

[1]   For accessible introductions to the theory of deconstruction see C. Norris, *Deconstruction: Theory and Practice* (1982); J. Culler, *On Deconstruction* (1983). See also Derrida, *Of Grammatology* (1977).

2   P. de Man, "The Epistemology of Metaphor" (1978) 5 *Critical Inquiry* pp. 13-30 and "The Resistance to Theory" (1982) 63 *Yale French Studies* pp. 3-20. See also C. Norris, *The Deconstructive Turn* (1983) chap. 2.

3   P. de Man, *Allegories of Reading* (1979) p. 115.

4   C. Norris, *op. cit.*, p. 3.

5   J. Finnis, *Natural Law and Natural Rights* (1980); all unattributed page references are to this work.

6   R. Rorty, *Consequences of Pragmatism* (1982) p. 141.

7   P. Goodrich, *Reading the Law* (1986) p. 91.

8   Keats, *Endymion* 1, pp. 665-69.

9   M. Aske, *Keats and Hellenism: An Essay* (1985).

10 *Id.*, p. 58.

11 *Id.*, p. 61.

12 R. Selden, *A Reader's Guide to Contemporary Literary Theory* (1985) p. 90.

13 R. Unger, *Knowledge and Politics* (1975) chap. 4 and *Law in Modern Society* (1976) pp. 192-242.

14 Constative statements describe (for example, a textbook); performative statements do by and in saying (for example, "I thee wed").

15 The philosopher's answer takes the form of *antanaclassis*, the repetition of the same words with different meaning.

16 "If one is not so fortunate in one's inclinations or upbringing, then one's conscience will mislead one, unless one strives to be reasonable and is blessed with a *pertinacious intelligence* alert to the forms of human good yet undeflected by the *sophistries which intelligence so readily generates* to rationalise indulgence, time-serving and self-love." (J. Finnis, *op. cit*, p. 125 – emphasis added).

17 For the history of rhetoric see Goodrich, "Rhetoric as Jurisprudence" (1984) 4 *Oxford J. Legal Studies* p. 88; T. Eagleton, *Walter Benjamin* (1981) pp. 101-13; P. Ricoeur, *The Rule of Metaphor* (1977) Studies 1 and 2.

18 Paul de Man comes to a very similar conclusion in his deconstructive reading of Rousseau's *Social Contract*, de Man, *op. cit.*, pp. 246-77.

19 See C. Belsey, *Critical Practice* (1980) p. 70.

20 *The Portable Nietzsche* (1976; ed. Kaufmann) p. 47.

21 See Derrida, *op. cit.* See also Culler, *op. cit.*, chap. 2.

22 Selden, *op. cit.*, p. 87.

23 It cannot be claimed that the death bed hour is merely a pedagogical vantage point and no more. All the values depend on knowledge. But we can only obtain the knowledge that is necessary to assess what our actions should be, and how to participate in any of the values, at this crucial last moment which by its own definition is too late. "Plato's Socrates teaches that philosophy (which for him is always contemplatively practical) is the *practice* of dying" (note, p. 130 – emphasis added). This practice of dying is the practical activity, not the educational prop of remembering, but the actual activity of dismembering of the finality of all flourishing possibilities.

24 Derrida, *op. cit.*, p. 15.

25 J. Derrida, *Margins of Philosophy* (1982) p. 270.

26 *Id.*, p. 247.

27 *Id.*, p. 248.

28 *Id.*, p. 271.

29 A conclusion that would not surprise Nietzsche: "*Actual philosophers . . . are commanders and law givers*: they say 'thus it *shall* be'." *A Nietzsche Reader* (1977; ed R. Hollingdale) p. 42.

30 de Man, *op. cit.*, p. 130.

31 "To solve everything at a stroke, with a single word – that was the secret desire." Nietzsche, *op. cit.*, p. 33.

32 Logopaignia: games (paignia, paidia) of language (logos) in other words puns. But also the formation (paideia) of reason (logos).

33 Nomopoieticon: the giving (poiesis) of Law (Nomos). But also the law (nomos) of poetry (poiesis).

Dworkin; Which Dworkin? Taking Feminism Seriously†

ANNE BOTTOMLEY,* SUSIE GIBSON** AND BELINDA METEYARD**

Feminism and critical legal studies are, of course, two entirely different creatures. Feminism is only partially and peripherally concerned with academic theorising. It is motivated by the dissatisfactions of a wide spectrum of both non-academic and academic women and by the everyday experience of such women. Critical legal studies, whilst it seeks to explore the interrelationship between theory and political practice, is a movement whose impetus springs from the dissatisfactions of legal academics. Amongst feminists there is unanimity about the need to alter the social dynamics of power between women and men in capitalist and other societies, and a diversity of explanations for and solutions to existing power structures. In critical legal studies little unanimity has been apparent. Both movements are revolutionary in the sense that they seek to bring about change. One of the objects of this paper will be an attempt to analyse what feminism might have to offer to critical legal studies.

This paper grew out of discussions within the women's caucus of the U.K. Critical Legal Conference and thus reflects some diversity of views. The authors themselves are all feminists who are also involved in the fruitful, but unresolved, dialogue between Marxism and feminism. In this paper, however, we have attempted to distinguish between the times when we can make broad feminist points and times when we would recognise a particular position within feminist theory. It cannot be over-emphasised that feminism covers an enormous range of diverse theoretical positions. It is part of the argument of this paper that too often that fact is ignored or not understood by those espousing the feminist project from within an academic arena. Feminism has grown out of and taken sustenance from a diverse gamut of political practices. It has not been built on a careful body of theory but rather on instances of the experience of power and lack of power. When, as feminists, we begin to talk about such concepts as 'patriarchal relations', we are not simply engaged in an academic search but giving expression to a set of experiences. Many feminists are wary of the academic project. It attempts to put 'us', as women, under the

* Department of Law, North East London Polytechnic, Longbridge Road, Dagenham, Essex RM8 2AS, England.
** The University of Kent, Canterbury, Kent, CT2 7NY, England.

† This chapter is dedicated to the memory of Viki Fisher, who will be sadly missed.

microscope. And it presumes to offer the possibility of validity, the development of a tested theory for feminism. Feminists do not seek to make themselves objects of study, neither will the fundamental validity of feminism be accredited in the academy. To lose sight of the lived political nature of feminism would be to betray the very nature of feminism itself. This is not to reject the academic project or to doubt that we can, and will, make a major contribution. It is merely to place it properly within the spectrum of feminist practice.

It is important, however, to ask why feminism has now become academically acceptable, indeed celebrated, by 'critical studies' movements. It is our contention that this has as much to do with the general political and academic climate as with a maturity in feminist theory which now demands recognition. At its most positive it is clear that space has been created for feminism by a more 'open' approach amongst critical scholars, including Marxists. At its most negative it is equally clear that many who now inhabit the space in academic work labelled 'critical' are at a loss, and having found traditional approaches no longer sustainable are searching for new doctrinal comforts which offer an 'ism' and yet do not call for too much rethinking on their part. There are also those who are searching for fresh credibility in what seems to be an intellectually bleak world. This seems to us the boyish enthusiasm for anything new combined with an age-old thrust to colonise, particularly if it looks like a field where no angel has yet trodden or at least registered a thesis topic.

These points may sound like a criticism of individuals. A little healthy scepticism persuades us that there are more fundamental issues at stake. We would diagnose an intellectual malaise and ask why it should arise at this specific historical juncture. We then wonder why generic feminism should be reckoned a ready remedy. We perceive that underlying our reception is a crisis in radical beliefs, manifest in both the political and academic spheres. We are not alone in recognising this incursion of uncertainty. We are, though, more aware than many that feminism's new allure may prove problematic.

In different phases of feminist theory support has come from different quarters and for a variety of reasons. Thus, liberals in the nineteenth century could understand and support demands from women for equality. In recent years support for feminism has been most vehemently voiced by those concerned with building broad political alliances. In both cases feminists either shared a political background with those with whom they aligned themselves or built strategies around mutually acceptable political positions, but neither necessarily reflects either a movement from within feminism or a true espousal of feminism. In both cases only certain aspects of feminism are regarded and incorporated; clearly those which most closely fit the pervading ideological stance of the host group. Feminist theory is not an hermetically sealed theoretical construct but it does offer key themes which must be engaged with, rather than glossed over in an attempt to adapt feminism for other purposes.

In so far as feminism is held together by an acceptance that women are subordinated and that their position must be changed, this, of itself, says little. It is like saying that we all like democracy. Feminists divide over many major issues. To conflate is not simply to confuse but to patronise and to attempt to control through simplification and caricature. We cannot merely be added to the agenda. We may actually be tearing the agenda up. We don't yet know. Feminism is much more threatening than it is comforting.

In academic terms, perhaps our greatest challenge is directed towards the construction of theory. Feminists claim that the very project of constructing theoretical argument is more value-laden and gender-specific than is ever accepted. Part of our concern must therefore be to tackle questions of methodology, which necessitates a critique of epistemology, methods of reasoning and argument, as well as problematising the search for grand theories. What languages are being used which might not merely silence women's experience, but also privilege men's? We cannot simply subject ourselves to the judgment of others (men) on constructs which they have developed. These constructs are the subject of critique.

In the study of law both feminist and critical approaches have made a relatively recent appearance. Hence the body of work published on critical legal studies from a feminist perspective is inevitably small. For those who read the few feminist writers in this field, with a limited knowledge of feminist writing in other areas, there is the danger of not recognising the different assumptions underlying the different strands of feminist thinking: the danger of tearing the work from its feminist context. Thus, with Catherine MacKinnon, reference to Dworkin (no, not him, her) and Rich are not really understood in the same way as they would be by feminists reading that material, for whom the citations are a signal of the particular brand of feminism favoured by the author.[1] Her feminist background is one associated with a particular and highly controversial form of feminism. This is not to dismiss the importance of her work but rather to place it in context, for the starting point, for us, is not in legal theory but in feminist theory. There are specific explorations to be made in the area of law but they spring from debates within feminism. The emphasis on these, for some unfamiliar debates, leaves us vulnerable to the 'go and bake a cake' brigade. These are the men who ask for a well-baked theoretical cake before they will engage in tasting the ingredients. The recipe must be tested, written up and have a proper bibliography.

One of the first trends to emerge in critical studies in other disciplines was a focus on women as a category, rather than a development of feminist theory *per se*. Much of the literature on law has also trodden this route, and we would characterise it broadly as women and law work.[2] It does seem to us that this work, while having performed a very valuable service, has its limitations, particularly as it is also reflected in curriculum development as being evidence of the inclusion of feminist theory within the curriculum. The greatest disadvantage is that it presumes that the contribution of feminists is simply that of placing women on the agenda. Thus, writers such as Sachs and Wilson, and Hoggett and Atkins have produced work concentrating on areas of law where so-called women's concerns may be seen to enjoy a high profile, such as family law, sex discrimination and so on.[3] Unfortunately, such work often takes as the categories to be studied discrete subject areas, as traditionally defined. Thus, women at work and women in the home are treated as separate areas and little attempt is made to connect themes. This becomes particularly crucial in relation to 'silences' in law. If proper space is not taken to overview the construction of gender relations in law then whether certain aspects of women's experience are or are not met within legal definitions is not addressed, neither is the choice of category. A simple example of this is the treatment of domestic violence. This area, to be understood, must be discussed both within public and private law terms. By this we mean from the provision of public resources to the question of its treatment within the category of criminal law. Thus, much of this work, in accepting the existing terrain, makes no attempt to construct new maps which might lead to greater insights. Further, by ghettoising the development of feminist theory into areas overtly concerned with women we do a major disservice to other areas which fundamentally pertain to women but less overtly. We were amused, for instance, when a colleague said that in her area of work feminist theory was not really relevant. This was consumer law. At other times we are not amused. In a paper on critical legal studies and the development of the curriculum it was said that, in recognition of the political nature of property, political theory should underpin the study of property law. Failure to recognise the political nature of the family, however, led that writer to suggest that family law could be adequately explained by reference to the sociology of the family. Such boundary definitions close the broader question of the construction of gender relations by law and the legal system as a whole.

A further problem is found in the type of critique which tends to emerge when such a focus is taken. It seem to us that too often it becomes reduced to a series of investigations into how the law operates in practice. Thus, in Sachs and Wilson the individual sexist attitudes of those who operate the legal system become the major focus of critique and there is no development of more structural arguments about the nature of law and the legal system. This takes place not in the context of a rejection of grand theory but rather in a failure to address it.

Finally, it should be noted that taking women as the entry point in this way may lead to two distortions. First, it presumes gender relations rather than analysing their construction and reproduction. Secondly, it takes as given a category which needs much more careful handling. For instance, in the criminal justice system it too easily leads to such questions as "Are women treated more or less harshly?" This is obviously important but may blind us to the fact that gender may not be the primary consideration but rather other factors which act indirectly on gender, for instance the family. Thus in Mary Eaton's work we are warned against asking simplistic questions and thereby missing the factors which feed into a criminal justice system to reproduce gender relations, other than by the process of differential treatment in relation to gender.[4]

To move forward in feminist theory we must move beyond women and law work. This is seen to some extent in the recent work of Carol Smart. In *The Ties that Bind* she first of all provides a cogent explanation for her reasons for looking at family law.[5] This is found in her argument that the family is still central to the gender construction of women. She therefore places her work within the context of an argument based on the oppression of women. Secondly, she faces the problem of whether to use such concepts as patriarchy in order to extrapolate from her work a theoretical understanding of the construction of gender relations in law. She examines the potential use and limitations of a concept of patriarchy, concluding that 'patriarchal relations' is a useful working tool but rejecting a trans-cultural, trans-historical and determinist model which suggests that the law as a mechanism of organised society operates to the advantage of men. Her approach is to examine the specific interrelations of one area of law at a given time to examine how far it has done so, the diverse ways in which it has done so and the space found in the contradictions of law and legal practice which allows women to achieve victories or at least compromises. This detailed work, both historical and contemporary, is obviously crucial, but we would query a position which comes in the end very close to rejecting a concept of patriarchal relations by looking for the wrong evidence. The flaw in her argument seems to us to be a classic 'women and law' flaw. It presumes that the evidence for patriarchal relations, and therefore the basis for a specifically feminist critique, is found by asking whether men benefit to women's detriment. It seems to us that the position of either individual men or even a category of men is not the determining factor for whether law is reproducing patriarchal relations. A concept of patriarchal relations does not have to be based in the search for a unitary, fixed, determined or immediate expression of male oppression or female subordination. So evidence that men, as individuals, lose out by paying maintenance or losing custody of children does not seem to us fatally to wound patriarchy as a concept and certainly not patriarchal relations. It simply warns us that it is not a simple set of practices. It also warns us that it is clear that state institutions are not addressed to one issue. Whether we accept Smart's contention of the need to work within the law and the possibility of that because it is neither a unitary system nor simply gives expression to men's interests, we must consider the interrelationship of factors that different agencies of the state address (class, race, etc.). Feminist work is fatally flawed if it loses sight of this.

This brings us to the recurring problem of the need for a feminist theory of the state. It is clear to us that to tear feminist legal theory out of its political context is very dangerous. The relationship between state and law is crucial and has not been sufficiently analysed by feminist lawyers. An example of this can be found in the theory and practice of MacKinnon. In her two articles on feminism, Marxism, method and the state she recognises the problems with a capitalist state, though she does not explicitly address the question of whether such a state is also, inevitably, patriarchal.[6] In her political practice she argues, with Dworkin, that women should seek improvement through recourse to a state-authorised right to censor pornography. MacKinnon and Dworkin identify pornography as one of the central means by which women are constructed as subordinate objects by depiction. The problem here is that arguably legal censorship of sexual matters may empower the twin forces of oppression – reaction and the state – more than it will empower subordinated women. MacKinnon and Dworkin suggest that this may be averted by casting anti-pornography measures in the guise of civil actions to be brought by individuals. It seems to us extraordinarily naive to imagine that the discursive potential of reactionary argument can be contained by demarcating the legal venue in which it may appear. Already, some of our sisters in the U.S.A. are disturbed by the extent to which MacKinnon and Dworkin, in pursuit of their purpose of seeing their measures made law, allied themselves with forces which were fundamentally opposed to the empowerment of women through other routes, such as abortion rights or the Equal Rights Amendment.[7]

The absence of a specifically feminist theory of the state should not lure us into the argument that the state is open. There is a major difference between analysing the contradictions within law and trying to use law without reference to other constraints. These constraints may be simply directed at women or they may emanate from patriarchal relations. The particular relationship between state agencies' concerns and practice may give some room for movement at legislative level, although we have grave doubts about it, but in any case, it is certain that legislative intervention is never value free. The major thrust of our argument, at this point, is that working within established categories and practices is essential to provide political strategies for the present but that accepting these definitions as the basis for theoretical development is too constraining. Establishing an agenda for the development of feminist theories of law is a project which cannot be hamstrung, whether by the need for immediate political action or by a confusion between feminist theory and work on women. Part of that project must be a feminist analysis of the role of the state and of law's relationship to the state.

We have stressed that there is little established orthodoxy to feminism. We have also pointed out that, in our view, it would be a mistake for feminist critical legal scholars to take law as their starting point for analysis. Law reflects and constructs power relations in society and it is those power relations between men and women which are the primary object of the enquiry. The concept of power itself is in any case problematic. It includes authority over the disposal of resources and of labour, economic independence/dependence, as well as control over women's reproductive capacity. Labour law, tax law and family law are some of the more obvious methods by which power relations in these areas are mediated, reflected and constructed in our society, but we need to understand the dynamics of both personal and public life and the hidden imbalance of power within the family and within the workplace if we are to understand the significance of law. In addition power relations produce their own forms of resistance, which are as crucial an aspect

52

of relations between the sexes as is class struggle from a Marxist perspective. In some cases resistance has taken the form of a struggle within law or campaigns about law. Which brings us back to the practical question; can struggle within law do more than simply protect women's vulnerable position or is this use of law, or legal discourse, in relation to family, crime or employment a means of empowering women? This question cannot be answered, we would suggest, without a feminist theory of state and of the relationship between state and law.

Some of the divisions within feminism, to which we have referred, spring from the amount of weight given to the various possible sites and expressions of women's oppression. Many feminists would argue that the family or kinship system is the prime arena for the construction of female subordination. They would argue that the sexual division of labour, which is not biologically determined but is socially constructed, has its inception within the family whence it affects the rest of social life, and becomes the principal mechanism for oppression. They would argue that it is the allocation of the primary responsibility for caring for others (whether children, the sick or the old) to women which perpetuates women's subordination and prevents their being able to act as autonomously as men, even taking into account all those constraints which limit the autonomy of men within capitalist societies.

For some feminists heterosexual relations provide the principal site for subordination and are always and inevitably oppressive to women. The fact that the line between definitions of seduction and definitions of rape in our culture, is so fine, seems to lead to the conclusion that penile penetration is the basis of men's dominance. This is, broadly, the approach adopted by MacKinnon. The argument has some force but unless we can explain why it is that power is required or sought in this arena it begins to look dangerously like a form of biological determinism. Another danger with such an approach is that it tends to locate power within individual heterosexual relationships without taking sufficient account of the total entity which may contain, unsurprisingly, its own contradictions. A patriarchal society, like a capitalist society, reveals itself as a dense social network of half truths and illusions.

Another strand of feminist thought concentrates on concepts of normality and the pervasiveness of what Judith Kegan Gardiner has called "binary thinking" as mechanisms of oppression.[8] Binary thinking is so firmly established in our system of thought, and cultural definitions are so powerful, that there is widespread consensus about the appropriate columns in which such oppositions as head/heart, reason/emotion, nurturance/achievement, community/individualism, subject/object, public/private, family/market, etc. should be placed. There is even a high degree of consensus about where feminine/masculine should be placed, at least in our culture. Disagreement arises when the labels 'positive' and 'negative' are attached to either column. Men recognise the value of nurturance and altruism but they prefer to ascribe these qualities to others. Hence the popularity of sociobiological theories which define such attributes as the property of women. Feminists have displayed a certain ambiguity in relation to these clusters of qualities. They have argued that, on the one hand, the so-called feminine attributes are superior – in other words the world would be a better place if men could be more like women – and, on the other, they have denied the validity of the oppositions, arguing that they are not immutable or biologically determined, and that, for example, there is nothing to stop women showing aggression or men developing attachment. Feminists have vacillated between attempting to change the positive and negative labels on the columns and attempting to overcome the duality in thinking by merging the columns.

The first tactic (label changing) is a necessary and valuable corrective to the dominant perception. Its danger lies in that it tends to reproduce and reinforce the polarities. In its extreme form it leads to a total rejection of men and a retreat into separatism. The second tactic (column merging) is appealing but difficult to put into practice, given the power of the *status quo*. To take one of the oppositions as an example: a classic case of binary thinking, and therefore binary living, is the old separation of the world sphere into public/private or, in the case of women, the family and the market. The common approach by feminists to this particular duality has been the use of the column merging tactic. The general argument is that the distinction, as conceived, is simply false, both as theory and in fact. Overcoming the pervasive problem of the distinction, however, has its difficulties. Olsen in her study of the ideology and implications of the family/market dichotomy, begins the attempt to suggest a solution, but her analysis disintegrates into idealism in her final paragraphs, where the only form of action she can suggest is individual attempts to alter consciousness. She argues that in order to transcend the male/female opposition we must increase the options available to each individual and we must allow human personality to break out of the present dichotomised system, so that women may be *less* like present men and men *less* like present women. She envisions a world of reds and greens and blues rather than a compromise of grey as an alternative to the present all black/all white gender opposition. It is an attractive vision but she gives no hint as to what material changes would be required to make it realisable.[9]

A possible third tactic which has as yet remained relatively unexplored would be to redefine entirely the terms of the debate. We are proposing here the utilisation of a different language. By this we mean language in the broad sense of finding adequate expression for women's distinctive encounters with, and understanding of, the social world. This leads us to Carol Gilligan and her suggestion that the new language of morality, for example, could privilege an understanding of responsibility and relationships rather than an understanding of rights and rules.[10] We anticipate that the impact of this reconceptualisation upon the order and privilege of legal principle and priority could be immense. Drawing out the implications of this is clearly a massive project which we have only the space to acknowledge here. We would suggest of Gilligan's work, however, that even if we now use it as no more than a fresh reference point in our enquiry – that is, as a tentative framework for exploring the limits of the old thought with the shock of the new – we are at least able to envisage its potential. Elizabeth Kingdom has warned of the problem of becoming trapped in the language of rights; inventing a new language may well open up our avenues of escape.[11]

An understanding that normality is not as settled as it seems has provoked feminists to question the methods by which theory, and hence our explanations of normality, are built. There are really two questions here. First, how has theory been constructed, and therefore how far can we accept its validity, and secondly, as feminists how should we tackle the project of our own theorising?

It has always been implicit in feminism that its critique of existing theory is based upon the disjuncture of women's lived experience of reality and men's representations of it. In this sense, then, feminism is an attack of the specific (women's knowledge) upon the universal (that is, what is represented as knowledge writ large). The point about male theorising is that if it has originated from men's lived experience this has never been explicitly acknowledged, so that specific theory becomes universal, in much the same way that 'man' has come to mean both man in particular and man and woman in universal. Gilligan's useful critique of theory building in the male mode contains some splendid examples of this kind of androcentric theorising, and demonstrates its pernicious effect upon the way in which judgment is constructed.[12] Instancing, for example, a series of studies by Kohlberg on the development of moral judgment, Gilligan points out that the research group upon which Kohlberg's initial 'findings' were based comprised eighty-four boys. In a theory outlining a six stage sequence derived from his observations of this group, a mature woman's judgment generally exemplified stage three, a point at which "morality is conceived in interpersonal terms and goodness is equated with helping and pleasing others".[13] Gilligan suggests, however, that Kohlberg's scale, based upon a study of *men's* maturation "reflects the importance of individuation in *their* development"(our emphasis). She further suggests that had the pilot study been based upon a group of women, the "moral problem" would be identified as arising:

> . . . from conflicting responsibilities rather than from competing rights, and would require for its resolution a mode of thinking that is contextual and narrative rather than formal and abstract. This conception of morality as concerned with the activity of care, centres moral development around the understanding of relationships, just as the conception of morality as fairness ties moral development to the understanding of rights and rules.[14]

Feminism's concern with the diffuse forms and subtle exercise of power places it in this arena, closer to post-structuralist theorising than to Marxian derived theorising on ideology. Whilst the authors of this paper would not necessarily endorse, in its every theoretical precept, the notion of discourse and its constructions, we have found it a useful tool of analysis. To merely question, however, the current official boundaries of our understandings and judgments of the world is clearly insufficient. The primary question must then become how to proceed. It is clear that we must take some initiative, for simply to present the deconstructive revelation and then stand clear is to leave a dangerous void defended by no more than the feeble forces of *laissez-faire* individualism. If oppression lies in a constructed normality, through which constructions do we pursue freedom?

The question of how, as feminists, we should set about the project of our own theorising raises the problematic of a feminist methodology. To some extent we have already referred to aspects of this: the assault of the specific upon the universal, the process of transforming practice to theory. MacKinnon raises the question in her work, and suggests that the true methodology of feminism is consciousness raising. While we recognise the value of consciousness raising for the empowerment of individual women, and the significance of this in raising feminist theory, we cannot accept that it is, or should be, the entire or only methodology. The first problem lies in the efficacy of consciousness raising itself. We have some doubt that it can be utilised to articulate the entire individual experience. Some women have argued that the group itself can be oppressive, in the sense that one orthodoxy, the orthodoxy of patriarchy, may well be replaced by another.[15] This in its turn goes on to impose limits upon the revelation and authentication of experience. This suggests to us the problem we have already recognised in the process of transforming authorised normalities. The orthodoxy that emerges within the group may well be as much reflexive as reflective; that is to say, it may emerge equally in the guise of committed individualism as in the form of a considered 'feminist morality'. We have grave doubt that liberal individualism contains any real potential for progressive change, so that if this is the political stance that emerges within the group, the capacity for change disintegrates. In addition, it is clear that to some extent the reinterpretation of experience, which is a necessary part of consciousness raising, relies upon theory itself.

The second problem is that we see consciousness raising as primarily a method of empowering individual women. If we are right that patriarchy is constituted in more than the sum of individual lives, then the response to it must be more than the sum of articulated individual experience.

We remain uncertain as to quite what the ideal of feminist methodology would be, although we suspect that the answer may lie in further considering the terms in which theory is built.[16] Thus, although we could then move beyond the individualist level of consciousness raising we could, too, avoid the trap of attempting to emulate male models. Like the anonymous scribes of a thousand walls, we consider that in this field, at least, women who want to be like men lack ambition.

In our discussion of the problems of theory building we referred to the problems feminists have encountered in dealing with the old distinction between a public/private, family/market sphere. We suggested that a common theme emerged from feminist writing which was to argue that the distinction was, in one way or another, false. Although there is this convergence in the way in which the problem has been approached, the detailed analysis itself is quite widely varied according to the political standpoint of the writer. Varied too, therefore, are the proposals for ways of change. Olsen argues that because the family is seen as natural and consensual, relations within the family are not deemed to require regulation.[17] Hence the inequality of power within the family is ignored. The state sees its role in the family as establishing what constitutes a family (marriage law, social security law – both private and public law) and as ratifying correct roles within the family (dependents, maintenance, responsibility for children). In certain crucial areas the state seeks to interfere as little as possible (domestic violence, marital rape) but reinforces the roles of 'good wife', 'deserving parent', etc. through family law and social work practice. The family is represented as a private domain, albeit one which has been publicly defined. That this paradox exists is not, for feminists anyway, in dispute, but as we remarked earlier it is when ways of overcoming it are sought that we run into difficulty. We suggested before that this is when Olsen's piece disintegrates somewhat, and one begins to see why, even in her introductory paragraphs. She opens by suggesting that it is only through interrogation of the ideological foundations of social reform that one may achieve an understanding of why reform strategies have manifestly failed to overcome the subordination of women. Identifying a clutch of significant dichotomous visions – state/civil society, male/female and, of course, family/market – she argues that the family/market dichotomy is one of the culpable, unexamined assumptions limiting the scope of reform. She indicates a way forward:

> All three dichotomies seem eternal, yet by transcending all those, by reconceiving the relationship between the two elements in each of those pairs and restructuring our thoughts and lives to create, reflect and reinforce their reconceptions, we have the greatest possibility for bringing about changes.[18]

This is all very well if our only problem, as feminists, is how to shatter set unexplained assumptions. Her argument that reforms are limited by their ideological foundations is fine as far as it goes, but in her article she seems to sidestep the issue of why we have these assumptions and not others. In examining the ideological foundations of reform she omits to examine the material foundations of ideology; the ideology which fathers social reform must itself have some birthplace. Ideology cannot simply arrive by a sort of spontaneous combustion or in the beak of a stock. That the paradigm is drawn up in the form of the family and the market indicates that the construction which defines the home as a woman's place may have as much to do with the market as the family itself. It is her failure to find the cradle of the ideological assumptions which leads to Olsen's failure to locate the grave.

Nancy Chodorow, having grounded binary definitions in child rearing practices, provides a more positive programme for change by advocating the dissolution of the sexual division of labour with regard to small children.[19] But, like Olsen, Chodorow pays insufficient attention to the material conditions which serve to perpetuate the polarities. If so-called binary living is to the benefit possibly of both capital and of men, it will require more than different consciousnesses to dissolve it. We would argue, with Nancy Hartsock, that it is crucial to take account of the totality of any particular social formation.[20] In a capitalist social formation there is an appearance of separation between public and private, market and family: the one political, regulated and alienating, and the other apolitical, unregulated and co-operative. But it is only an appearance. The reality is that the spheres of production and reproduction are intimately interrelated and interdependent. In addition, women suffer by being regulated in and through the family where official definitions mean that there is considerably more control than is formally recognised. To the extent that the law formally adopts a non-interventionist stance *vis à vis* the family, that apparent non-regulation simply serves both to draw a veil over more discreet state intervention and to abandon women to control inherent in the nature of the family institution itself.

Marxists would argue that non-alienated human existence, that is an existence in which everyone can achieve their full potential, is only possible when production and exchange have been fully socialised. Feminists fear that patriarchal tendencies will not necessarily be eliminated by a revolution in these spheres alone.

At the beginning of this paper we cautioned against the mistake of reading feminist texts out of context. Equally, it would be foolhardy to ignore the foundations of jurisprudence. Just as feminist theory cannot be laid, like a grid, over the contours of existing jurisprudential concepts, so these concepts should not simply be laid over one or another feminist theory. We must attempt to make feminism and jurisprudence mutually fruitful and enlightening. To take one specific example, feminist analysis of the development of the rule of law ideology in the nineteenth century would throw further light upon the demarcation of the category 'woman'. It would also highlight the way in which law, and theories about law and critiques of jurisprudence and of bourgeois legality have all been markedly androcentric whilst claiming a spurious universality. Maine, Marx and MacPherson, in company with many others, all stress the idea that under capitalism the individual gains in significance in contrast to the community or collectivity.[21] Status gives way to contract in law, the individual increasingly becomes the unit of which civil law takes account, and in criminal law individual responsibility predominates. Progressive individualism, it is claimed, is the characteristic of a competitive market economy. Commodity fetishism results in alienated individuals. The 'individual legal subject', bearer of rights and potential owner of alienable private property is a commonplace of political and legal analysis of the nineteenth century and is associated with the emergence of an apparently 'autonomous' legal system. But in all this wealth of theory about forms of law in nineteenth century Britain there is no recognition that it is adult men who are constructed as separate, individual, legal subjects. Women, and more especially married women, are not so constructed in nineteenth century law or in nineteenth century ideology. They are constructed as unequal legal objects rather than equal legal subjects.

Of course, we are fully aware that the realities of class inequality in a capitalist social formation expose legal equality as a mask for economic inequality. Such a realisation is the stuff of the Marxist critique of the rule of law. But unless that critique can also explain married women's total absence even from the ideology it seems to us to be inadequate. We think the answer to the question "how was it possible for married women to be excluded from the ideology of the rule of law at a time when that ideology was at its most powerful?" may involve an examination of nineteenth century patriarchal ideologies, their class specific character, and the material conditions for women in the labour force and in the bourgeois family which gave rise to them. Is there a connection between married women's exclusion from the market as fully acting subjects and their exclusion from the rule of law? There is a need for more work to be done on this question which has been hitherto largely ignored in the body of 'rule of law' writing.

We do not wish the task of feminism in law to be the task of feminising jurisprudence. The project of feminism may indeed be to redefine the concepts with which we have hitherto been theorising law. In this paper it should have become clear that we are not seeking feminist grid references but rather a new topography of legal theory. The task is immense but already under way, and we welcome the increasing body of work, published and unpublished, which is emerging to offer us directions for change.

In April 1986 we participated in the first major European Conference on Feminism and Law.[22] From many interesting papers and discussions three issues became manifest which we regard as crucial absences from this article, although they are now very much present in our thinking. First, our concerns clearly reflect the specific academic and political contexts in which we all work. The conference revealed significant differences between our debates and those of Scandinavian women, for example. Secondly, as a separate but related issue we found that these differences become even more marked when we come to compare the work arising from our position of relative privilege as white academic women in this country with the work of our sisters in the Republic of Ireland or Greece, for instance. It was also clear that our black sisters had distinct and vital demands and initiatives to place on the agenda. The relationship between gender and religion or gender and race, and the practical struggle for law reform must be central to our thinking. Finally, we are constantly drawn back to the imperative link between theory and practice. Feminism, within the academy, is as much about *how* we teach as it is about *what* we teach. Feminist legal practice constantly poses the question of theory in praxis; we, as academic women, must take that debate on board.

The struggle continues.

NOTES AND REFERENCES

1   MacKinnon, "Feminism, Marxism, Method and the State: an Agenda for Theory" (1982) 7 *Signs* p. 515 and "Feminism, Marxism, Method and the State: Towards a Feminist Jurisprudence" (1983) 8 *Signs* p. 635.
2   This must not be confused with the 'women's law' position developed in the Scandinavian countries. For an introduction to the Scandinavian material see the special issue on *Feminist Perspectives on Law*(1986) 14 *International J. Sociology of Law.*
3   A. Sachs and J. H. Wilson, *Sexism and the Law* (1978); B. Hoggett and S. Atkins, *Women and the Law* (1984).

⁴ M. Eaton, "Documenting the Defendant: Placing Women in Social Enquiry Reports" in *Women in Law* (1985; eds. J. Brophy and C. Smart) p. 117. This point is also made by S. Edwards in "Gender Justice: Defending Defendants and Mitigating Sentence" in *Gender, Sex and the Law* (1986; ed. S. Edwards) p. 129, and, rather differently, by M. Cousins in "Mens Rea: A Note on Sexual Difference, Criminology and the Law" in *Radical Issues in Criminology* (1980; eds. P. Carlen and M. Collison) p. 109.

⁵ C. Smart, *The Ties that Bind* (1984).

⁶ MacKinnon, *op. cit.*, 1982 and 1983.

⁷ For references to these measures see MacKinnon, *op. cit.*, 1983.

⁸ J. Gardiner, "Power, Desire and Difference: Comment on Essays from Signs Special Issue on Feminist Theory" (1983) 8 *Signs* p. 733. See also K. O'Donovan, *Sexual Divisions in Law* (1985) for a discussion of the public/private dichotomy.

⁹ F. Olsen, "The Family and the Market: A Study of Ideology and Legal Reform" (1983) 96 *Harvard Law Rev.* p. 1497 at p. 1578.

¹⁰ C. Gilligan, *In a Different Voice* (1982).

¹¹ E. Kingdom, "Legal Recognition of a Woman's Right to Choose" in J. Brophy and C. Smart (eds.), *op. cit.*, p.143.

¹² Gilligan, *op. cit.*

¹³ *Id.*, p. 18.

¹⁴ *Id.*, p. 19.

¹⁵ C. Vance (ed.), *Pleasure and Danger: Exploring Female Sexuality* (1984).

¹⁶ See some of the considerations given to this question in (1986) 14 *International J. Sociology of Law*.

¹⁷ Olsen, *op. cit.*

¹⁸ *Id.*, p. 1499.

¹⁹ N. Chodorow, "Family Structure and Feminine Personality" in *Woman, Culture and Society* (1974; eds. M. Rosaldo and M. Lamphere) p. 43.

²⁰ N. Hartsock, "Feminist Theory and the Development of Revolutionary Strategy" in *Capitalist Patriarchy and the Case for Socialist Feminism* (1979; ed. Z. Eisenstein) p. 56. For this point see also D. Harvey, *The Limits of Capital* (1982) and W. Lazonick, "The Subjection of Labour to Capital: the Rise of the Capitalist System" (1978) 10 *Review of Radical Political Economics* p. 1.

²¹ H. Maine, *Ancient Law* (1930); K. Marx, *Capital*, Vol. 1; C. B. MacPherson, *Political Theory of Possessive Individualism* (1975).

²² This conference was organised by the women's caucus of the U.K. Critical Legal Conference on behalf of the European Conference on Critical Legal Studies. Entitled "Theory and Practice: Feminist Perspectives on Law", it attracted some three hundred participants from the U.K., Europe and North America and a selection of papers from the conference is published in (1986) 14 *International J. Sociology of Law*. The women's caucus convenors of the U.K. Critical Legal Conference are Joanne Conaghan and Susie Gibson, both of the University of Kent. Anyone who would like further information is welcome to contact Susie Gibson at Darwin College, University of Kent, Canterbury, Kent CT2 7NY, England.

Beyond the Public/Private Division: Law, Power and the Family

NIKOLAS ROSE*

Over the past ten years, the intellectual machinery which radical social analysts have used to produce political intelligibility has begun to fall apart. Faced with the inadequacies of most social theory to cope with the problems of contemporary social reality, two strategies of repair have been noteworthy. The first is to shift the issue of power to the forefront of investigation. Power is no longer seen as the automatic by-product of economic exploitation or social stratification; it is itself the focus of analysis and the stake in political contestation. The second is to use 'history' rather than 'grand theory' as a way of taking apart the self-evidence of the present. The past is used to reveal the socially constructed nature of the present, implying that it can be transformed by conscious political strategy. Yet studies carried out under these auspices find it difficult to abandon the comfort provided by old forms of explanation. Historical investigation often merely projects conventional radical wisdom back onto the past. Power often appears in the repetitive guise of denial, control and repression. The old theories reappear as solutions to their own failure.

The aim of this paper is to recommend a use of the past, and an analysis of power which would disrupt these certainties. I term this approach 'genealogical' in that it uses the analytical devices developed in the 'genealogical' studies of Michel Foucault and his co-workers. Genealogy is not a methodology, but a means of distancing oneself from certain conceptual tools which have a powerful hold over critical thought. I will counterpose genealogy to the most popular radical strategy of all, that of critique. I will focus upon the area where the arguments seem to me to be most advanced: feminism and the critical analysis of 'the family' and 'family law'.

Feminism exploded the boundary lines of traditional socialist politics, and re-inserted questions of family, sexuality, children and domestic life into the heart of progressive political discourse. The analysis of domination was no longer confined to the market, the workplace or the formal institutions of the criminal justice system. A multiplicity of infra-state powers were made visible and contestable. Feminist studies of law and legal regulation often succeeded

* *Department of Human Sciences, Brunel University, Uxbridge, Middlesex UB8 3PH, England.*

This paper was originally given at the First Annual Critical Legal Conference, University of Kent, September 1986. I would like to thank Alan Hunt and Phil Jones for comments and criticism.

61

almost uniquely in tying up concrete, contingent and local instances of oppression and domination with, on the one hand, more general networks of social power and, on the other hand, specific and immediate strategies for reform.

Recently, however, a certain language of analysis has come to the fore which promises to confer a unity upon the investigations of the diverse social, legal and economic practices within which women are subordinated.[1] Each of these, it is suggested, can be understood in terms of the division and opposition of public and private spheres. In this paper I examine this claim in order to illustrate some basic weaknesses in much contemporary critical analysis of law and politics. I argue that critical analysis must abandon the analytic strategy of critique and rethink some of its fundamental concepts – state, interest, ideology and power. I conclude by sketching out some characteristics of a genealogical approach to family powers, identifying regulatory mechanisms which raise difficult problems for political evaluation.

PUBLIC POWERS AND PRIVATE FREEDOMS?

Contemporary disputes over the boundaries of public powers and private freedoms in issues of morality, sexuality, marriage, reproduction, child care and divorce follow familiar lines. How much should the state intervene into private life? How successful are public authorities in making decisions on care, custody and so forth? What aspects of personal morality are public concerns and what are not? Is there a sphere of private life and personal morality that is, in brief and crude terms, not the law's business? Have welfare professionals colonised the family at the expense of personal liberties and formal legal protections? The debate has been going for a long time; the problems seem both crucial and interminable.

Recently feminist lawyers and critical legal scholars have proposed a new approach to these old disputes.[2] They have argued that the key to resolving the analytical and practical problems lies in understanding the division between public and private spheres. Thus Freeman suggests that "at the root of a critical theory of family law is the public/private dichotomy".[3] It is claimed that such a dichotomy both underpins the present organisation of legal regulation of family relations and that:

> ... many of the reform strategies in the recent past which are conceived within this particular world view are 'cabined, cribbed and confined' by it and that their effectiveness is accordingly limited.[4]

Critical analysis of the public/private distinction is hardly new in legal thought. Throughout the first half of this century jurists attacked the premises lying behind the classification as it underlay the division of law into public and private realms, arguing that so-called 'private' categories of law such as contract actually represented a delegation of public power, entailing a policy decision and enforced by state imposed sanctions.[5] Extending this critique, contemporary critical legal scholars in the U.S.A. argue that the public/

private division is one of a number of homologous distinctions that:

> ... taken together, constitute the liberal way of thinking about the social world. These distinctions are state/society, public/private, individual/group, right/power, property/sovereignty, contract/tort, law/policy, legislature/judiciary, objective/subjective, reason/fiat, freedom/coercion ....[6]

These oppositions, it is argued, shape our consciousness. When incorporated into legal discourse they induce beliefs that existing social arrangements are just, natural, inevitable, legitimate, thereby denying our capacity to conceive of new forms of human relations and to challenge existing forms of domination.[7] Critical legal scholars in the U.S.A. have sought to demonstrate that the public/private distinction has no determinate content in law, that it functions more as an image or metaphor which is able to suture judicial argument to existing values and beliefs, and that it serves less as an analytic tool or means of deciding cases than as a form of political rhetoric used to justify value choices.

These authors argue that the distinction serves or seeks to maintain the belief that social and economic life – business, education, community, family – are outside government and law, simultaneously denying the role of political processes in constituting and maintaining them, and legitimating these arrangements by implying that they have arisen from decisions and choices freely made by individuals. This protects existing hierarchies yet delegitimises alternative forms of group solidarity – unions, universities, communities – which cannot fit within the public/private divide. Hence critical legal theorists regard the public/private distinction as inimical to the construction of democratic, self-governing group life which would transcend the distinction between the state as the *locus* of all legitimate power and the individual as the isolated atom of freedom and rights.

This analytic machinery is deployed by Olsen in her critique of the dichotomies underpinning the subordination of women to men.[8] The central opposition, she claims, is that between the market and the family, which was consolidated in the nineteenth century. This is less a real division of zones and relations than a set of powerful beliefs that structure our ways of conceptualising and evaluating different types of activity. The family/market dichotomy embodies the idea that the market structures our productive lives whilst the family structures our affective lives. This division of experience into two separate and interdependent spheres must be transcended.

Olsen argues that the free market combines an egalitarian ideology with an individualist ethic, whilst the private family combines an hierarchical ideology with an altruistic ethic. When our consciousness is structured by the public/private division we conceive of reforms only in terms of making the market more like the family or the family more like the market. Thus reforms to the market have sought to mitigate individualism but only at the price of creating new hierarchies, and reforms of the family have sought to undermine hierarchy but at the price of creating a spurious equality which promotes individualism, undermines solidarity and altruism, and obscures the real differences in power between women and men. The solution is to transcend the

63

public/private divide, transforming both family and market, and simultaneously transcending the male/female dichotomy – creating what she terms "a new referential system for relating men and women to the world . . . allowing the human personality to break out of the present dichotomised system".[9]

English critics of the public/private divide as it relates to the family have tended to draw upon a different language of critique but come to similar conclusions.[10] The division between public and private is traced back in political and social philosophy at least as far as Aristotle's distinction between *polis* and *oikos* and up to the natural rights theories of John Locke. However, in the eighteenth and nineteenth centuries the distinction is reposed in terms of the division between home and market. It is given a philosophical foundation in the liberal political philosophy of J. S. Mill and his followers, with the opposition between the realm of legitimate public regulation and the realm of freedom from intrusion, personal autonomy and private choice. Writers point to the particular associations in these texts between the public sphere – the world of work, the market, individualism, competition, politics and the state – and men, and the corollary association of women with the private, domestic, intimate, altruistic and humanitarian world of the home.

These feminist histories argue that notions of the home and family relations as private so far as the law was concerned pre-date the constitutional theories of the nineteenth century. Similarly, these authors refuse the earlier Marxist account of the division as a function of the change in production relations associated with the rise of capitalism, arguing not only that it pre-dates capitalism but that its primary function was to support and reinforce male, patriarchal control over women, both in the formulation of laws and regulations pertaining to the public sphere, and in the powers allowed to men in the home and family to control women. It is argued that, in law as elsewhere, this public/private divide, and the conception of the private which it uses, has always functioned to sustain a particular and oppressive set of relations between men and women.[11]

However, most of the authors suggest that the developments within capitalism in the nineteenth century reworked this public/private divide to suit the interests of a ruling, property owning male elite. This can be seen in the emergence of a cult of domesticity with its idealisation of motherhood. Whilst allowing that this allotted certain powers to women, these authors suggest that it did so only in their status as mothers confined to the private sphere, and hence failed fundamentally to challenge either the patriarchal separation of realms, or the economic power which men wielded over the family unit.

Analyses of the legal regulation of marriage, divorce, sexual behaviour and domestic violence are deployed to show that the ideology of individual choice and personal freedom in the private domain of home and family legitimates a refusal by public authorities to intervene into certain places, activities, relationships and feelings. Designating them personal, private and subjective makes them appear to be outside the scope of the law as a fact of nature, whereas in fact non-intervention is a socially contructed, historically variable and inevitably political decision. The state defines as 'private' those aspects of life into which it will not intervene, and then, paradoxically, uses this privacy as the justification for its non-intervention.

Like *laissez faire* in relation to the market, the idea that the family can be private in the sense of outside public regulation is a myth. The state cannot avoid intervening in the shaping of familial relations through decisions as to which types of relation to sanction and codify and which types of dispute to regulate or not regulate. The state establishes the legal framework for conducting legitimate sexual relations and for procreation and privileges certain types of relation through rules of inheritance. Further, the state, through public law, has established complex welfare mechanisms, especially those surrounding the proper development of children. And however potent is the legal ideology of family privacy, in decisions as to the best interests and welfare of children in cases concerning care and custody, and in the division of family property and other aspects of family disputes, legal functionaries operate according to ideological and patriarchal beliefs as to morality, responsibility and family life and what is best for children. On the one hand, the state, representing dominant male interests, chooses the nature and objectives of public regulation; on the other, a domain is constituted outside legal regulation where welfare agencies enforce the ideology of motherhood, and where male power is not even subject to limited protections of the rule of law. The public/private division mystifies these processes.

Amongst the reform strategies discussed and criticised because of their commitment to the public/private dichotomy are those which seek to increase regulation of family relations by public law, those that try to decrease legal regulation of family conflicts by encouraging informal, non-legal forums for dispute resolution such as conciliation and family courts, proposals which advocate that the powers, duties and responsibilities of parties to domestic arrangements should be specified in private contracts enforcible at law, and those that seek to protect the family from excessive state intrusion by establishing a framework of family rights.[12]

For example, conciliation and family courts are frequently advocated as techniques and institutions which will increase the powers, capacities, autonomy and responsibility of the private parties involved, reducing damaging conflict between the parties and respecting their interests.[13] However, the critics of the public/private divide argue that the consequences of the reduction of such controls as flow from formal legal hearings – legal representation, due process and so forth – will be different: ignoring real conflicts in capacities, situations and wishes, denying inequalities in power and, in general, increasing the powers of welfare professionals over family members and of men over women. And the development of conciliation and family courts are viewed as part of a general increase in mechanisms of informal justice whose benign rhetoric disguises an increase of state power, establishing new, less visible channels through which the social control capacities of the state are extended and dispersed.[14]

Arguments for family rights can be similarly undercut. Thus, in an influential book, Goldstein, Freud and Solnit argued:

> The child's need for safety within the confines of the family must be met by law through its recognition of family privacy as the barrier to state instrusion upon parental autonomy in child rearing.[15]

The critical rejoinder is that such proposals gloss over, ignore or obscure the different powers and interests of different members of the family: family privacy is all too often a licence for men to dominate women and children.[16] The very notion of family privacy thus mystifies the extent to which the family is constructed and controlled by the state and its agencies, and obscures the power differences and conflicts amongst family members. Reform proposals which operate in terms of the public/private divide, or which seek to increase an unproblematical family privacy, are thus fundamentally flawed. Critical legal theory must expose the ideological nature of the dichotomy; critical family politics must transcend it in practice.

CRITICISM AND CRITIQUE

The arguments which I have been discussing conceptualise the public/private division as an ideology and subject it to a critique. As in other critiques of ideology, this has a particular form. It seeks to demonstrate the *falsity* of the dichotomy. It aims to reveal the *function* of the dichotomy. It thus appears to *explain* the falsity *in terms of* the function it serves. The public/private division is false because the private realm is not natural but is itself a construction within a particular set of beliefs. And it has at least four functions. It mystifies the fact that the state itself constructs both the boundaries and the limits of privacy. It legitimates the extent to which the state refuses to intervene into certain places or relations through its legal mechanisms. It masks the fact that privacy is all too often the right of men to dominate women and children. And it obscures the degree to which the state empowers welfare professionals to impose social norms on the family lives of certain sections of society, expecially controlling women in their roles as wives and mothers.

This critique of the public/private division is frequently revealing and insightful. But it is hamstrung by the analytic strategy it uses. This limits our understanding of the relations between regulatory systems and conjugal, domestic and child-rearing arrangements and forms of habitation. It fails to grasp the ways in which the private family has, on the one hand, been linked into new forms of political rationality which have developed over the last century, and, on the other hand, has been central to transformations in subjective realities and desires. It thus leads to over-simple criticisms of family policies and proposals for reform. If we are to understand the politics of familialisation, and the transformation of political concerns into personal and familial objectives which it entailed, we need to fragment, disturb and disrupt some of the central explanatory categories of critique.

The first fragmentation must be of 'law' itself. The 'legal system' is neither totalised nor enclosed. There is no unity to the complex of written codes, judgments, institutions and agents and techniques of judgment which make up 'the law'. 'Law' does not operate on 'the family': family law is a creation of textbook writers and legal pedagogy. Different laws – in relation to inheritance, marriage, divorce, custody, the protection of children and so forth – specify their objects and powers in terms of varied statuses which cannot be simply translated into each other: husbands, wives, parents, spouses and so forth. Legal regulation of each of these different relations and processes has emerged at different times and in relation to different concerns. They have defined their terms differently and utilise diverse forms of judgment and mechanisms of enforcement. They do not operate according to a single division of 'public' and 'private' - spaces, activities and relations which are within the scope of regulation for one purpose are outside it for another. Unities and coherences must be analysed in terms of outcomes rather than origins or intentions. Rather than conferring a false unity upon the diversity of legal regulation, critical analysis should treat this diversity as both a clue to the social intelligibility of the law and, perhaps, as the key to a political strategy in relation to law.

Further, law does not exist in isolation from other regulatory systems. Over the past hundred and fifty years we have seen the construction of a new form of 'government', one in which the family was central – or rather in which certain desirable states of affairs – profit, tranquillity, security, health, virtue and efficiency – were to be brought about by governing residential, domestic, sexual and child rearing arrangements in the form of the private family. Government here should be seen in an extended sense, as all those interdictions, urgings, interventions, techniques and evaluations which seek to shape up events towards desired ends. Legal mechanisms need to be relocated within this far wider field of regulatory mechanisms ranging from taxation, through welfare to the design of domestic space. Critical approaches to law must face up to the paradox that, in many cases, analysis of law is the wrong place to start if one wishes to understand regulatory strategies.

Critiques of the law appear ineluctably drawn to a concept of the state which reproduces the terms of constitutionalist doctrines. The state is conceived as the single sovereign source of authoritative regulation in a given, bounded national territory. Power is the state and the law is its voice. What the state does not prohibit, it commands. Power is construed as centralised, wielded by a political elite and directed outwards through the various organs of social control. But we need to take the category of the state as a problem and not a solution. The programmes of regulation of domestic, conjugal and reproductive arrangements, and the projects for the reform of habitation, did not originate with 'the state'. Their initiators, supporters and allies were heterogeneous, the problems which they posed themselves were diverse. They were certainly bound up with systems of domination, if one takes this term in its sense of ruling or governing, shaping events to certain ends. But the ends they sought were not in any simple way functional to the state, to men or to the economy. We should see 'the state' not as the origin but as the outcome of these programmes. Rather than seeing an expansion of state control we should seek to analyse what one might term 'the governmentalisation of the state': a transformation of what could be governed, by whom and in what ways.

We need to take the arguments of political and legal 'pluralism' seriously. Modern societies are shifting networks of agencies, associations, corporations and domestic units, with many distinct and differentiated *loci* of decision, criteria of judgment, bodies of knowledge and expertise. This 'pluralism' entails genuine conflicts of interest, struggles for political ascendancy and labile alliances. Familialised concerns have arisen in relation to different issues across these networks: inheritance of property or of pathology; vice and delinquency; health and efficiency; motherhood and femininity. They have issued in diverse laws concerning anything from testation to video nasties, and have been incorporated into varied regulatory apparatuses ranging from taxation and social security through architecture and town planning to the decisions of judges in relation to the disposal of female offenders. This 'pluralism' is not a mere surface which we must aim to unify through critique; it must be the field of analysis not least because it must also be the sphere of political judgment and policy evaluation.[17]

The new vocabularies and programmes which emerged in the nineteenth and twentieth centuries do, indeed, entail the formation of sectors and zones which are not merely creatures of state power or means of it extending its control. 'Familialisation' was crucial to the means whereby personal capacities and conducts could be socialised, shaped and maximised in a manner which accorded with the moral and political principles of liberal society. It is inadequate to regard the languages of regulatory strategies, the terms within which they thought themselves, the ways in which they formulated their problems and solutions, as ideological. Little will be understood about their rationale or consequences through 'interpreting' them to reveal fundamental processes or contradictions which they dissimulate or suppress.[18] Instead we need to examine the new ways of thinking and acting which these languages of the family have introduced into our reality. Rather than obscuring or legitimating, they actually constituted new sectors of reality, new problems and possibilities for personal investment as well as for public regulation. The familialisation of society operates because it has managed to command considerable subjective commitment from citizens who have come to regulate their own lives according to its terms. To analyse the private family in terms of illusion, mystification or false consciousness is to avoid examining how this new system of regulation operates, the relations of power it installs and, indeed, how we might seek to transform it, if at all.

Finally, we need to re-conceptualise 'power'. It is now a commonplace to assert that power is not merely negative, repressive and inhibitory. But too often this recognition is merely a means of claiming that a given subject of power – the state, capitalism, patriarchy, men – extends their control by ever more wily means into even more nooks and crannies of existence. But power – the ability to exercise mastery over others, to pursue goals against resistance, to mobilise natural or human forces individually or collectively around aims, aspirations and beliefs – does not have any such single subject or repetitive form. Power cannot be calibrated in zero-sum terms, where what is gained by one side is lost by another. The sources of power are multiple – from control over economic, political, cultural or military resources to charisma, erotic attraction and desire.[19] The mechanics of power vary from physical coercion, through the inertial properties of multiply secured social circuits of exchange or hierarchy, to the micro-organisation of technical forms such as military organisation or domestic architecture. And amongst the modes of operation of power, the shaping of wills, desires, aspirations and interests, the formation of subjectivities and collectivities is more typical than the brute domination of one will by another.

If these arguments are accepted, we must recognise that the critical apparatus of radical thought needs more than repair. Indeed, the demarcation of theoretical resources conducted by radical theorists over the past two decades itself needs to be junked. We will find as much insight in Max Weber as in Karl Marx, in Emile Durkheim as in Evgeny Pashukanis, in Robert Dahl as in Antonio Gramsci. If the work of Michel Foucault has been the stalking horse for this rethinking of the role and nature of radical theory, it is perhaps in large part because he posed these problems to us in their starkest form.

THE GENEALOGY OF FAMILY POWERS

What might an alternative critical analysis of family powers look like? Whilst such a task cannot be undertaken here, some important themes can be drawn out of recent genealogical studies which highlight the differences between genealogy and critique.[20]

1. Beyond the State

Katherine O'Donovan concludes her examination of developments in family law from feudalism to the nineteenth century by arguing that, by the end of this long period, although public regulation provided a legal form for conjugal relations, the content of those relations continued to be ordered by patriarchy – the control of women and children by men. Despite the changes in the law bound up with what she terms "the elevation of domesticity", she concludes: "Rather than intervene directly to regulate family relations publicly, the state delegates its power and authority to the husband."[21] The state is seen as, on the one hand, the enunciator of regulation in the form of law and, on the other hand, the embodiment of male interests.

But the ways of thinking about and acting on family life which have developed over the last century do not have the sources, the functionality or the unity which is here ascribed to them and used for evaluating them. To suggest that these transformations originate in the state, and amount to allotting powers to husbands and fathers, or to coercive welfarism rendered benign by ideology, is to obscure the new types of powers and relations between individuals, experts, professionals and authorities which have taken shape over the last century, and the ways in which the subjectivities, responsibilities and aspirations of both women and men have been transformed.

The emergence of an institutionally distinct political domain, the sovereign state, entailed the gradual concentration of formal political, juridical and administrative powers which had hitherto been dispersed amongst a range of authorities – guilds, justices, landowners, religious authorities – and which had contained extensive mechanisms for specifying, monitoring and sanctioning detailed aspects of personal, conjugal, sexual and domestic conduct.[22] This concentration, and the concomitant legitimation and delimitation of political authority by the doctrines of 'rule of law', entailed the conceptualisation of certain domains which were freed from the threat of punitive sanction and detailed internal regulation. In general terms, one sees here the formation of the domains of the economy and the social, as new sectors of existence.

In the same movement as the political domain separates itself out in this way it defines the limits of the social and economic domains and polices certain of their key elements. If the contract is fundamental to the economy, so the family is fundamental to the government of the social. The family, as Donzelot points out, appeared as a positive solution to the problems of the regulation of morality, health and procreation posed by a liberal definition of the limits of legitimate state action.[23] It has been both distinguished from political life, yet defined by law and permeable to both compulsory and voluntary interventions.

Throughout the nineteenth century and into the twentieth one sees a proliferation of hundreds of little and large projects which sought to shape, mould, regulate and utilise the family and 'what goes on' in it, for social ends and to secure social objectives. Thus 'family reform' was central in programmes for the reform of morality, for the elimination of crime and for the maximisation of efficiency through promoting hygiene of body and mind. A wide variety of problems and possibilities were thought about in terms of the family and acted upon by seeking to affect domestic, conjugal and child rearing arrangements. Public authorities were not often the originators of these programmes, but were involved in various ways, for example by providing a legal framework for voluntary action, by establishing key institutional sites, and by supporting private campaigns with funds and information. One needs to think of 'socialisation' less as an anthropological universal than as an historically specific outcome of such diverse programmes for constructing the capacities, habits, ambitions and subjectivities of citizens. These programmes of socialisation were not simply targetted upon evident social threats – prostitutes, vagrants, lunatics, criminals – but also upon those who were not of 'society' in its earlier sense, that is, who were not persons of property and civility. The familialisation of society was a central instrument in constituting what one might call a subjectivity of citizenship.

By the start of the twentieth century, the family is administered and policed by practices and agencies which are neither private – in that their powers are constructed legally, they are the recipients of public funds and their agents are publicly accredited by some form of licensing – nor organs of political power in that their operations and objectives are not specified by the decrees and programmes of political forces but operate under the aegis of moral principles and, increasingly, by professional expertise underpinned by the power of a claim to truth. To claim that the content of family relations is either unregulated or delegated to husbands is to fundamentally mistake the nature of the modern family and its political role, it is to fall victim to the public/private dichotomy not to transcend it.

2. Whose Interests?

These new programmes of government thus cannot be attributed to the actions of an agency termed 'the state'. The state is not a unified and internally coherent entity which is the *locus* of all social power, but a complex set of agencies which are involved to different extents in projects for the regulation of social and economic life whose origins, inspirations and power often come from elsewhere. Nor can one see all these new programmes of government as unified in the interests they served or the objectives they sought. The issues around which forces were mobilised were often surprising and the groupings promoting reform were complex and heterogeneous. For example, moral and sexual scandals such as those over masturbation in the eighteenth and nineteenth centuries or over the breakdown of marriage in the cities in the mid-nineteenth century operated as important relays through which the wishes of individuals could become linked up with the concerns of population regulation. The campaign against masturbation constituted parents as responsible for the supervision and government of the petty habits of children in the names of their own future health.[24] In the campaign for marriage, the legal relation was to promote emotional and economic investment by both men and women into the home, cathecting domesticity at the expense of street life, public bawdiness and vice.[25] But these campaigns were not organised or orchestrated by the state nor by groups seeking to impose the interests of one class or gender upon another. The anti-masturbation campaign was medically inspired and directed primarily towards the bourgeois family concerned about its own lineage. The campaigns to get the urban poor to marry, to reform domestic architecture and to promote domestic hygiene were waged by bourgeois women who sought to extend the benefits of domesticity to their working class sisters and to further their interests by increasing their powers *vis-à-vis* their menfolk.

Women have not been passive victims or duped collaborators in the family reforms of the last century. They have frequently been active campaigners for such reforms, arguing for them from explicitly radical and feminist positions, and conceiving them as in their political interests, in the interests of their sex, or those of children, or vital for the pursuit of more general moral or social objectives. Increasingly over this century, campaigns for family reform have been initiated by professionals and experts, backing their proposals with a claim to authority based in science. Indeed, many of the current campaigns to increase the autonomy of the family have actually reversed this relation between family members and expertise: family members have organised reforming campaigns, and have called upon expertise to back their criticisms and proposals.

71

Of course, it is still possible to 'interpret' these campaigns, to reveal underlying class, gender or occupational interests. But it is difficult to see what intelligibility is conferred by such *ex post facto* 'explanations' upon the issues, forces, alliances and methods involved. To seek to explain these events *in terms of* interests – as if these interests pre-existed the events and determined their course and pattern – is to miss the point. What is involved is the emergence of new ways of constituting one's own and others' interests, and new mobilisations of forces around them.

3. Power and Control

Critical legal scholars conceptualise the new networks of power which link up the private family and personal life with authoritative judgment as extension of the social control apparatus of the state disguised by the ideology of the family as a realm of privacy. For example, recent moves to informalism in the resolution of family disputes are often seen as actually extending the monitoring and controlling of family relations. This is supported by the argument that:

> ... informal justice increases state power. Informal institutions allow state control to escape the walls of those highly visible centers of coercion ... and permeate society .... But it is possible – and essential – to penetrate the comforting facade of informalism and reveal its political meaning.[26]

The object of critique, then, is to penetrate the facade of privacy and free choice, to reveal the hidden mechanisms of control and to expose the interests served.

But, as I have already argued, there is little empirical evidence for such linkages between strategies of the state, interests in control and the establishment and operation of regulatory systems.[27] Further, social control is a somewhat meagre explanatory device. It 'explains' only at the cost of unifying a vast range of mechanisms, techniques and objectives. It must 'explain away' not only the varied ethical, political and technical motives of social reformers, but also the subjective commitments of the individuals involved to the values and practices which 'control' them.[28]

It is often suggested that women's apparent investment in family matters is actually forcibly imposed upon them.[29] Women are forced into the private domain by the inequities of the structure of the labour market, the wage system and other institutions from education to child care; domesticity and motherhood are portrayed as the sites of female satisfaction, and women's rejection of this role is portrayed as the origins of all sorts of personal and social ills from juvenile delinquency to unemployment. But we can contest the constraints upon choice in domestic arrangements, the lack of child care facilities, the social representations of women and so forth without reducing personal commitments to domestic life, or to the pleasures and pains of caring and intimacy, to a 'coercion of privacy'.

It is misleading to analyse social representations of motherhood, fatherhood, family life and so forth as if they distort experience or impose false consciousness; they are crucial aspects of the processes by which individuals constitute their selves and their lives, and come to establish certain 'personal' aspirations and evaluations. Of course, the construction of subjective values and investments was the aim of many familialising projects of the nineteenth and twentieth centuries. It was an explicit rationale in the moralising philanthropy of the nineteenth century, and in the arguments for universal education. It was also evident in the concern for the health and welfare of children in the early twentieth century. This certainly sought to utilise 'the family' and the relations within it as a kind of social or socialising machine in order to fulfil various objectives: military, industrial and moral. But this was to be done not through the coercive enforcement of control under threat of sanction, but through the construction of mothers who would want their homes and children to be governed according to hygienic norms. The promotion of hygiene and welfare could only be successful to the extent that it managed to solicit the active engagement of individuals in the promotion of their own bodily efficiency. Perhaps the final instalment in the construction of a subjectivity of citizenship comes only with the Second World War and its aftermath, in which films, television and propaganda interpellated those of all ages, sexes and classes as engaged in a common struggle in defence of their country, in which each had their value and each their part.

If the family came to serve social objectives, it was not in spite of the wishes of women and men, but because it came to work as a private, voluntary and responsible agency for the rearing and moralising of children and promoting their physical and mental welfare. Domestic, conjugal and parental conduct is increasingly regulated not by obedience compelled by threat of sanction but through the activation of individual guilt, personal anxiety and private disappointment. Husbands and wives, mothers and fathers themselves regulate their feelings, desires, wishes and emotions and think themselves through the potent images of parenthood, sexual pleasure and quality of life. In the necessary gap between expectation and realisation, between desires and satisfaction, anxiety and disappointment fuel the search for expert assistance. It is this pleasure/anxiety relation that drives the government of personal life; it is this which is both installed by the tutelage of expertise and which provides it with its voluntary relation to its subjects. These kinds of mechanisms, not those of social control, domination and subordination, link up the private family with social, economic and political objectives through the maximisation of consumption, the promotion of subjectivities and the construction of social solidarity through the rituals of personal life.

Indeed, the contemporary family is not the subject of perpetual scrutiny or of totalitarian policing. The repetitive 'scandals' of abused children reveal how diverse and unco-ordinated are the agencies which surround even the 'problem' family, how varied are their values and techniques, how ineffective is their scrutiny. More generally, the variety of expert discourses, the range of sources of advice, the competitiveness of pressure groups, lawyers, psychologists, psychiatrists and other professionals, the proliferation of advice on all aspects of personal relations means that pluralism is more than a myth. What unifies the family machine, as it were, is not the solutions posed to the problem of living healthy, well adjusted and fulfilled life, raising happy children and forming satisfying relationships – it is the terrain established by the problem itself.

CONCLUSION

Critical analysis of family law must relocate legal regulation within the complex network of powers which link up domestic, sexual and parental relations with social, economic and political objectives. Laws and statutory duties, statuses and obligations are very important here, but are neither primary nor constitutive. Certainly coercive regulation of familial relations needs to be understood as just one modality amongst many differentiated modes by which privacy is scrutinised, judged and normalised: we need to analyse its place without regarding it as paradigmatic or determinant. Legal relations and legal sanctions are bound up in different ways in the varied regulatory apparatuses by which social life has become familialised, but an analysis of family policies cannot privilege family law.

In particular we need to appreciate the forms of power flowing from claims to knowledge concerning family life, child rearing, sexual pleasure, health and hygiene, happiness and contentment. The power of expertise installs a new type of relation between authority and its subjects. Expertise is a form of authority bound up with the development of new regulatory techniques. It certainly cannot be compartmentalised according to the public/private opposition but nor can it be evaluated in terms of *state* regulation, social *control* or *male* power. The term 'tutelary' captures the nature of this relationship rather well, with its implications of dependence, subservience, guardianship and instruction.[30]

Characterisations of the family as a site of female subordination, however accurate, fail to capture the complexity of familial powers, of the duties, obligations, pains and pleasures which have been constituted through the familialisation of the subjectivities of both women and men. The programmes for the government of the conduct of families, parents and children, husbands, wives and sexual partners over the last hundred years have actually constituted new forms of social subject committed to a project of subjective fulfillment in which familialism has a central role. This is not to deny the extent to which many aspects of familial relations disadvantage women, or the failure of legislation and enforcement to rectify this disadvantage. But feminist critiques and proposals will be of limited value unless they can provide a positive analysis of the new types of power and authority which have come into existence over the last century and the ways in which they operate. In analysing these forms of subjectification from the perspective of power we need to free ourselves from the belief that this entails only the submission of self to others and allow the possibility that it also involves the way in which we – modern women and men – have become tied to a project of our own identities, a project which binds us to others at the same moment as it binds us to ourselves.

More generally, I have suggested that social analysis needs to break from the techniques of critique which have underpinned its explanatory strategies for so long. Critique has certain advantages for radicals: for it appears simultaneously to explain, to judge and to proffer an alternative. Breaking with critique makes visible a complex of practices and powers that do not lend themselves to global analysis and evaluation. Hence they do not suggest the task of constructing a general theory of power or a programmatic politics of social transformation. Rather, they suggest a more modest task that, starting from definite problems or concerns would seek to uncover the conditions and assumptions which have made them possible and the relations of advantage and disadvantage they entail. Such investigations pose us questions of judgment which cannot be answered by political slogans but require ethical choices that are both difficult and compromising.

NOTES AND REFERENCES

1   For some of this literature see M. Stacey, "The Division of Labour Revisited" in *Development and Diversity: British Sociology 1950-1980* (1981; eds. P. Abrams *et al.*); M. Stacey and M. Price, *Women, Power and Politics* (1981); E. Gamarnikow *et al.* (eds.), *The Public and the Private* (1983). Much of the recent debate refers back to M. Rosaldo, "Women, Culture and Society" in *Women, Culture and Society* (1974; eds. M. Rosaldo and L. Lamphere).

2   F. Olsen, "The Family and the Market: a Study of Ideology and Legal Reform" (1983) 96 *Harvard Law Rev.* p. 1497; K. O'Donovan, *Sexual Divisions in Law* (1985); M. Freeman, "Towards a Critical Theory of Family Law" (1985) 38 *Current Legal Problems* p. 153; A. Bottomley, "Resolving Family Disputes: A Critical View" in *State, Law and the Family* (1984; ed. M. Freeman).

3   Freeman, *op. cit.*, n. 2.

4   *Id.*

5   M. Horwitz, "The History of the Public/Private Distinction" (1982) 130 *University of Pennsylvania Law Rev.* p. 1423.

6   D. Kennedy, "The Stages of the Decline of the Public/Private Distinction" (1982) 130 *University of Pennsylvania Law Rev.* p. 1349.

7   Cf. K. Klare, "The Public/Private Distinction in Labour Law" (1982) 130 *University of Pennsylvania Law Rev.* p. 1349.

8   *Op. cit.*

9   *Id.*, p. 1578.

10   *Supra*, n. 1.

11   See O'Donovan, *op. cit.*, p. 11 and Freeman, *op. cit.*, p. 169.

12   *Supra*, n. 2.

13   E.g., L. Parkinson, "Conciliation: a new approach to family conflict resolution" (1983) 13 *Brit. J. Social Work* p. 19; M. King, "Child Protection and the Search for Justice for Parents and Families" in Freeman, ed., *op. cit.*, n. 2, p. 139.

14   E.g., Bottomley, *op. cit.*, n. 2, pp. 293-300 and Freeman, *op. cit.*, n. 2, pp. 163-65. Cf. R. Abel (ed.), *The Politics of Informal Justice* (1982) 2 Vols.

15   J. Goldstein, A. Freud and A. Solnit, *Beyond the Best Interests of the Child* (1983).

16   Freeman, *op. cit.*, n. 2, p. 171.

17   See the paper by Hirst and Jones in this volume.

[18] This is the task Olsen sets herself, wrenching the language of reforming strategies from their context and reinterpreting them in terms of the family/market opposition. What is gained in elegance is lost in intelligibility as to what was at stake in these debates. See Olsen, *op. cit.*, n. 2.

[19] For a thought-provoking historical study of power relations with a productive conceptual basis see M. Mann, *The Sources of Social Power* (1986) Vol. 1.

[20] See J. Donzelot, *The Policing of Families* (1979); M. Foucault, *History of Sexuality* (1978) Vol. 1; D. Riley, *War in the Nursery* (1983); N. Rose, *The Psychological Complex* (1985); P. Miller and N. Rose (eds.), *The Power of Psychiatry* (1986) especially chap. 2; J. Minson, *Genealogies of Morals* (1985); D. Garland, *Punishment and Welfare* (1985).

[21] *Op. cit.*, n. 2, p. 57. See also Freeman, *op. cit.*, and, in a stronger form, C. MacKinnon, "Feminism, Marxism, Method and the State: Towards Feminist Jurisprudence" (1983) 8 *Signs* p. 635.

[22] Minson, *op. cit.*, n. 20 has a good discussion drawing on J. Strakosch, *State Absolutism and the Rule of Law* (1967).

[23] *Op. cit.*, n. 20.

[24] See Foucault, *op. cit.*, n. 20 and Donzelot, *op. cit.*, n. 20, and the discussion in Minson, *op. cit.*, chap. 8.

[25] *Id.*; see also Rose, *op. cit.*, n. 20, chap. 6.

[26] Abel, *op. cit.*, n. 14, p. 6. Cf. Bottomley, *op. cit.*, n. 2, p. 300; O'Donovan, *op. cit.*, n. 2, p. 195; Freeman, *op. cit.*, n. 2, pp. 163 and 173.

[27] See also R. Gordon, "Critical Legal Histories" (1984) 36 *Stanford Law Rev.* p. 57 and D. Sugarman's introduction to *Law, Economy and Society* (1984; eds. G. Rubin and D. Sugarman).

[28] Even those sociologists most committed to explanations in terms of social control now have doubts about the utility of the concept; see, for example, A. Scull and S. Cohen (eds.), *Social Control and the State* (1982). But they end up offering revamped versions of social control as a solution to its own failure: see the criticisms in Miller and Rose, *op. cit.*, n. 20.

[29] Freeman, *op. cit.*, n. 2; C. Smart, *The Ties That Bind* (1984); T. Dahl and A. Snare, "The Coercion of Privacy" in *Women, Sex and Social Control* (1978; ed. C. Smart); S. Hall, "Reformism and the Legalisation of Consent" in *Permissiveness and Control* (1979; ed. National Deviancy Conference).

[30] Cf. Donzelot, *op. cit.*, n. 20.

Power, Property and the Law of Trusts:
A Partial Agenda for Critical Legal Scholarship

ROGER COTTERRELL*

Much uncertainty still surrounds the enterprise of critical legal studies. What does it mean to undertake 'critical' study of any particular area of legal doctrine or institutions? This paper will sketch out elements of a conception of critical legal scholarship as an enterprise and then apply some of its methods and precepts to a preliminary and tentative 'critical' exploration of the legal conception of the trust in English law. My aim is to suggest parts of an appropriate agenda for critical study of English property law and, within it, especially trust law.

It should be said immediately that the conception of critical legal scholarship adhered to in this paper is substantially different from – and in many respects opposed to – that which has been developed in the important recent American Critical Legal Studies Movement.[1] The view taken in this paper is that critical legal scholarship in the U.S.A. has crucial inadequacies which make it an inappropriate model for a form of legal scholarship now widely sought; one with the intellectual strength to endure and build progressively a more adequate understanding of law while, at the same time, radically challenging existing forms of legal study.

There are three major reasons for this. First, critical legal scholarship in the U.S.A. is too narrow in its vision of appropriate scholarship in the field of law. It puts great emphasis on the need for radical analysis of legal doctrine and of the processes of its professional interpretation. But in general it does not give enough serious attention to the equal need for systematic analysis of the social, economic and political context within which legal doctrine is developed, interpreted, invoked and applied. It ignores or dismisses the claim that legal doctrine receives its practical meaning and significance only from that wider context and that, therefore, it is self-defeating to engage in critical study of doctrine without seeing this doctrine (and the use made of it) as an integral element in a larger social, political and economic environment which itself requires systematic empirical and theoretical analysis. Secondly, critical legal scholarship in the U.S.A. is theoretically inadequate because of its failure to

*Faculty of Laws, Queen Mary College, University of London, Mile End Road, London, England.

I am grateful to Alan Hunt for comments on a draft of this paper.

address seriously a number of fundamental questions about the nature of the knowledge critical scholarship seeks (the epistemological foundations of critical legal studies) and about the objectives of critical scholarship (which necessitates a theory of the nature of critique).[2] Thirdly, critical legal scholarship in the U.S.A. is inadequate because it largely ignores what is most needed as a practical pre-requisite for the development of rigorous critical scholarship in law. What is needed is an escape from the 'intellectual ghetto' of the law school in which legal knowledge typically exists in a world substantially isolated from wider currents of systematic knowledge associated with other intellectual disciplines (especially the social sciences and philosophy). The understanding of law today requires that legal knowledge be continually confronted with, challenged by and eventually integrated with forms of knowledge developed in 'non-legal disciplines'. Critical legal scholarship in the U.S.A. remains, however, above all a law school movement; it offers the latest in an historical succession of movements of critique of law 'from within'; that is, critique which occurs almost entirely within the professional world of law. The preoccupation of critical legal studies in the U.S.A. with the 'internal' critique of doctrine (of legal doctrine's shifts and failures of logic, casuistry and U-turns) stresses only a part (a small part) of what is needed to reorient legal scholarship in genuinely radical directions. Having found what they have taken to be 'social science' wanting, critical legal scholars in the U.S.A. have fled back to the security of the law school and refined their lawyers' techniques of doctrinal dissection. There is no reason to hope, however, that use of these techniques to subvert some lawyers' assumptions about doctrine can substitute for the complex task of systematic empirical study of law as a social phenomenon.

CRITIQUE OF LAW

This paper begins, then, from 'first principles' and considers that many basic questions about the nature of critical legal scholarship remain to be addressed. What is the guiding motivation behind critique of law? Above all it is explicitly to refuse to accept legal doctrine on its own terms; that is, to refuse to accept it in the terms in which it justifies itself (as the unfolding of legal logic; as the self-evident embodiment of rationality; as the purely technical instrument of policies originating from 'non-legal' (political) sources). Critique of law asks of legal doctrine in a radical questioning: why does this doctrine exist? What is it for? Why has it taken its particular form and content? All these questions have, and in critical analysis must receive, answers which make sense not just as extrapolations from other elements of doctrine: that is, not just in terms of a legal 'logic' of the form rule X combined with rule Y allows us to deduce rule Z; or rule A confronted by rule B and seen in the light of principle P 'rationally' results in rule C; or rule E confronted by new fact situation F leads 'logically' (or plausibly) to rule G. None of these kinds of reasoning is adequate for critical analysis of law. All such reasoning involves assumptions of various kinds which are often glossed over or ignored in traditional legal analysis.[3]

78

Critical analysis can accept no such assumptions but must bring them to light for examination. It follows that adequate critical explanations of legal doctrine can never be explanations in terms of other legal doctrine. Legal doctrine is to be seen not as a self-justifying edifice but as a social construct. The critical logic of legal doctrine is a logic in terms of social and political causes and effects of doctrinal developments. The form and content of legal doctrine is to be explained in terms of the empirical conditions in which law as doctrine and legal institutions exist in society. Thus *critique of law is in its fundamentals a sociological analysis of law*: the patient quest to explain its doctrinal and institutional characteristics as social phenomena having empirically identifiable social causes and social effects.

It is impossible here to explore properly the ramifications and problems of such a project, although some further comments must be made. First, no suggestion is being made here that legal doctrine and its characteristics can in some way be 'read off' from a more general study of economic or political developments. Law is one of the major elements by which social life is constituted (as critical legal scholars in the U.S.A. have properly stressed). It cannot be seen as a reflection or derivation of other social phenomena. As a social phenomenon itself, however, it is to be understood as obtaining all its specific characteristics from its place within a broader social environment.

Secondly, the kind of analysis of this broader social environment which is necessary to advance the project of critical legal scholarship is different from that which has so far characterised much 'law and society' research. Empirically oriented socio-legal studies have been of great value in highlighting previously misunderstood or unrecognised aspects of law as a social phenomenon. However, these studies have often not escaped (but rather reinforced) certain features of traditional legal study which critical study needs to challenge.[4] Among these are: (i) *empiricism* (in this context, the assumption that 'the facts speak for themselves' and need little or no theoretical interpretation); (ii) *positivism* (in this context, the assumption that law is an objectively identifiable social fact, a datum whose fundamental nature is basically understood or, at least, not capable of being analysed except through unscientific, untestable, unprovable speculation); and (iii) *pragmatism* (in this context, the assumption that the test of success in research or scholarship is the production of information or ideas with demonstrable immediate practical significance).

Critical legal scholarship needs to challenge positivism, in the sense in which the term is used above, because this scholarship cannot take for granted the conceptions of law which are presupposed in legal doctrine itself and in legal practice. A radical critique of law must put all taken-for-granted assumptions about the nature of law in issue. This requires an escape from the tyranny of the need to be 'immediately useful' because what is commonsensically understood to be 'useful' or 'practical' is also given by assumptions which require critical examination. These are assumptions about the nature and functions of law, about the social context in which law exists and which it is held to regulate and influence, and about the way legal doctrine is developed and legal institutions operate. When these assumptions are challenged what is useful or practical may be decided by quite different criteria. Hence it is necessary to reject pragmatism in the sense referred to above. Finally, and most fundamentally, in order for the project of critique to achieve the rigour which is absent from 'commonsense' argument relying on wholly unexamined assumptions it must replace empiricism with theoretical analysis. Facts never speak for themselves. Meaning is always imposed on them. Theory is necessary to examine the coherence of the meanings we attach to what we observe about law and the context in which it exists. Thus, empirical study of law in its broader social context depends upon and should contribute to social theory – theory which seeks to explain systematically and in the broadest perspective the structure of societies and the empirical conditions of social order and stability and of social change.

It might be wise to be satisfied with a general conception of critique expressed only in these sketchy terms. However, many legal analysts of radical or critical persuasion seek more than this today. They demand a consistent and rigorous *moral* and *political* critique of law; a critique which not only opens our eyes to understand why and with what consequences law takes the form it does but also tells us what is wrong with it (and why). Such a critique aims to provide a *systematic vocabulary of censure* to apply to legal doctrine and institutions. To derive such a vocabulary is to go beyond sociological interpretation and demystification of law. Its basis is in a *moral vision* – a conception of the 'good' which gives criteria of moral evaluation – rather than in sociological theory. Sociological (or social) theory must progress by tentative, sceptical, systematic analysis of empirical experience. But what can provide the intellectual foundation of a moral vision? More fundamentally, what can adjudicate between competing opposed moral visions? Philosophy has not yet found an unassailable intellectual foundation for the assertion of moral values.

It is equally true that the competing perspectives of different kinds of social theory are far from any reconciliation or harmonisation. However, the sociological study of law – grounded in a faith in systematic and sceptical empirical inquiry – must presuppose as a working hypothesis the eventual possibility of a rational unity of social theory and seek as its ultimate aim to promote that unity. The systematic empirical analysis and interpretation of historical experience in a continually broadening perspective is its means of moving a little way towards realising this aim even though we may doubt it will ever be fully realised.

What lodestar, however, beyond a faith in one's own personal values, can be found to guide moral critique? If there is a way of finding an answer to this dilemma it is perhaps most likely to be by developing 'Critical Theory' - the unfinished original project of the Frankfurt School. For the moment, complex and problematic as the Frankfurt School project is, certain strands only can be grasped as elements of a moral vision to guide critique of law. They are inadequate and because of their inadequacy the *sociological* critique of doctrine and institutions appears to this writer as having an overriding priority in current critical work. Sociological critique is, indeed, a prerequisite of effective moral critique – although no substitute for it. Sociological analysis is indispensable to explain the social setting in which moral dilemmas present themselves and so to show the range of practical choices and the social costs and consequences of moral and political decisions.

Critical theory has given little beyond the vaguest outlines of a foundation of moral critique. Such as they are, these outlines are nonetheless of great importance.[5] Two pervasive themes can perhaps be drawn from them: (i) the duality of human subject and social object (the isolated individual confronted by 'society' or social institutions in relation to which she or he seems powerless and uncommitted) and the alienation and oppression which result from this duality; and (ii) the responsibility of the critical scholar to evaluate all action and institutions in terms of the need to confront and undermine this duality. Thus critique is aimed at helping to free the subject as an autonomous actor in the social world, to humanise a dehumanised society; and, correspondingly, to explain the necessarily social, collective dimension of all individual lives, the responsibility of the individual to a wider collectivity beyond self and family, beyond locality and nation, beyond race and class, and perhaps even beyond humanity to other aspects of nature. If we seek to develop rigorously critical legal scholarship as a political and moral critique, as well as a sociological critique founded in and contributing to social theory, we have no choice but to swim in these deep waters. But sociological critique must be the starting point and is the essential foundation of all else.

CRITIQUE OF THE TRUST CONCEPT

A useful strategy in developing a critical analysis of any area of doctrine is to start from its most central and fundamental ideas and to ask what social (as contrasted with professional legal) significance they may have, and what resonance such ideas may have beyond the world of professional legal practice in the consciousness of ordinary citizens. Legal doctrine has obviously *instrumental* aspects – it guarantees and structures the exercise of power, facilitates governmental and private administration, allows for reliable calculation and accounting in economic and other transactions by citizens, state agencies and public and private institutions of all kinds, and provides a framework for the resolution or containment of disputes and the channelling of expectations to avoid conflict. It only does these things, however, when it lives in the consciousness of those who are supposed to be affected by it or who are entrusted with its application. How significant doctrine is depends on how it is interpreted and applied (if at all) in a wide variety of circumstances of which traditional legal scholarship often takes little or no account.

Equally, however, legal doctrine contains concepts and principles which relate in direct or indirect ways to wider currents of thought, to ideas which are part of the everyday climate of thought of citizens. The concept of 'freedom of contract' is not just reflected in legal doctrine but is part of the fabric of thought of a free enterprise society – an element of *ideology* in such a

81

society. Legal doctrine thus reflects and contributes to wider currents of ideology. Critical legal scholarship needs to show how and with what consequences it does this. In showing this, critical scholarship portrays doctrine as a social phenomenon inseparable from the wider social context in which it exists, as an aspect of society.

The legal concept of the trust is a particularly interesting area of legal doctrine to examine in this way. A thoroughly familiar, commonplace idea of Anglo-American legal thought, it still remains alien to other legal traditions lacking the distinctive relationship of law and equity established in English legal history. Behind the concept of the trust, however, stands an even more fundamental one of great and universally recognised ideological significance – the concept of property. In the remainder of this paper I want to suggest a way of looking at the concept of the trust which makes it possible to relate clearly (i) the ideological significance of the concept of property, and (ii) the legal doctrine which centres on the notion of the trust in English law.

1. Property

Legal doctrine is ideologically important not only for what it expresses but also for its 'silences'; for the apparent fact that it *avoids* explicit recognition of certain features of social life which are familiar from experience. Through the use of the concept of property, elaborated in legal doctrine, it becomes possible to banish almost entirely from the discourse of private law recognition of one of the most dominant features of life in a society of material inequalities – that of *private power*. How is this possible? It is fundamental to modern western legal doctrine and legal ideology that human beings appear as equal subjects before the law.[6] They relate to each other typically on the basis of free agreement between legal equals, through contract. Outside the realm of law and legal ideology we experience the fact that individuals (and families, groups, organisations, social classes, etc.) are *not* equal, but grossly unequal in power and capacities. Yet the concept of property makes it possible for the law to accommodate and guarantee these inequalities while maintaining the ideology of equality. This is because the idea of property treats those attributes which make human beings grossly unequal as separate from them and conceptualised as 'things' which they own. Legal subjects (*persons*) who are equal before the law are thought of as owning assets (*things*) which can be conceptualised as distinct from them. Subjects are equal (in legal doctrine and ideology) but the distribution of assets is not. Nevertheless, however much more one person may own than another, the general freedom of transactions and the equal security of property which the law affords to all subjects makes it possible for legal ideology to affirm that *the equality of legal subjects is in no way compromised by inequalities in the nature and amount of assets which they are said (in legal doctrine) to own.*

Law and ideology thus turn attributes of human beings into 'things' which they own. The transition is reflected in the varying meanings of the term 'property' which can refer to (i) an attribute or characteristic of someone or something, (ii) an entitlement, or (iii) an asset owned (strictly speaking an object of property). Such a transformation of attributes into things makes private power all but invisible in legal doctrine and legal ideology. The property concept makes it possible to portray the attributes of power as separate from the holder of power. As (objects of) property those attributes seem natural – a part of the natural world – 'things'. It is this regime of things which gives some people power over others. Private law does not give this power, or even recognise it. It merely guarantees the equal right [7] of all citizens to own property and engage in lawful transactions with it. Inequalities arise from the free exercise of uniform rights which all subjects have because of their fundamental legal equality. In Nozick's "justice of entitlements"[8] grounded in the concept of property is the ideological foundation *par excellence* which justifies the inequalities of capitalist societies.[9]

Of course, (public) power is recognised in so-called public law but the ideological significance of the distinction between private and public law is to affirm the existence of a private sphere (civil society) distinct from the state and unaffected by the public law which structures the state; a private sphere in which individuals deal with each other as equal subjects and in which the existence of private power is legally unrecognised. Thus in legal doctrine and ideology the concepts of property and of power become separated from each other. This is a truly remarkable ideological feat since property encapsulates precisely those attributes of human subjects (knowledge, reputation, ability to control human and material resources, etc.) which give them power over others, and property is the legal form which embodies most directly – and makes possible the orderly and efficient exercise of – power in everyday life.

A major concern of the sociological critique of property law should be to show how these ideological mechanisms work in the law; how the concept of property is manipulated in legal doctrine. Nevertheless, property law is not just a matter of ideology. Law has, above all, technical functions. It structures the distribution and use of power even when it avoids all recognition of the concept of power; and (the obverse of this) it provides the possibility of security by limiting and making predictable the exercise of power. It will be necessary to return later to this point.

2. *The Trust*

If the concept of property allows an ideological separation of the human actor from those characteristics or attributes which give such an actor power, the device of the trust can be seen as a further distancing. The trust provides a way of freeing the property owner from constraints which the ideology of property otherwise imposes on her or him through its logic.

As has been seen, the property-form (the expression of relationships in terms of the concept of property) depends as a commonsense idea on our being able to conceptualise a 'person' owning a 'thing'.[10] It is because of this conceptualisation that the separation of owner and owned is established with the consequence that the attributes of power are seen as separate from the owner and attached to the assets which are owned.

To achieve these effects the property-form requires clear identification of a person - the being who can be conceptualised as a property-owner – and of the thing owned. As Pollock made clear nearly a century ago, English law has been able to recognise as a thing capable of being owned any asset which is regarded as having value. Any benefit or attribute which can be recognised as of commercial value is a potential object of property.[11] Nevertheless, if commonsense conceptions of property rights and property relationships depend on this 'thing-owner' relationship, the stability of these rights and relationships depends on the continuing stable existence of identifiable things and identifiable owners of things. Plainly the disintegration or transformation of the thing or the death, disappearance or lack of clear identity of the thing-owner may pose threats to the continuance of these rights or relationships. It seems possible, however, that with such threats the limitations of property as an ideological framework of power begin to emerge. Power in society is often the attribute of *collectivities* or groups – families, organisations of many kinds, elites, classes, etc. Because of this there may be some inherent limitations in the property-form as an embodiment of social power because of its requirement of a clearly identifiable thing-owner. It may sometimes be difficult to conceptualise particular kinds of collectivity as thing-owners and it may even be counter-productive to try. For example, social classes (however defined) are not known to the law and ideologically it is most important that the notion of social class be rigidly and, if possible, totally excluded – law's conception of capitalist society is essentially that of a society of equal citizens. Again, the conception of the 'family' is usually too imprecise for legal use, though law has to recognise family relationships in numerous ways. If an attempt were made in modern law to conceptualise the family as a thing-owner, the legal devices for protection of family power would probably be far too rigid and, again, perhaps ideologically transparent.

Modern legal doctrine can and does, of course, deal with the problem of recognition of certain kinds of collectivities by the device of constructing a 'corporate person' alongside or around the group of 'natural' persons (human individuals) to which it relates. The device of corporate personality does, however, seem to have some enduring problems (despite its ubiquity as a framework for many aspects of the organisation of contemporary economic life). At base is the problem of the exact nature of the relationship between the 'artificial' corporate person and the human individuals associated with it, for example, as shareholders or employees of a business corporation. This is not just a technical question of legal doctrine. At least in earlier times, it has been a matter of very great ideological importance: how far could the 'reality' of the corporate body be reconciled with individualist ideology which emphasised the individual human being as the fundamental *locus* of responsibilities and rights?[12]

As Maitland suggested long ago, it was, above all, the device of the trust which made it possible for English law to recognise many forms of property ownership by collectivities without attracting some of the technical difficulties and ideological conflicts centred on aspects of the doctrinal problem of corporate personality in continental civil law systems.[13] Today, however, adopting a critical perspective on doctrine, we can see more clearly how this doctrinal device of the trust has served to extend the ideological utility of the property-form. The trust makes possible the maintenance of permanent, easily identifiable property-owners (explicitly recognised as such by law) in the form of replaceable trustees, together with an indefinite range of beneficially entitled individuals or collectivities (for example, groups of children or other issue, classes of discretionary beneficiaries, members of associations, organisations and interest groups of numerous kinds) who, having beneficial entitlements guaranteed in equity, can share in property-power but remain invisible to law as property-owners as such. The limitations which the property-form as an ideological form imposes on the nature of the property-owner (that is, basically, that such an owner should be a clearly identifiable 'person' and not an indefinite collectivity) are overcome. Equally, the trust makes possible the creation of enduring objects of property ('things', clusters of value) in the form of funds which can be invested in various ways to preserve and enhance their value. In this way the trust greatly facilitates the concentration and preservation of capital – and thereby helps guarantee the power and security which the property-form embodies. The recognition of the trust fund, in many trusts, as the embodiment of *abstract value*, a 'cluster of value', rather than tangible assets (for example, land)[14] is a sophisticated recognition in legal doctrine of the ideological nature of property as an embodiment of power. Ultimately what is important is not the particular assets which are owned at any given time but the abstract value of what is owned which determines the degree of power of the property-holder. Only in certain (usually family) trusts, in which what is being provided for beneficiaries is security of use of real or personal property or the preservation of specific assets rather than power as such, is the asset held in trust important in itself. In other cases all that is fundamentally important is the maintenance of the value which presently held trust assets represent.

The extension of the property-form which the trust allows can be illustrated as in Figure 2. What is made possible is an extension of both elements in the commonsense (ideological) 'thing-ownership' property relationship (Figure 1); that is, an extension of the nature and range of those who own and also of what can be owned.

FIGURE 1 'Commonsense' (ideological) conception of ownership

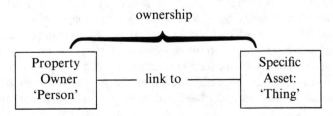

FIGURE 2 Conceptualisation of (ideological) 'thing-ownership' property
relations typically made possible by trust

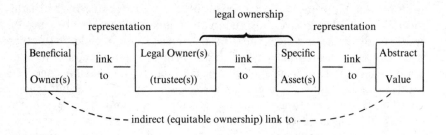

The major ideological significance of this structure is the far greater flexibility in manipulation of property-power which is made possible by it, and a further 'disguising' in ideological forms of the nature of that power. An illustration of that disguising can easily be given. The trust form tends to disguise the actual nature of the power relationship between trustees and beneficiaries. The ideology of the trust is such that the legal owner (trustee) is the person who 'looks most like' an owner since she or he is the one who (usually) can carry out most of the ordinary legal transactions possible to an owner[15] – sale, mortgage, lease, exchange, etc. The beneficiary under a trust is seen as passive. Typically the beneficiary cannot interfere in management of the trust property except by procuring the intervention of the courts (for example, in claiming breach of duty by the trustee). During the existence of the trust, control of capital typically rests with trustees. In discretionary and protective trusts, and in the exercise of powers of maintenance and advancement, the trustees may exert significant control over the situation of beneficiaries. Again, it is in some family trusts in which what is at stake is the property-security of dependents (the preservation of trust assets rather than use of the property-form as an instrument of power) that this control by trustees is often greatest.

This apparent power of trustees and passivity of beneficiaries is, however, misleading. It is the beneficiaries – often collectivities – unrecognised directly as legal owners who actually have access to the property-power embodied in the trust. This is ultimately admitted in, for example, the very strict rules governing trustees' duties with regard to investment, profit-taking by trustees and conflicts of duty and interest, and in the rule in *Saunders v Vautier*,[16] which allows the trust device to be set aside if the beneficiaries so wish where all of them are identifiable persons having full legal capacity and hence easily recognisable as property owners within the orthodox commonsense conception. Yet the very fluidity of beneficial entitlements which the trust makes possible hides from view even more effectively than the property concept in its simple form the actual structure of power which private law guarantees and perfects.

86

How can this view of the ideological significance of property and trust help us to analyse trust law from a critical perspective? First, by looking at the trust in terms of its ideological significance in helping to exclude the element of power from recognition in legal doctrine we can begin to put the element of power back into our picture of law and its workings. It is, indeed, impossible to understand law's relationship to power without analysing the way in which legal ideology is often able to exclude all recognition of private power. It follows, however, that an approach such as this requires an historical perspective which, in this short essay, cannot even be sketched. Historians have shown how understandings of the nature of property have changed over time and have associated the formation of the idea of property rights as exclusive entitlements with the emergence of capitalist society. Debate still rages as to when such changes in conceptions of property became significant.[17] All that it is necessary to say here is that in sketching out some ideological dimensions of the concept of property, which have been extended through the conception of the trust, no claim is being made here that these ideological aspects are timeless. They undoubtedly became and remain important as part of a wider complex of ideological currents within capitalist societies.

It follows that the critical analysis of property and trust is in no way exhausted by following up this line of enquiry about aspects of their ideological significance in contemporary British society. Thus, as has been said earlier, law, in this area as in others, needs to be understood in terms of its obviously instrumental aspects (above all concerned with the channelling of power rather than the obscuring or disguising of it), although it seems likely that these aspects often cannot be separated from the ideological aspects touched on here. Further, a concentration on understanding property as a framework and mystification of power should not make us ignore the importance of property as *security* – as a form of protection. The reason why much discussion of property as the basis of 'liberty' is misleading is because it often makes no adequate distinction between these two dimensions of property. Generalised talk about 'liberty' usually reflects directly the ideology of property which has been discussed in this paper, seeing property as the fulfilment and exemplification of the equal freedom of all citizens – the equal right of each and every person to acquire and keep whatever is available to her or him for acquisition by lawful means. Thus property-power and property-security are undifferentiated in legal ideology. Both are seen as accidental by-products of the equal distribution of rights. But the security of access of all citizens to the basic resources of well-being might be thought to be a more secure foundation of equal freedom than is the ability of some to exercise unlimited property-power over others. A major part of the project of critical study of property law (and of trust law as a part of it) must surely be the exploration of the relationship between property as power and property as security. The reason for concentration on the relationship between property and the exercise of power in this paper is that it seems reasonable to claim that in capitalist society this relationship has been most striking in its legal and social consequences.[18]

A second reason for looking at the trust concept in terms of its ideological significance is that this emphasises that what appears as a highly technical and esoteric part of property law doctrine is actually a conception of wide influence in popular consciousness. The idea of fiduciary obligation of the trustee harnesses to legal doctrine a moral conception of great social significance [19] and induces us to see the trust beneficiary not as the possessor of property-power but as a person meriting protection; a person to whom moral as well as legal obligations are owed. The trust-form, concentrating and guaranteeing property-power, not only fails to impose moral obligations on the powerful, but actually encourages us to think of *moral obligations owed to them* because of their beneficial entitlements.

The best (and ultimately the essential) reason for viewing the trust in terms of its ideological significance is that such a view helps us to understand particular problems of legal doctrine. Compare, for example, the recognition of public (charitable) purpose trusts in legal doctrine and the great and remarkable difficulty in recognising private purpose trusts as legally valid. Private purpose trusts run into difficulties since by their nature they have no human beneficiaries. Although the problem is said to lie in the lack of means of enforcement of such trusts,[20] some judges have doubted that this is a serious problem since indirect means of judicial control often exist.[21] From the standpoint adopted in this paper, however, the real difficulty is that property necessarily represents in ideological form the attributes of power of someone or some collectivity. Ultimately the ideological form must be consistent with what it represents. Thus the law cannot comprehend property without any beneficial owner. Assets cease to be property if they lack an owner. In cases in English law where no property-owning subject can be found the Crown typically takes the asset as *bona vacantia*.[22] The 'reality' which grounds the ideology 'rebels', so to speak, at the idea of 'disembodied', unowned property. In private purpose trusts there are, of course, legal owners (the trustees) but the ideological form of property does not play here the role it plays in all other areas of property law – that of expressing, in relation to 'things' (property objects), the attributes or characteristics of individuals or collectivities which give them power or security. Perhaps it is thus unsurprising that courts have tended to see private purpose trusts in general as fulfilling no purpose deserving of the protection of law.

With public (charitable) purpose trusts the situation is wholly different and, from the perspective of this paper, even more interesting. Property put into a charitable trust is not 'disembodied' property. Not only is it technically owned by charity trustees but its protection is in various aspects the responsibility of public officials (the Attorney General, the Charity Commissioners). The crucial factor here is that property settled on charitable trust is given for the 'public benefit'. Its ultimate beneficial owner is 'the public' or, we might say, 'society'. Charitable trusts provide a rare, perhaps unique, instance of the construction of society as a collective subject – a property owner – within private law. Small wonder that property once dedicated to charity remains perpetually so dedicated. Society as beneficial owner can never die. There are profound and far reaching ideological dimensions of the law which cannot be explored further in the space available here. But one important reason why charity is such an attractive notion in a framework of individualist thought characteristic of capitalist society is because social welfare can be reduced by means of this notion to no more than the working out of private transactions, and 'society', as beneficiary under a charitable trust, appears as no more important than any individual beneficiary of a private trust arrangement.

By illuminating and exploring sociological aspects of legal doctrine and legal ideology such as these, critical legal scholarship can dig deep beneath the bland surface of traditional forms of legal enquiry. The concern of this paper has been merely to illustrate aspects of an approach to and agenda for critical legal scholarship in one important area of English legal doctrine.

NOTES AND REFERENCES

[1] See generally, for example, Unger, "The Critical Legal Studies Movement" (1983) 96 *Harvard Law Rev.* p. 563; special issue on critical legal studies (1984) 36 *Stanford Law Rev.* Nos. 1 and 2; Hunt, "The Theory of Critical Legal Studies" (1986) 6 *Oxford J. Legal Studies* p. 1.

[2] These matters of theoretical inadequacy are discussed in Cotterrell, "Critique and Law: The Problematic Legacy of the Frankfurt School" (1986) 3 *Tidskrift foer Raettssociologi* No. 2, p. 1. See also on other aspects of theoretical difficulties of critical legal studies, Hunt, *op. cit.*

[3] For convenience I use the term 'traditional' in contrast to 'critical' following Horkheimer's terminology in contrasting traditional and critical theory. Cf. M. Horkheimer, "Traditional and Critical Theory" in *Critical Sociology* (1976; ed. P. Connerton).

[4] Perhaps this is especially true of 'law and society' research in the U.S.A. for complex reasons connected with the nature of social science traditions there. See Cotterrell, "Law and Sociology: Notes on the Constitution and Confrontations of Disciplines" (1986) 13 *J. Law and Society* p. 9, at pp. 20-29. Given this situation, America critical legal scholars' hostility to or distancing from 'law and society' research seems understandable.

[5] Their importance for critical legal scholarship is discussed in Cotterrell, *op. cit.*, n. 2.

[6] The best discussion of the sociological significance of this is in E. B. Pashukanis, *Law and Marxism: A General Theory* (1978).

[7] Of course in contemporary English law this is far from perfect legal equality. Special statuses, for example of children, mental patients and several other categories of person are important, but none of this upsets the fundamental general legal principle of equality of subjects.

[8] R. Nozick, *Anarchy, State and Utopia* (1974) pp. 150ff.

[9] It must be stressed that, no claim is being made here that the concept of property in all times and all societies is necessarily to be understood as a general ideological foundation and embodiment of power. In capitalist societies it has especially assumed this character because of the emphasis in such societies on equal rights of all legal subjects to acquire and exploit property-assets with little or no restriction.

[10] Sophisticated legal analysis recognises, of course, that property rights can entail legal relationships only between persons and not between persons and things. Commonsense property conceptions seem to assert the thing-ownership basis of property, however. See B. A. Ackerman, *Private Property and the Constitution* (1977). This seems to be an example of the way legal doctrine and its professional interpretation can and do diverge from some aspects or implications of the broader ideological conceptions (reflected in 'commonsense' thought) which they nevertheless serve to support and express. Legal doctrine and legal ideology are thus intimately related but not the same.

11   F. Pollock, "What is a Thing?" (1894) 10 *Law Quarterly Rev.* p. 318.

12   R. Cotterrell, *The Sociology of Law: An Introduction* (1984) pp. 130-34.

13   F. W. Maitland, "Introduction" in O. v. Gierke, *Political Theories of the Middle Age* (1900); Maitland, "Trust and Corporation" in his *Selected Essays* (1904; eds. H. D. Hazeltine, G. Lapsley and P. H. Winfield).

14   For aspects of the history of this gradual recognition see M. R. Chesterman, "Family Settlements on Trust: Landowners and the Rising Bourgeoisie" in *Law, Economy and Society 1750-1914: Essays in the History of English Law* (1984; eds. G. R. Rubin and D. Sugarman).

15   Cf. G. W. Paton, *Textbook of Jurisprudence* (4th ed. 1972) pp. 517-18.

16   (1841) 4 Beav. 115; affirmed Cr. & Ph. 240.

17   See, for example, D. Sugarman and G. R. Rubin, "Introduction" in *Law, Economy and Society, op. cit.*, n. 14, pp. 23-42.

18   R. Cotterrell, "The Law of Property and Legal Theory" in *Legal Theory and Common Law* (1986; ed. W. Twining).

19   For an examination of the sociological significance of the idea of trust which suggests quite different aspects from those indicated here see N. Luhmann, *Trust and Power* (1979) Part 1.

20   *Morice v Bishop of Durham* (1804) 9 Ves. Jr. 399.

21   See, for example, *Pettingall v Pettingall* (1842) 11 L. J. Ch. 176 and *Re Thompson* [1934] Ch. 342 (indirect enforcement envisaged through residuary legatees' entitlement to claim property in absence of fulfilment of trust); *Re Dean* (1889) 41 Ch. D. 552 (unenforceability not a reason for invalidity). In *Re Astor's Settlement Trusts* [1952] Ch. 534 it was emphasised that, apart from certain "anomalous" cases, those private purpose trusts which the courts had upheld were ones in which a residuary legatee was available to "indirectly enforce". But the untenability of the argument about indirect enforcement is shown in *Re Endacott* [1960] Ch. 232 where it was accepted (at p. 246 by Lord Evershed M.R.) that there would be no difference between "enforcement" by residuary legatees and by next-of-kin. If so, virtually all private purpose trusts are "indirectly enforceable" since there will be next-of-kin with an interest in the property on failure of the purpose trust. Thus in *Re Endacott* the lack of human beneficiaries is regarded as, in itself, a sufficient ground of invalidity (irrespective of questions about enforcement) and the court relies also on the narrower ground of insufficient certainty of the purpose of the trust.

22   See, for example, *Cunnack v Edwards* [1896] 2 Ch. 679.

The Decline of Privacy in Private Law

HUGH COLLINS*

Privacy is primarily a political value. It addresses not the morality of behaviour but its suitability for state control. A society may accept the moral principle that promises ought to be kept, but out of respect for the value of privacy object to the application of legal sanctions for breach of every promise. The principle of privacy delineates a realm of conduct which the state cannot justifiably regulate. This principle plays a central role in liberal political theory, since it colours many liberals' conceptions of personal freedom.

Isiah Berlin identifies this link in his description of the predominant conception of liberty in liberal philosophy:

> . . . there ought to exist a certain minimum area of personal freedom which must on no account be violated; for if it is overstepped, the individual will find himself in an area too narrow for even that minimum development of his natural faculties which alone makes it possible to pursue, and even to conceive, the various ends which men hold good or right or sacred. It follows that a frontier must be drawn between the area of private life and that of public authority.[1]

Thus privacy, in the sense of freedom from public regulation, provides the essential condition for liberty. Although liberal philosophers have been primarily concerned with encroachments upon individual choice by the criminal law, the argument in favour of an area of private life immune from legal interference applies equally to contractual and tortious obligations, but with one significant difference. In the context of criminal and constitutional law, the individual's right to privacy can be enshrined in law with the consequence that the state is under a correlative legal obligation not to interfere with an individual's chosen way of life. In private law, however, where the dispute lies between individuals, appeals to the value of privacy always contemplate the rejection of all legal rights and duties.

This paper has several aims. The first section distinguishes two conceptions of privacy in private law, which are united in their purpose of providing justifications for the exclusion of legal rights, yet quite separate in their fundamental vision of freedom of the individual. The paper then notes the frequency of judiial appeals to both of these conceptions of privacy. It is then argued that these rhetorical appeals to the value of privacy conceal a fundamental incoherence in legal reasoning. This incoherence indicates that

---

* Fellow of Brasenose College, Oxford, England.

91

we must dig beneath the rhetorical justifications for judicial decisions in order to grasp the instrumental purposes which they serve. Finally, the paper notices that the realm of private conduct beyond the regulation of private law has diminished significantly during this century. Some tentative explanations are then put forward to account for this apparent decline in the value of privacy in private law.

TWO CONCEPTIONS OF PRIVACY

The first conception of privacy insists that an individual owes no legal obligations to a stranger. This 'estrangement' conception of privacy confines obligations to those persons who have deliberately chosen to bind themselves towards one another. Thus contractual obligations created by agreement between the parties must constitute the paradigm form of legal obligation.

This estrangement conception of privacy views suspiciously any claim for breach of duty where the duty has not been voluntarily assumed. Its most startling invocation occurs in the denial of a general duty to rescue a drowning person. This example, however, merely illustrates the absence of a general duty in the common law either to provide assistance to a stranger or to intervene to prevent a stranger from suffering physical or economic harm caused by the acts of a third party.[2] A more commonplace example of the implications of the estrangement conception of privacy arose in the law of tort in the nineteenth century on account of its resistance to the imposition of liability on manufacturers for defective products towards the ultimate consumer because of the absence of a contractual relation between them. Although this restriction upon negligence liability, often dubbed the "privity of contract fallacy" or simply the "contractual fallacy",[3] was decisively rejected in *Donoghue v Stevenson*,[4] it had effectively limited the scope of legal obligations for the preceding century.

Similarly, in the law of contract, by virtue of the doctrine of privity, an agreement cannot give rise to legal obligations owed to third persons, even though these persons may have been intended to benefit from the performance of the contractual undertaking. One reason given for the denial of contractual rights to third parties is that such "rights and duties remain personal to those who create them; all contracts resemble a marriage in so far as no third party can claim the right to share the intimate relations established between the spouses".[5] This first conception of privacy thus regards both the ultimate consumer and the third party beneficiary as a stranger to whom no private legal obligations can be owed. But this estrangement conception of privacy jostles with another in private law.

The second conception of privacy insists that an individual owes no legal obligations to intimates. Again, respect for the value of privacy prevents any legal obligations from arising, but this 'intimacy' conception of privacy gives as its reason the principle that legal rights and duties are inappropriate for social and domestic relations. Few commentators doubt that the courts will refuse to enforce such agreements as invitations to dinner and agreements to

92

pay a fixed sum of housekeeping money to a spouse. Often the courts achieve this result by declaring the absence of consideration to support such agreements. For example, courts normally refuse to treat a wife's domestic services during marriage in keeping house, shopping, gardening and bringing up the children as constituting consideration for any express or implied agreement to share the legal ownership of property acquired by the husband.[6] In a few cases of social and domestic arrangements, however, the courts cannot resist the conclusion that the plaintiff has established the presence of consideration and in these circumstances they invoke a further doctrine that they will not enforce agreements if the parties do not intend to create legal relations.[7] Thus, an agreement to come to dinner, or to do the shopping, or to mow the lawn made between friends or a cohabiting couple will not incur legal sanctions for breach of promise despite the presence of agreement and consideration. Similarly, in the law of tort, although the modern law imposes a broad liability for negligent misrepresentations, the courts decline to find such an obligation when the misleading advice or information was given on a social occasion, such as a doctor or a lawyer giving her opinion about a case at a party.[8]

As well as these traditional examples of the limits of private law, even in modern legislation governing contracts we can discern similar regulatory abnegation inspired by the intimacy conception of privacy. For example, under British legislation employees receive protection against sex discrimination with regard to recruitment, terms of employment, training, promotion and dismissal, but s.6(3)(b) of the Sex Discrimination Act 1975 exempts small firms employing five people or less. Although the European Court of Justice has recently found that this exemption violates E.E.C. standards,[9] the amended legislation tenaciously clings to an exemption for domestic households.[10] A similar limitation applied to the Race Relations Act 1968 s.2(1) which excluded both domestic arrangements and private clubs.[11] The Race Relations Act 1976 reduced the scope of privacy, but retained an exclusion from prohibited discrimination for employment in private households[12] and for membership of clubs with less than twenty-five members which also apply an acceptability test before admitting a person.[13] Once again, therefore, we discover a marked unwillingness to regulate domestic transactions, even where the conduct violates such an important value as equality. A common motive of respect for privacy appears to bind these examples together. The worry is that excessive legal regulation will distort intimate social relations by forcing people to act as strangers to each other.[14]

These two conceptions of privacy focus on the same question: is a particular relationship a suitable target for private legal obligations? Yet they suggest two very different reasons for declining to grant a legal remedy. The estrangement conception of privacy insists that legal obligations should be denied unless the parties have formed a close relationships by agreement or some other voluntary assumption of responsibility. The intimacy conception of privacy, in contrast, excludes legal obligations unless the parties are dealing at arm's length, in the stance of self-interested strangers.

93

When courts decline to find legal obligations on the ground of privacy, they frequently employ a group of rhetorical words and phrases which express this perspective on the situation. In this section of the essay, we will first identify some of the typical phrases used to justify results embodying the value of privacy, and then question the coherence of this rhetoric.

In the context of the estrangement conception of privacy, the courts often use the word 'stranger' itself to describe the person to whom no legal obligations are owed. Consider, for example, this formulation of the doctrine of privity:

> Although I may regret it, I find it impossible to deny the existence of the general rule that a stranger to a contract cannot in a question with either of the contracting parties take advantage of provisions of the contract, even where it is clear from the contract that some provision in it was intended to benefit him.[15]

Alternatively, the estrangement conception of privacy can be expressed by stressing the intimacy of the parties, thereby asserting a justification for cloaking them in legal obligations towards each other. The growth of a duty of care owed to persons other than parties to a contract was expressed in the rhetoric of neighbours in order to overcome the objection grounded in the estrangement conception of privacy that these strangers were insufficiently close for private law obligations to arise. In Lord Atkin's famous formulation the word 'neighbour' translates the stranger into an intimate:

> The liability for negligence . . . is no doubt based upon a general public sentiment of moral wrongdoing for which the offender must pay. But acts or omissions which any moral code would censure cannot in a practical world be treated so as to give a right to every person injured by them to demand relief. In this way rules of law arise which limit the range of complainants and the extent of their remedy. The rule that you are to love your neighbour becomes, in law, you must not injure your neighbour . . . .Who, then, in law is my neighbour? The answer seems to be – persons who are so closely and directly affected by my act that I ought reasonably to have them in contemplation as being so affected when I am directing my mind to the acts or omissions which are called in question.[16]

In contrast, in order to express the intimacy conception of privacy, the courts frequently stress the informal and social nature of the relations. The sentiments of love and affection exclude the law of contract in another of Lord Atkin's famous judgments:

> Agreements such as these are outside the realm of contracts altogether. The common law does not regulate the form of agreements between spouses. Their promises are not sealed with seals and sealing wax. The consideration that really obtains for them is that natural love and affection which counts for so little in these cold Courts . . . .In respect of these promises each home is a domain into which the King's writ does not seek to run, and to which his officers do not seek to be admitted.[17]

Another way of expressing the intimacy conception of privacy is to label a relationship as a private one in contrast to the public relations between citizens. Hence in the statutes against discrimination which we noted above, the principal exclusionary phrase speaks of "services offered to the public",[18] with its implicit contrast of private, secluded, domestic and social relations.

These few examples convey some of the themes of judicial rhetoric. Yet they exhibit a disturbing characteristic. Our initial distinction between the two conceptions of privacy appears to melt away before our eyes. We said that the estrangement conception of privacy insists that strangers and remote actors cannot have legal obligations thrust upon them, for that would violate their private autonomy. Yet we have also noted that friends and intimates cannot have legal obligations imposed upon them, for that would subvert the bonds of trust and affection which sustain their private relationship. The estrangement conception of privacy restricts legal obligations to intimates, whereas the intimacy conception only permits obligations between strangers. At one moment in judicial rhetoric, words and phrases denoting intimacy, proximity and neighbourliness provide a reason for the imposition of legal obligations but at the next the same words justify the denial of a legal remedy. Similarly, the emphasis upon the distance between the litigants, their self-interested independence, and the absence of ties of sentiment, authority or dependence provides a reason both for granting legal rights, as in domestic contracts, and for refusing rights, as in the privity of contract doctrine. Is this a contradiction lurking in the rhetoric of privacy?

I think that to speak of contradictions in legal rhetoric is a mistake. This kind of legal discourse expresses values and political principles which provide generalised justifications for decisions rather than precise legal rules which may conflict in a contradictory way. Tensions in legal rhetoric are often better described as "dangerous supplements".[19] Like the green and black colours on the monitor before me, the terms strangers and intimates define themselves in opposition to each other. Their meaning depends upon the sense of contrast or *différance*.[20] One term cannot be understood without reference to the other: to be a stranger one must not be an intimate; to be an intimate, one must not be a stranger. Where the meaning of terms depends upon such fragile contrasts, rhetorical justifications necessarily employ both terms, if only by implication. Hence the assertion that a third party is a stranger implies a meaning for intimacy at the same time as it identifies the stranger. But each term also presents a danger to the other on account of the two conceptions of privacy. An assertion that persons are intimates rather than strangers in order to justify the imposition of legal obligations always runs the risk of running foul of the second conception of privacy in which intimacy abhors legal obligations. To take concepts such as intimacy or estrangement to their logical conclusion would have the effect of depriving the other of any content. For example, it was suggested above that the estrangement conception of privacy generates a justification for the doctrine of privity in contract. The principle that obligations can only be created between close associates requires that third parties cannot gain rights under a contract because they are strangers. By virtue of the intimacy conception of privacy, however, it is precisely the fact that third parties are strangers and not intimates which provides a reason for legal protection of their interests. The interplay of the two conceptions of privacy thus produces apparent incoherence in the law of privity of contract, for whilst the estrangement conception restricts legal obligations to parties to the agreement, the intimacy conception perceives the importance of attaching legal obligations to dealings between strangers. In this realm of legal rhetoric, the concepts of intimacy and estrangement threaten to subvert each other's values, yet they depend upon each other implicitly for their meaning. In this sense, they function as dangerous supplements to each other.

It is important to notice that this relation of dangerous supplement operates only at a rhetorical level. Although judicial appeals to privacy as grounds for their decisions always contain the seeds of self-destruction, this does not relieve them from the practical task of isolating an appropriate sphere of conduct for the application of private obligations. Without such a terrain for contract and tort, it is hard to imagine how a market economy would operate. By revealing how one conception of privacy functions as a dangerous supplement to the other, we merely cast doubt on the coherence of legal principles and justifications for decisions framed in the rhetoric of privacy.

That conclusion drives us to look more closely at the decisions to find deeper motives for the results. In each successful case the court creates a space for legal obligations, and in so doing, constitutes the realm of social and economic relations in which individuals must treat each other with the dignity of citizenship and respect the other's economic interests. By examining particular cases, we can identify the immediate grounds for expanding or contracting the sphere of citizenship and economic interdependence.

In the following two sections, we will consider the law at both the rhetorical and instrumental levels. We will notice how justifications framed in terms of privacy tend to rebound upon themselves. Then, leaving aside the rhetoric, we can identify the particular reason for placing the social or economic relation inside or outside the sphere of private law. In the course of this brief review, we shall notice how the scope of private obligations has expanded at the expense of the value of privacy.

STRANGERS AND NEIGHBOURS

With regard to the first conception of privacy, which excludes legal obligations on the ground that the parties are insufficiently intimate, during the last half century the courts have translated strangers into intimates by a variety of doctrinal techniques, so that little force has been left in the objection to legal obligations based on the requirement of intimacy. Of course, at the same time legal doctrine has had to avoid the danger of characterising the relation as so intimate that no legal obligations can arise.

In the law of contract, the courts have forged an increasing number of exceptions to the doctrine of privity through such devices as agency, collateral contracts and the protection of reliance through promissory estoppel. One theme which runs through many of these exceptions to the doctrine of privity is the insistence that the third party in fact enjoys an intimate relation with the others. One key strategy involves the assertion that the stranger has become in law a party to the agreement by virtue of an artificial device such as agency, a collateral contract, or an assignment of rights. By this route a court can claim that two parties have attained the intimacy of an agreement even though they have never communicated with each other and may even be unaware of the other's existence.[21] Alternatively, through the concept of privity of estate, the stranger becomes entitled to legal rights because she or he is bound by a proprietary interest in real property shared with the defendant. In *Junior Books Ltd. v The Veitchi Co. Ltd.*,[22] potentially the greatest threat to the doctrine of privity, the House of Lords permitted the plaintiff owner of a building to sue a sub-contractor in tort for negligent performance of his contract with the main contractor. The requirement of intimacy or proximity was satisfied by the crucial assertion that the parties were so closely linked (because the sub-contractor had been nominated by the plaintiff's agent) that they were almost in a contractual relationship:

> The appellants, though not in direct contractual relationship with the respondents, were as nominated subcontractors in almost as close a commercial relationship with the respondents as it is possible to envisage short of privity of contract . . . .[23]

It is no accident, I suggest, that the exceptions to the doctrine of privity are expressed in terms which stress the intimacy of the relation between the parties. On the estrangement conception of privacy, this intimacy is a prerequisite of private law obligations. Yet, in order to avoid the dangerous supplement of the intimacy conception of privity, these cases stress at the same time how the relations between the parties possess a commercial quality, so that the parties are acting as self-interested strangers. "The relations of all parties to each other are commercial relations entered into for business reasons of ultimate profit."[24]

Similarly, as the law of negligence has become established, at each stage when further expansion was countenanced, the courts have returned to the requirement of intimacy, which Lord Atkin originally expressed in the terminology of neighbours, in order to justify their conclusion. Thus, in *Hedley Byrne & Co. v Heller & Partners*,[25] when the House of Lords expanded liability for damages to include negligent misrepresentations which cause economic loss as well as acts causing physical harm, they insisted that the parties should be in a special relationship akin to the intimacy required by privity of contract:

> [T]he categories of special relationships, which may give rise to a duty to take care in word as well as deed, are not limited to contractual relationships or to relationships of fiduciary duty, but include also relationships which . . . are "equivalent to contract" that is, where there is an assumption of responsibility in circumstances in which, but for the absence of consideration, there would be a contract.[26]

Yet at the same time the courts hasten to insist that the relation between the parties be not too intimate or informal, for then the second conception of privacy would defeat legal obligations:

> Quite careful people often express definite opinions on social or informal occasions, even when they see that others are likely to be influenced by them; and they often do that without taking the care which they would take if asked for their opinion professionally, or

in a business connexion. The appellants agree that there can be no duty of care on such occasions . . . .[27]

In these examples of judicial rhetoric in contract and tort, we see the dangerous supplement at work. As soon as strangers become intimates, because they are constituted as parties to an agreement or are treated as neighbours, they must become strangers again in order to escape the objections to legal invasions of intimacy. Only when they can be regarded as both strangers and intimates at the same time can they escape the rhetorical concern for privacy and enter the world of private legal obligations. The potential incoherence of this rhetoric suggests that other reasons guide the judicial decisions which chart the scope of private law obligations.

Why, then, have the courts pressed back the frontiers of intimacy in order to encompass an increasingly wide range of persons formerly regarded as strangers in the web of contractual and tortious obligations? Elsewhere, I have argued that the pressure for extension of the realm of legal obligations beyond the parties to the contract stems from the increasing division of labour.[28] Through specialisation of economic function and the need for larger groups to co-operate in productive and distributive activities, market transactions cannot be neatly divided into isolated exchanges between individual traders. In order to protect and sustain these economic relations, the common law has had to expand the scope of contractual and tortious obligations. Strangers become integrated both vertically and horizontally into the enterprise to such an extent that they can be recharacterised as intimates and then the doctrine of privity can be ignored or sidestepped. Strangers thus become neighbours, to whom a duty of care is owed. But these neighbours must not be members of the family, for then the intimacy conception of privacy would threaten the creation of private law obligations.

In addition to this significant response to a more complex division of labour, it is possible to discern paternalist values leading the courts to push back the frontiers of liability to include increasing numbers of persons, who hitherto had been regarded as strangers. Inequalities of skill, knowledge and resources create relations of dependence which may be counteracted for paternalist reasons by an imposition of duties of care and liability for reliance losses. Cane argues that:

> The idea of relationships of dependence goes a long way to explain why the courts have been prepared to reject the contract fallacy and impose tortious liability on professional advisors for purely economic loss whether caused by misfeasance or nonfeasance and regardless of whether the plaintiff had a contract with the profesional or gave value for his services.[29]

Certainly the expansion of tort liability dovetails well with the concept of relations of dependence, though other kinds of reliance liability in contract do not appear to be so limited.[30] Paternalist concerns lead judges to counteract imbalances of power by treating the subordinate party as a person sufficiently dependent upon the other to establish the necessary intimacy to satisfy the estrangement conception of privacy.

Equally, we must dig below the rhetoric of privacy in order to understand the reasons why the courts and the legislature have fixed those boundaries of legal obligations which reflect the intimacy conception of privacy. We noted above that the rhetoric in which intimacy shuns legal obligations pervades decisions in which courts exclude contractual relations from social and domestic arrangements. Yet no sooner has this been said than the contradictory theme contained in the estrangement conception of privacy rears its head in order to explain that some intimates are entitled to behave as strangers: "The fact that a contracting party is in some circumstances unlikely to extract his pound of flesh does not mean that he has no right to it."[31] Without this concession that intimates can sometimes insist upon their legal rights, the courts might undercut the law of private obligations altogether. But, if intimates can demand legal enforcement of obligations, this destroys the rhetoric based upon the intimacy conception of privacy. In the light of the incoherence produced by the way each conception of privacy functions as the dangerous supplement to the other, plainly this rhetoric should not be accepted as the true reason for the absence of legal obligations. Hence we must search for a deeper explanation for the limitation upon contractual relations in social and domestic contexts.

The underlying reason for legal abstention in domestic relations is not to be found in appeals to intimacy but in reflection upon the effects of the denial of legal obligations. In practice, legal abstention leaves the matter to be regulated by other social norms which often establish the dominance of men over women, thereby reinforcing the material domination which men normally enjoy through superior physical power and control over the major source of income.[32] Similarly, legal abstention guarantees the power of adults over children. Viewed in this light, abstention from legal regulation of social and domestic arrangements serves the function of buttressing the position of those who hold power already. This alternative perspective suggests that far from abstaining from regulating social and domestic arrangements for reasons of privacy, this limit upon the law of contract is designed to endorse and legitimate certain structures of power. Thus, the unwillingness of courts to recognise that domestic labour performed by women can count as consideration for an exchange of property rights serves the purpose of maintaining the hegemony of the wage earner over the household. In short, this realm of social relations unregulated by law has been constituted in order to leave certain kinds of domination unfettered by legal regulation and appeals to the sentiments of community simply mask institutions of domination.

Yet this instrumental account of privacy provides only a partial explanation of the case law. We should avoid a commission of what we may call 'the green field fallacy'. This fallacy suggests that whenever courts decline to find a species of legal right, their abstention leaves the parties without legal rules to govern their relation. In practice, however, the scope of the outlawed sphere remains much smaller than commentators normally suppose. For example, economic relations between husband and wife are closely regulated. The real issue in *Balfour v Balfour*,[33] a case often used to illustrate the limits of the law of contract in domestic relations,[34] lay not in whether the husband and wife could create a binding agreement, but rather whether the deserted wife's ordinary rights to support and maintenance could be altered by contrary agreement. Far from deliberately leaving the relation unregulated, thus putting the wife at the husband's mercy, the court viewed its decision as one which preserved the paternalist framework of rights accorded to the deserted spouse.[35] The seamless web of the common law ensures that truly green fields, where no legal rights and obligations pertain to the matter, are extremely rare. Whilst this argument does not destroy the thesis that legal abstention buttresses informal power relations, it does suggest that the function served by the denial of contractual rights often comprises the restriction of autonomous choice in favour of paternalist mandatory regulations.[36] Each instance of legal abstention must therefore be examined closely in order to discern whether these paternalist values, which contain the antithesis of legal abnegation, in fact determine the result.

Indeed, paternalist considerations have in recent years led to a rapid decline in the size of the realm of private unregulated conduct. Courts are increasingly unwilling to treat informal arrangements as none of the law's business. One symptom of this change of attitude can be found in the use of proprietary estoppel to secure the economic interests of deserted women. In *Pascoe v Turner*,[37] for example, when a man deserted his mistress, he asserted: "The house is yours and everything in it." No formal transfer of rights was accomplished, however, and subsequently the man brought an action for possession. The Court of Appeal refused to give the man possession of the house and instead granted the mistress title to the property. Although earlier cases had refused to countenance such an informal transfer of rights in a domestic situation, clearly the court believed that protection of the economic interests of the mistress justified a diminution in the scope of the unregulated private sphere. In the absence of legislative regulation of the proprietary rights of cohabiting couples, the courts have ingeniously found contracts and equitable rights to secure the position of the weaker party.

The argument that relations are too intimate to bear legal regulation has been applied outside domestic contexts. It applied to a tenancy in *Ramsden v Dyson*.[38] Here a landlord allowed factory workers to enter his land and build a shanty town (which became Huddersfield) following a written memorandum inscribed on the manorial rolls for an annual rent of four pounds. The landlord's heir challenged the tenants' right to remain upon the property and in response the tenants brought an action for either formal leases for sixty years or restitution for the value of their houses. The House of Lords declined to find that the tenants had acquired any rights to remain on the property other than a tenancy at will, arguing that the landlord had acted out of motives of beneficence rather than commercial advantage. Any greater obligations than a tenancy at will were binding in honour only. In other words, the landlord's implied permission to build the houses was regarded as a symbolic

100

act of patronage and authority, and therefore one which could not create legal obligations. The court thus reinforced a relation of authority by declining to award the tenants any contractual right to remain on the land. Almost certainly, however, these days the case would be decided rather differently. We can draw an analogy with *Crabb v Arun District Council*[39] where, perhaps appropriately, the private landowner is replaced by the officers of a local authority. The officials led the plaintiff to believe that he would be granted a right of access to his land from an adjacent road, but the council subsequently refused to complete the formal conveyance. The Court of Appeal granted the plaintiff's request for a right of access in the light of the economic damage which he had suffered from being unable to enter his land. We can surmise that the court was interested in protecting the citizen against arbitrary actions of government in a way in which the nineteenth century court was unwilling to challenge the authority of a knight of the shire with regard to his dependants.

In any event, contract law, whether based upon consideration or detrimental reliance, has gradually confined the scope of the intimacy conception of privacy to a vestigial theoretical limit rather than a practical constraint upon the creation of private obligations. In the pursuit of legal techniques by which to assist economically vulnerable groups, the courts have pushed back the frontiers of private law. Intimate relations have been redefined as relations between citizens in which each party should treat the other with respect and dignity. Relations of authority have been replaced by the formal equality of the marketplace.

A similar development has occurred in the law of tort. The common law prohibited actions in tort between husband and wife, and indeed at one time expressly endorsed a man's right to beat his wife,[40] but the Law Reform (Husband and Wife) Act 1962 abolished this rule. Hence a woman may now sue her husband for negligent and deliberate personal injury.[41] Yet the second conception of privacy retains some force, since under s.1(2)(a) of the Act the proceedings may be stayed in the case of trivial domestic disputes if it appears that no substantial benefit will accrue to either party from their continuation.[42] With regard to the protection of children from physical violence from parents and schoolteachers, the common law permitted reasonable chastisement, but this private realm has been substantially reduced through the effect of care proceedings to remove children from their home into the custody of local authorities and the recent statute prohibiting corporal punishment in publicly funded schools.[43] Once again, therefore, relations of dependence and subordination have been reconstituted by the law in the form of relations between citizens.

THE DECLINE OF PRIVACY

The pattern which emerges from this overview of the value of privacy in private law is a striking reduction in the importance attached to both conceptions of privacy with a consequential enlargement of the scope of private legal obligations. At the level of rhetoric, each conception of privacy has proved the dangerous supplement of the other. Strangers have been redefined as intimates such as neighbours or parties to a contract in order to broaden the range of liability in tort and contract. At the same time, intimates have been recategorised as citizens, that is, strangers to whom respect is owed and to whom dignity must be accorded, with the effect that contractual and tortious obligations can regulate domestic relations. Beneath the rhetoric of the two conceptions of privacy, however, we have observed diverse policy considerations which press back the boundaries of private law obligations. The purpose of revealing the incoherence of appeals to the value of privacy has been to enable us to discount this rhetoric and to proceed to a more detailed examination of the motives for the decisions.

What emerges from this overview of the decline of privacy in the common law is a developing faith in private law to govern the whole gamut of social and economic relations found in modern society. This decline signifies the collapse of earlier differentiations of social relations between the marketplace which is suitable for private law and the family and political authority which must be handled either by mandatory public norms or left entirely unregulated. But with this reorientation of the way in which the common law interprets social and economic relations comes a new understanding of the paradigms of private law. The double transformation of strangers into intimates and *vice versa* symbolises the emergence of a communitarian perspective in which individuals owe duties of care and responsibility to a much wider group of persons than hitherto. The paradigm for private law obligations switches from agreement or voluntary assumption of responsibility to a general duty to respect the interests of others and a special duty to sacrifice one's own interests for the sake of dependents. The general duty substitutes closer bonds of social solidarity than those recognised by the ideal of private autonomy, and the special duty emphasises trustworthiness at the expense of authority and discretion. This transition in legal thought implicitly contains a rejection of the traditional liberal view that privacy is essential for human flourishing. It seems instead that the common law, both in its rhetoric and its practice, seeks the good and the right in the values of trust and solidarity.

NOTES AND REFERENCES

[1]   Berlin, "Two Concepts of Liberty" in *Political Philosophy* (1967; ed. A. Quinton) p. 143.
[2]   For the exceptions to this principle see: P. S. Atiyah, *Accidents, Compensation and the Law* (3rd ed. 1983) pp. 95-112.
[3]   W. V. H. Rogers, *Winfield and Jolowicz on Tort* (12th ed. 1984) p. 71, n. 11.
[4]   [1932] A.C. 562.
[5]   H. Collins, *The Law of Contract* (1986) p. 106.
[6]   K. O'Donovan, *Sexual Divisions in Law* (1985) p. 118, discussing *Cowcher v Cowcher* [1972] 1 W.L.R. 425.
[7]   *Jones v Padavattan* [1969] 1 W.L.R. 328.
[8]   *Hedley Byrne & Co. Ltd. v Heller & Partners Ltd.* [1964] A.C. 465, 529.
[9]   *E.E.C. Commission v United Kingdom* [1984] I.R.L.R. 29.
[10] Sex Discrimination Act 1986 s.1.
[11] *Charter v Race Relations Board* [1973] 1 All E.R. 512.

12 Section 4(3).
13 Section 25; see D. Pannick, *Sex Discrimination Law* (1985) p. 73.
14 Lon Fuller explains this limit upon contract as a functional necessity, for the strict measurements of obligation which are characteristic of legal discourse would destroy the sentiments which establish communities; Fuller, "Human Interaction and the Law" in *The Rule of Law* (1971; ed. R. P. Wolff) at p. 204. See also: K. Davis, *Human Society* (1948) p. 470. K. O'Donovan, *op. cit.*, pp. 5-8 points out the importance of privacy in this context, but fails to draw the distinction between the two conceptions of privacy. The text follows Unger in perceiving privacy as a political principle: Unger, "The Critical Legal Studies Movement" (1983) 96 *Harvard Law Rev.* p. 561, p. 620.
15 *Per* Lord Reid, *Scruttons Ltd. v Midland Silicones Ltd.* [1962] A.C. 446, 473.
16 [1932] A.C. 562, 580.
18 Sex Discrimination Act 1975 s.29(1).
19 This terminology, derived from the post-structuralist critical theory of Jacques Derrida, has been employed in a similar way by Frug, "The Ideology of Bureaucracy in American Law" (1984) 97 *Harvard Law Rev.* p. 1276, pp. 1277-96; and Dalton, "An Essay in the Deconstruction of Contract Doctrine" (1985) 94 *Yale Law J.* p. 997, p. 1017.
20 This term is used by Derrida, as explained in J. Culler, *In Pursuit of Signs* (1981) p. 41.
21 For example, *New Zealand Shipping Co. Ltd. v A. M. Satterthwaite & Co. Ltd. (The Eurymedon)* [1975] A.C. 154.
22 [1983] 1 A.C. 520.
23 *Per* Lord Roskill, [1983] 1 A.C. 520, 542.
24 *Per* Lord Wilberforce, [1975] A.C. 154, 167.
25 [1964] A.C. 465.
26 *Per* Lord Devlin, [1964] A.C. 465, 529.
27 *Per* Lord Reid, [1964] A.C. 465, 482-3.
28 H. Collins, *op. cit.*, pp. 44-45. Collins, "Contract and Legal Theory" in *Legal Theory and Common Law* (1986; ed. W. Twining) pp. 148-49.
29 Cane, "Contract, Tort and Economic Loss" in *Studies in Tort Law* (1986; ed. M. Furmston) pp. 124-25. See also Reiter, "Contracts, Torts, Relations and Reliance" in *Studies in Contract Law* (1980; eds. B. J. Reiter and J. Swan).
30 H. Collins, *op. cit.*, n. 5, p. 121.
31 *Per* Salmon L.J. in *Jones v Padavattan* [1969] W.L.R. 328, 334.
32 Olsen, "The Family and the Market – A Study of Ideology and Legal Reform" (1983) 96 *Harvard Law Rev.* p. 1497, p. 1510; K. O'Donovan, *op. cit.*, pp. 15-19, 107-25; Dalton, *op. cit.*, p. 1095ff.
33 [1919] 2 K.B. 571.
34 Hedley, "Keeping Contract in Its Place - *Balfour v Balfour* and the Enforceability of Informal Agreements" (1985) 5 *Oxford J. Legal Studies* p. 391.
35 "In order to establish a contract there ought to be something more than mere mutual promises having regard to the domestic relations of the parties. It is required that the obligations arising out of that relationship shall be displaced before either of the parties can found a contract upon such promises." *Per* Duke L.J. in *Balfour v Balfour* [1919] 2 K.B. 571, 577. See also Swan, "Consideration and the Reason for Enforcing Contracts" in *Studies in Contract Law* (1980; eds B. J. Reiter and J. Swan) p. 57.
36 H. Collins, *op. cit.*, n. 5, pp. 127-30.
37 [1979] 1 W.L.R. 431.
38 (1886) L.R. 1 H.L. 129.
39 [1976] Ch. 179.
40 W. V. H. Rogers, *op. cit.*, n. 2, p. 698.
41 *Church v Church* (1983) 133 *New Law J.* p. 317.
42 W. V. H. Rogers, *op. cit.*, n. 2, p. 690.
43 Education (No.2) Act 1986, s. 47.

Critical Criminal Law

David Nelken*

To come to criminal law in a spirit of criticism is to find a subject full of paradoxes. It is an area where there is both an abundance of criticism and yet where critique has hardly started. It is *the* branch of law where most social studies have been done of the 'law in action' and where the gulf between ideals of equality and the reality of differentiation has been shown to be glaring and recurrent, and where official arbitrariness and repression are most obvious. Yet in Britain the law schools do not even have a 'law in context' textbook to relate legal doctrine to studies of criminal justice and criminology. The standard textbooks hold their own.[1] On the other hand, even the mainstream commentators on the criminal law are highly critical of the development of this branch of law, stigmatising it as indefensible and incoherent, challenging its most basic conceptual categories and backing a codification project designed to rein in the judges (when not conducting almost continual guerrilla warfare).

There are some signs of new approaches to the study and teaching of criminal law but these lie mainly in the area of philosophical reflection on fundamental aspects of criminal doctrine and the justification of punishment. It is uncertain whether any new explicitly critical text would draw more on the heritage of contextual studies or the more recent unorthodox form of legal scholarship associated with the U.S.A. critical legal studies movement. Even in the U.S.A., however, criminal law seems to have been strangely neglected by critical scholars. Thus the special issue on critical legal studies put out by the *Stanford Law Review* contained nothing on criminal law but a bitter attack on a paper by Mark Kelman, a paper which represents one of the few explicitly critical discussions of substantive criminal law.[2] Likewise, the Kairys volume, *The Politics of Law*, contained three articles on criminal law (including one by Kelman) but these dealt only with the causes of crime, crimes of the powerful and police deviance.[3] Yet critical discussion of substantive legal doctrine in this area is all the more important because of recent trends in which those on the left have emphasised the importance of taking crime seriously as a blight on the lives of those living in working-class neighbourhoods. This must surely also entail seeing how far the concepts and categories of the *criminal law* can

* *Faculty of Laws, University College, 4-8 Endsleigh Gardens, London WC1H 0EG, England.*

serve to further rather than hold back their political goals. From this perspective the teaching of criminal law in Britain needs to change not only to incorporate insights developed in contextual studies of crime and the criminal process but also by beginning to confront the problem of exploring legal doctrine and the nature of criminal law's specificity.[4] How far can critical legal studies be used to construct an interpretation and critique of law which manages in this way to be both 'internal' and 'external' to law's self-understanding?[5] Going on from this, what are the possibilities of getting beyond the 'deconstruction' of criminal law's various incoherences and 'closures' to the development of what Unger has described as "deviationist doctrine"?[6]

It is obvious that not all criticisms made of the criminal law come under the heading of critical legal studies. It is therefore necessary, on the one hand, to avoid covering all existing critical discussions of the content, values and operation of the criminal law without, on the other hand, entering into an endless debate about what is critical about critical legal studies. I shall be particularly concerned with the approach(es) adopted by the critical legal studies movement in the U.S.A. This may be characterised, somewhat cavalierly, as a left-leaning, unorthodox form of legal scholarship which challenges what is taken to be the mainstream liberal consensus concerning the nature and purpose of law. To do this it draws on diverse strands of modernist social, political and literary theory. Amongst its targets are the idea that law is to be explained in terms of the functional and instrumental purposes it serves, the attempt to present law as rational and coherent, and the effort to separate legal discourse from moral and political argumentation.

But to distinguish critical legal studies in this way raises the question of whether the required critical work has not already been covered by other approaches under other headings. The paucity of specifically critical studies in this area of law may suggest that the approach is in fact redundant. Alternatively, it could indicate that there are particular difficulties in furthering the critical legal studies project with criminal law materials. Thus, my task in this paper is to examine whether there is intellectual space for critical legal studies in the area of criminal law and consider what its contribution might be.

I shall organise my discussion around a series of hypothetical arguments attempting to deny the value of introducing this critical approach here and some of the possible replies which may be given. I begin by examining some special features of criminal law which might explain and even justify the way it has been comparatively neglected by critical scholars. I then discuss whether there is a need for a critical approach in this area in relation to the other approaches which are available and I conclude by considering the applicability of the critical methods of deconstruction and reconstruction used in other branches of law.

106

WHAT'S SO SPECIAL ABOUT CRIMINAL LAW?

There are at least three features of criminal law which may help to account for its comparative neglect by critical legal scholars. The first, which is again something of a paradox, is that criminal law is too obviously part of the *repressive* armoury of the state. Criminal law plainly contains the sanctions to enforce its definitions of right and wrong. It seems fatuous and insubstantial to offer to 'deconstruct' criminal law in the face of the solid facts of punishment and degradation. Although, as will be seen, this reflects at best only a partial view of criminal law, it is possible that it has discouraged critical legal studies interest in this area. But even in its own terms the argument is flawed. It is easy to find examples where criminal and civil law are inseparable – as in the law of theft. Thus a critical approach finds itself bound to give some explanation of these areas of criminal law. It must also concern itself with cases where the grounds of culpability in criminal and civil law are different – as in the definition of consent. Is Kelman correct in arguing that consent in criminal law parallels the requirements of consent in the market place?[7] Should we impose stricter or more lenient principles in the criminal law? What are the dangers of following Box's suggestion that "rape could be defined as sexual access gained by any means where the female's overt genuine consent is absent"?[8] These problems cannot be dismissed by assuming that criminal law as a vehicle of repression is different from civil law. The case must be argued for in terms of a postulated theory of crime and the criminal law. Should critical legal studies endorse the Durkheimian view that the blaming feature of criminal law serves quite different functions from civil law so that conditions of culpability must reflect the special stigma involved in being penalised for an offence?[9] Or should they concentrate on the harms the law is trying to prevent and so be willing to extend the boundaries of criminal conduct as in Celia Wells' call for the criminal law to impose liability on those "knowingly marketing dangerous products or ignoring safety hazards"?[10]

A second reason why critical writers may have been wary of the criminal law is almost the opposite of the previous argument. Criminal law is not worth discussing, it is said, because it is too *essential* a feature of the social order, including any realistic alternative order. Thus, the contingency and arbitrariness of legal doctrine to which critics are keen to draw attention are less in evidence here. There can be argument over what should or should not be subject to the criminal law, and critical writers may well be expected to take distinctive positions in these debates. But the liberal view of law as a 'necessary evil' can hardly be in doubt here. On this view, critical experiments with other forms of legal and political arrangements, as in Unger's suggestion of a "no-structure structure", cannot be extended to criminal law but rather pre-suppose its basic prohibitions. The choice that is offered is between being "realistic" in this way or being categorised as a "Left idealist",[11] preoccupied with "crimes of the powerful" and neglectful of the effects of the standard textbook crimes on the working class neighbourhoods which should be the natural constituency of critical writers.[12] This position is not uncontroversial.

107

But, if anything, critical writers, including those writing from a feminist perspective, now seem to be arguing for more rather than less use of the criminal law, which makes it rather hard to doubt its necessity.

One way of replying to this argument would be to stress the point that a critical approach to criminal law should not be mistaken for a lenient one. (This helps to explain some of the misunderstandings which arise when some liberal writers insist that critical criminologists should be their natural allies in the fight against Conservative law and order policies.)[13] But a better answer would, I think, urge critical writers to focus precisely on the ideological significance of criminal law's claim to be essential. In fact, whereas the problems dealt with by criminal law may often be real enough, it does not follow at all that criminal law is the only or best way of dealing with them. (Mis)behaviour now treated as criminal has been dealt with or may even now be handled also as sin, disease, tort, deviance, dispute or a matter of administrative rearrangements.[14] Criminal law has been used, *inter alia*, to reinforce slavery, to secure the labour force, to maintain religious and political hierarchies, to convert customary rights into 'poaching' and so on. Even the definition and redefinition of standard offences like rape, theft or criminal damage reflect the particular interests which lie behind the formulation and application of law. The process is most easily visible when new forms of criminality are discovered.[15]

These somewhat obvious sociological truths are given more point when contemporary changes in responding to offences are examined. When compliance strategies replace punishment as a goal and mediation is substituted for adjudication it becomes questionable whether we are still in the realm of criminal law (which is defined as a proceeding which can be followed by punishment).[16] The present trend amongst some radical criminologists to take crime seriously thus takes criminal law too seriously. Its conditions of culpability may be questioned, its processes suspected, its necessity in relation to other types of social control put in doubt. Criminal law may do more to perpetuate than to reduce the phenomena with which it engages.

However, there is also a third argument for leaving criminal law alone which requires careful consideration. This concentrates on the role of criminal law in a liberal polity as a restraint on power and a bulwark against government's awesome capacity for violence. It might seem that, in this area at least, the importance of liberal values and procedures, reflecting the distrust of power and the need of specified rules announced in advance, can hardly be denied. It is no accident that criminal law served as the site in which western Marxist writers recently rediscovered the value of the 'rule of law', as in E. P. Thompson's celebrated if controversial conclusion to his study of the Black Acts in eighteenth century England.[17] Even the liberal tendency to limit an individual's legal responsibility to others seems to have more appeal when it protects the individual from the intrusive control of the state or the intolerance of other people than when, more typically, it supports individual property rights against redistributive projects carried out in the name of fairness or altruism.

Not surprisingly, this feature of criminal law is exactly what is stressed by the respected student textbooks. Writers such as Glanville Williams, Smith and Hogan, Ashworth and others seek to enlist students in their explicitly liberal struggle for a 'subjectivist' interpretation of criminal law and criminal responsibility. They see themselves as holding the line against judicial willingness to offend against liberal ideals by inventing new crimes, by changing the definitional requirements of offences too often and haphazardly, and, more recently, by introducing more objective standards of responsibility into the required mental element of crime. Such concerns also lie behind the increasing pressure for codification in the criminal law.

There are a number of points which critical scholars could make in relation to this view of the criminal law. In the first place, the fury of the battle between 'the subjectivists' and the judges suggests that the textbooks may be as much concerned with *changing* as describing the law. It has even been claimed that some of these writers misrepresent the extent to which the law (still) incorporates their liberal ideals.[18] There are manifest weaknesses in the argument that criminal law does restrain the state, as the methods used in policing the riots, Northern Ireland, the miners' strike, Wapping and so on make clear. Both military policing and policing by the military remain amongst the options available to government. But even in the enforcement of mundane crime, it has been shown by McBarnet and others that legal protections for the accused are formulated or applied by judges in a way which helps the police and prosecution to achieve their high levels of conviction.[19] Close investigation of the doctrinal development of the law also shows that hitherto, at least, there has been sufficient inconsistency and complexity about, for example, the definition of defences within and between offences as to make an account of criminal law as a haven of certainty somewhat unbelievable.

Critical writers have already made some useful comments here. One of the major themes running through Kelman's article is the *unpredictability* of criminal law because of its vacillation between "broad" and "narrow" "time-frames" on the criminal incident, "disjointed" and "unified" accounts of the criminal act and extended and limiting perspectives concerning intent and the offender.[20] What has not been sufficiently discussed, perhaps, is the question whether critical writers themselves are interested in supporting liberal attempts to increase certainty in the criminal law or whether they have other priorities. On one view critical legal scholars are certainly committed to a form of 'supra-liberalism' which transcends, but does not sacrifice, the achievements of 'bourgeois legality'. But they may be no better than anyone else at reconciling individual rights with the demands of substantive justice so as to create both a more just and more participatory society.[21]

THE NEED FOR CRITICAL LEGAL STUDIES

We have seen so far that assertions that the criminal law is straightforwardly repressive, that it is unavoidable, or even that it serves to restrain governmental power should function as only the beginning rather than as the end of critical discussion. But it remains to be made clear whether there is a need for the critical legal studies approach to be brought to bear or whether these issues are already receiving satisfactory consideration.

The major rival contender available is the extensive research which has been carried out by scholars of criminal justice and critical criminology. It might be thought more important to encourage the production of teaching materials which incorporate some of their approaches and findings rather than set off on a new form of critical enquiry. At present the standard textbooks make little or no reference to the factors which shape the making and enforcement of criminal law. They say little about the frequent irrelevance of doctrine to the way many criminal cases are handled and show only limited appreciation of the manner in which legal rules are redefined in the course of the criminal process.[22] There is certainly a danger that critical legal scholarship may repeat some of these mistakes; despite calls to the contrary, there is no good reason to think that unorthodox doctrinal scholarship will be any more interested than the mainstream in asking and answering empirical questions.[23]

The answer to these doubts is to see that critical legal scholars put legal doctrine on the research agenda in a way which differs both from 'law in context' writers and from mainstream writing. They do so because they adopt neither the 'external' approach characteristic of contextualisers nor the 'internal' position of those concerned to ensure that their arguments count as such within the existing legal framework. There are a number of points of contrast. Whereas 'law in context' writers may be taken as showing how 'context determines meaning', the writings of critical legal scholars are designed to reveal the context in law by describing how legal texts and practices attempt to create coherence out of the competing and contradictory social influences and arguments which animate them. 'Law in context' writers often adopt empirical methods and typically draw on external perspectives, or perspectives on what goes on outside the courtroom, to demonstrate the 'gap' between law's pretensions and achievements.[24] But the division of labour between them and orthodox commentators on the law is too neat because it leaves legal doctrine and its development largely unexamined. Critical legal scholars, on the other hand, take issue with the values and the concealed and congealed preferences incorporated into the law itself, and excavate doctrine to discover the stereotypes and assumptions which shape its 'solutions'.

In fact, the concerns of critical legal scholars and 'law in context' writers will sometimes overlap. But even when they examine similar problems they will tend to generate interestingly different insights. Both 'law in context' and critical discussions of strict liability, for example, reach the same conclusion that much of the mainstream liberal anxiety about these offences is misplaced. Carson and others, however, concentrated on showing the 'working logic' of factory inspectors; they demonstrated that this led them to prosecute only where warnings had been given – so that *mens rea* requirements were in fact usually satisfied.[25] Critical writers, by contrast, offer the argument that strict liability offences often do turn out to be "intentional" provided a "broader time frame" is adopted which reaches back before the criminal incident.[26] Such a broader view is already taken by legal doctrine in resolving the problems set by attempts, omissions and withdrawals. More controversially, they go on to argue that taking a broad view of some standard crimes might sometimes undermine the appearance of intentionality which is given by limiting the time-frame to the criminal incident itself.

Having distinguished the critical approach from that of 'law in context' writers it may still be objected that the required intellectual work is already in progress in another quarter. For mainstream criminal law teaching and writing has made a particularly strong alliance with *philosophy* (rather than with the social sciences). Could it not be said that all that critical writers have to offer is a variant of social theory which offers little original that cannot be achieved by the mainstream and radical philosophical critiques of criminal law now being advanced?[27] This argument receives unexpected support when we find that one of the most developed British attempts at critical exegesis and reconstruction of another branch of law, Hugh Collins' re-examination of contract law, looks for a model to Hart's (liberal) analysis of the conditions of criminal responsibility.[28]

It must be acknowledged that here, too, there will be an overlap between existing approaches and what is offered by critical writers. But the latter are likely to participate mainly in long-standing debates concerning the justifications and limits of punishment because these draw on wide-ranging discussions of moral and political philosophy; they will tend to be less interested in the more technical 'ordinary-language philosophy' exercises which have become almost a standard technique of the 'internal' criticisms made by mainstream criminal law commentators. The critical approach is distinctive, however, in its 'post-structuralist' recognition of the *reflexivity* of all such doctrinal reform. In basic terms, although keenly interested in the changing nature of social relations, critical writers are cautious about putting forward suggestions for change as something made 'necessary' by social developments. Moreover, they are concerned to bring about more awareness of what is special about law even whilst remembering the artificiality of the separation between legal and other types of discourse.

So far I have argued that there is scope for a critical approach which cannot be reduced to what is already on offer. But the need for critical legal study of criminal law may also be questioned in a different way. It has been asserted that criminal law is no more than a *residual* method of handling trouble and misbehaviour. As such, to give so much attention to the reconstruction of criminal doctrine is to endorse its totally inappropriate sense of self-importance and neglect the far more important practices and discourses which have inherited its mantle.

If Spector is to be believed, recourse to criminal law to deal with "troublesome individuals" reached its apogee in the nineteenth century.[29] As Foucault, Donzelot and Garland have shown us, juridical techniques have in any case since given way to surveillance and the "normalising" strategies which Foucault termed "the disciplines" of modern society.[30] This has obvious significance for criminal law as a form of social control. But it is also important for its alleged role as a restraint on power. Criminal law does little or nothing to restrict the intrusive efforts of the various professionals now responsible for preventing and reshaping deviant behaviour. Rather it is they who have colonised its territory, as in the welfare and rehabilitative approaches to justice. These forms of microcosmic power escape legal restraint because of the professional authority which legitimates them, because they represent constellations of what Foucault calls power/knowledge and because they enter into the *enabling* role of the state as dispenser of benefits. This is to say nothing of other forms of market and bureaucratic power and social control exercised by groups other than government. Under these conditions the alleged protections of the criminal law seem premised on a nineteenth century view of the state and society; those interested in the rule of law in the twentieth century must look to the potential of administrative law rather than to criminal law. Either way critical writers would be wasting their time here.

Whilst there is a lot of truth in this picture of the declining importance of criminal law, it is sensible not to exaggerate its loss of functions.[31] From a critical point of view it would seem to retain a crucial ideological significance as being *the* form of law in closest touch with the public, which reinforces their belief in the need for 'law' and incorporates basic assumptions about intention, fault and individual responsibility. It is hard to credit the idea that these central liberal/bourgeois notions have been displaced by the newer disciplines and strategies. On the contrary, critical scholars must investigate the way law maintains its boundaries in the face of these competing views of human behaviour and the compromises and forms of co-option which result. Recognition of the growth of alternative discourses does not mean that we have to side either with or against them in their struggle to undermine or bypass legal discourse. Indeed, some of the contextualising approaches to criminal law may be treated as part of this battle, and therefore as further data for a critical approach to unravel rather than a reason for it to abandon interest in the criminal law.

THE CONTRIBUTION OF CRITICAL LEGAL STUDIES

This defence of the need for a critical legal studies approach to criminal law has led, appropriately enough, to the question exactly what it is such writers are likely to have to say about this subject. But again, because of the limited literature yet available, we must start with a ground-clearing operation designed to test the value here of the critical methods and arguments characteristically used in studying other branches of law. This indicates that there are dangers in an undiscriminating application of methods appropriate elsewhere (although there are also some useful techniques which can be adapted).

A typical method used by critical legal scholars is to try and uncover the deeper roots of contradictory doctrinal strands within the law. Instead of working to harmonise and reconcile them in the manner of mainstream writers, these are rather referred to contrasted conceptions of social relations. At the basis of all stands the fundamental contradiction between the individual and the community (although Kennedy has lately abandoned this formulation). But this method runs into trouble when applied to criminal law because its contradictions lie very much on the surface. Criminal law, for its part, is quite explicit about the struggle to reconcile individual freedom and community interests, even if the clash between altruism and selfishness is not always so recognisable in the interstices of private law. Not surprisingly, therefore, Schwartz attacks Kelman's paper by arguing that the existence of conflicting policy choices in the criminal law is hardly newsworthy.[32]

Critical scholars could reply to this argument by claiming that it mistakes the point of their method. Whether or not contradictions are acknowledged as the *raison d'être* of a branch of law is less important than how this then structures legal discourse. Criminal law is a particularly good example of the way liberal legal argument moves between seemingly irreconcilable opposite goals such as justice and welfare, retribution and reform and formal and substantive justice. At the level of doctrinal detail these potential contradictions are mediated by oscillation between the different time-frames and conceptions described by Kelman, as well as by other antinomies he does not discuss such as the contrasts between 'mitigation' and 'culpability', 'harm' and 'blame' and even 'objective' and 'subjective' responsibility. The law also responds by developing separate rules and procedures for different categories of offenders and the variable circumstances of offences as well as by compromising with competing discourses. In addition, as has been noted, criminal law is sufficiently interwoven with civil law for there to be some relevance in applying established methods used in the critique of civil law categories (for example, in examining the distinction between public and private in the definitions of sexual behaviour and pornography).

On the other hand, there is still much that is unclear and unsatisfactory about this method of critique. We need to know how to tell which tensions in law count as real contradictions, which contradictions are enduring and which are remediable, and, above all, which reflect the underlying forms of social relations and social structures and which are the more prosaic result of such factors as judicial inconsistency in resolving 'hard' cases within a common law system. Part of the problem here arises from the critics' ambivalence about the extent to which legal rules can be said to 'express' rather than actually 'constitute' social relations. In deliberate contrast to the contextualisers, they stress law as an independent rather than dependent phenomenon, or rather they deny the point of talking in this way. Some critical writers think that admitting the dependence of law on specified social functions or purposes is at odds with their insistence on law's "contingency".[33] This means (if Kelman is representative of such writers) that they are unnecessarily cautious about relating contradictory rules and doctrines to the different historical periods and circumstances in which they were developed, which would help to distinguish more adequately between the kinds of contradictions they identify.[34]

Even if critical writers do have something like a shared *methodology* for describing and deconstructing law, there is still some difficulty in imagining how this could lead them to any shared *prescriptions* for the future shape of the law. Is there any reason to expect a pattern to emerge in their recommendations for the reconstruction of criminal law and the criminal process? How can the possible contribution of critical legal studies in this area be made clear unless we can be clear what it is?

So far, certainly, writers who describe themselves as having critical or radical perspectives on criminal justice and criminology may be found on *both* sides of the varied debates in these subjects. There are arguments for rights *and* for welfare, for rules *and* discretion, for greater community involvement (provided it is 'empowering') *and* for distrust of such developments in favour of preserving the existing legal protections ostensibly part of the present criminal process. Some of these apparent disagreements can be reconciled by showing that self-styled critical protagonists at least share similar values but disagree about the implications for them of given developments or proposed changes in criminal justice. Even this may not always be taken for granted, however, and the dividing line is often precisely over how closely to adhere or return to liberal political arrangements and 'process-values'. For example, some otherwise critical writers have warned that the currently popular drive to make the police more accountable to local communities carries the risk of encouraging a "tyranny of the majority" who will be unsympathetic to the rights of unpopular minorities.[35] Whereas some radical criminologists urge that 'working class' demands for crime control be given priority, others are concerned that these demands may reflect ideas about crime shaped by the wider hegemonic culture.

Critical writers also differ over the relationship between the descriptive and prescriptive parts of their project. Some see themselves as attempting, above all, to change the objects of the criminal sanction – so as to bring under control exploitative corporations and exploitative people and frame laws which can get at structural violence, and reduce various forms of discrimination and breaches of human rights. They accept that the criminal law may be as clumsy an instrument for achieving their goals as it is at present. But they explicitly advocate its *symbolic* role by which they intend to alter the accepted stereotype of criminality (if necessary by the creation of new 'folk devils' for a socialist society).[36] Others point out that criminal law *already* performs this task inasmuch as criminals can be seen as exemplars of the 'possessive individualism' to which socialism is most opposed. A third group, on the other hand, the so-called 'abolitionists', would encourage as much reduction as possible in the ambit of criminal law (replacing it by civil and administrative remedies) and cut punishment to the minimum.

This diversity of views amongst critical writers may not be altogether a bad thing. It would be too much to expect that they could be in possession of the key to crime or even the solution to a progressive approach to crime control in the transition to a better society. Given the officially perceived 'overload' on the criminal courts at present, there is considerable scope for experimentation with the forms and forums of the criminal process. As a result there may be genuine opportunities for critical *praxis* designed to learn about the potential of different social arrangements for dealing with crime and the constraints they must overcome.

However, in considering possible critical prescriptions in this area of law it is again necessary to be careful in borrowing from suggested reforms elsewhere. A common tendency of critical writers is to argue that increasing social interdependence justifies a more openly interventionist approach to private law which will help secure desired redistributive outcomes and tame bureaucratic and market forms of power. But the relevance of this to criminal law seems uncertain. Some critical writers, impatient with what they see as a lenient approach to such varied matters as crimes of the powerful or rape, do already advocate a reduction in the requirements of culpability in terms of the mental state of the offender, consent of the victim and so on.[37] But, unfortunately, they fail to discuss the question whether they are also willing to accept the considerable increase in the number of criminals from less advantaged backgrounds who will be pulled into the net as the likely result of such reforms.

By way of conclusion, consider the question whether or not critical writers should welcome the *Caldwell* decision because it imposes higher levels of responsibility on "heedless" conduct.[38] It could be argued that the *Caldwell* trend is more progressive than the opposition led by the liberal textbook writers. The judges could be said to be responding to the increased danger represented by fecklessness in a complex society where there is a need for a higher level of mutual consideration – this is assuming that it is neither right nor efficient to leave all such matters to insurance remedies. The textbooks, by contrast, could be seen as reflecting a nineteenth century *Gesellschaft* approach to law with its stress on limiting responsibility to individually chosen obligations.[39] On the other hand, the textbook writers are surely right to fear the encroachment of judicially defined forms of attributed responsibility in the criminal law. These will often have little to do with requirements of modern interdependence. And it should not be assumed that critical writers do equate progressiveness with matching the law to modern conditions. Unlike many other previous sociological or Marxist approaches to understanding law, including the assumptions built into 'law in context' work, their post-structuralist methodology leaves them free to argue for a role for law in which it is capable of resisting or regulating other social developments and not merely following their lead.[40] Criminal law is therefore not *forced* to turn into a form of bureaucratic-administrative regulation.

It remains to be seen, however, whether critical writers will agree that the main task of criminal law is to serve as a restraint on power or whether they will also assign it a more positive role in prefiguring and building a society based on less exploitative forms of social relations.

NOTES AND REFERENCES

[1]   C. M. V. Clarkson and H. M. Keating, *Criminal Law: Texts and Materials* (1984) represents a partial exception. But they reserve most of their 'sociological' comments for the crime of rape, offer no analysis in terms of class or race and entirely exclude any consideration of theft offences.

[2]   See L. Schwartz, "With Gun and Camera through Darkest CLS-Land" (1984) 36 *Stanford Law Rev.* p. 413 at pp. 450-61; and Kelman, "Substantive Interpretation in the Criminal Law" (1981) 33 *Stanford Law Rev.* p. 591.

[3]   See in D. Kairys (ed.), *The Politics of Law* (1982): M. Kelman, "The Origins of Crime and Criminal Violence" p. 214; W. J. Chambliss, "Towards a Radical Criminology" p. 230; and D. Rudovsky, "The Criminal Justice System and the Role of the Police" p. 242.

[4]   See parts I and II of D. Nelken, "Criminal Law and Criminal Justice: Some Notes on their Irrelation" in I. Dennis (ed.), *Criminal Law and Justice* (1987).

[5]   See Alan Hunt's paper in this volume.

[6]   Unger, "The Critical Legal Studies Movement" (1983) 96 *Harvard Law Rev.* p. 563.

[7]   Kelman, *op. cit.*, n. 2, at pp. 615-16.

[8]   S. Box, *Power, Crime and Mystification* (1983) p. 125.

[9]   E. Durkheim, *The Division of Labour in Society* (1984; trans. W. D. Halls); N. Christie, "Crime Control as Drama" (1986) 13 *J. Law and Society* p. 1.

[10] Wells, "Restatement or Reform" (1986) *Criminal Law Rev.* p. 314 at p. 319.

[11] J. Young, "Left Idealism, Reformism and Beyond" in *Capitalism and the Rule of Law* (1979; eds. B. Fine *et al.*) p. 1, and J. Lea and J. Young, *What Is To Be Done About Law and Order* (1982).

[12] Could this label be applied to Kelman's contributions to the Kairys volume, *op. cit.*, n. 3?

[13] F. Cullen and J. Wozniak, "Fighting the Appeal of Repression" (1982) *Crime and Social Justice* p. 29.

[14] Spector, "Beyond Crime: Seven Methods to Control Troublesome Rascals" in *Law and Deviance* (1981; ed. H. L. Ross).

[15] For example, D. Nelken, *The Limits of the Legal Process: A Study of Landlords, Law and Crime* (1983).

[16] D. Nelken, "Community Involvement in Crime Control" in (1985) 38 *Current Legal Problems* p. 239.

[17] E. P. Thompson, *Whigs and Hunters* (1975) p. 252, but cf. A. Merrit, "The Nature and Function of Law" (1980) 17 *Brit. J. Law and Society* p. 194.

[18] N. Lacey, "The Territory of the Criminal Law" (1985) *Oxford J. Legal Studies* p. 453.

[19] D. McBarnet, *Conviction* (1981).

[20] Kelman, *op. cit.*, n. 2.

[21] But see T. Campbell, *The Left and Rights* (1983).

[22] See n. 4.

[23] O. Trubek, "Where the Action Is: Critical Legal Studies and Empiricism" (1984) 36 *Stanford Law Rev.* p. 575.

[24] D. Nelken, "The Gap Problem in the Sociology of Law" (1981) 1 *Windsor Yearbook of Access to Justice* p. 35.

[25] W. G. Carson, "White-collar Crimes and the Enforcement of Factory Legislation" (1970) 10 *Brit. J. Criminology* p. 383.

[26] Kelman, *op. cit.*, n. 2.

[27] See, for example, A. Norrie, "Freewill, Determinism and Criminal Justice" (1984) 3 *Legal Studies* p. 60, and A. Duff, *Trials and Punishments* (1986).

[28] Collins, "Contract and Legal Theory" in *Legal Theory and Common Law* (1986; ed. W. Twining) p. 134, and see H. Collins, *The Law of Contract* (1986).

[29] Spector, *op. cit.*, n. 14.

[30] M. Foucault, *Discipline and Punish* (1977; trans. H. Sheridan); J. Donzelot, *The Policing of Families* (1979); D. Garland, *Punishment and Welfare* (1985).

[31] D. Nelken, "Is There a Crisis in Law and Legal Ideology?" (1982) 9 *Brit. J. Law and Society* p. 177; R. Dahrendorf, *Law and Order* (1984).

[32] Schwartz, *op. cit.*

[33] R. Gordon, "Critical Legal Histories" (1984) 36 *Stanford Law Rev.* p. 57.

[34] Cf. J. Hall, *Theft, Law and Society* (1952), and G. P. Fletcher, *Rethinking Criminal Law* (1978).

[35] R. Reiner, *The Politics of the Police* (1984).

[36] I. Taylor, *Law and Order: Arguments for Socialism* (1981).

[37] Box, *op. cit..*

[38] *R. v Caldwell* [1982] A.C. 341 (H.L.).

[39] E. Kamenka and A. Tay, "Beyond Bourgeois Individualism: The Contemporary Crisis in Law and Legal Ideology" in *Feudalism, Capitalism and Beyond* (1975; eds. E. Kamenka and R. Neale) p. 126.

[40] See T. O'Hagan, *The End of Law* (1984), and Nelken, "Beyond the Study of 'Law and Society'" (1986) 2 *American Bar Foundation Research Journal* p. 323.

Racism and the Innocence of Law

PETER FITZPATRICK*

> ... with us there is nothing more consistent than a racist humanism since the European has only been able to become a man through creating slaves and monsters.[1]

INTRODUCTION

In liberal views of the world, law is manifestly incompatible with racism. Where racist practice infects law that can only be something aberrant and remediable. Exploring the British situation as a case, I will argue that on the contrary racism is compatible with and even integral to law. I try to show that the very foundational principles of law as liberal legality import racism into law, those principles of equality and universality which stand in their terms opposed to racism. The aim is not to dismiss law, nor to expose liberal legality as a sham. But nor is it to retrieve law and add to the list of obviously desirable variants on how to combat racism through law, such as recent "left strategies".[2] The point is, rather, to make such "acts, gestures, discourses which ... had seemed to go without saying become problematic, difficult, dangerous".[3] A note on the term racism: I will use it in an extended way to cover both belief and practice.

LIBERAL CAPITALISM AND THE SPECIFICITY OF RACISM

Initially, I will set the argument in contrary Marxist views of racism. One, usually attributed to Marx, sees a fundamental incompatibility between racism and capitalism of a developed, liberal variety. With its integral assertions of equality and universalist morality, such a capitalism stands opposed to racist divisions and this for good economic reasons.[4] Far from seeing such capitalism and racism as opposed, the alternative Marxist tradition finds them compatiable, even symbiotic. In economic terms racism operates to provide cheap labour and to constitute a sector of 'the reserve army of labour'. Politically, racism divides the working class and counters the transformative potential of that class. There are numerous dimensions to this.

*Darwin College, The University, Canterbury, Kent, CT2 7NY, England.

Thanks to Fiona Kinsman, Lydia Pepple, Guy Smith and staff of the Central Office of the Industrial Tribunals for a lot of help with the cases. Thanks to Dave Reason for much else.

119

In the annals of war and imperialism, race has often served to unite a 'white' working class and bourgeoisie. Racial division has been a powerful strategic tool of employers both in undermining white workers and in gaining their support.

These abrupt accounts may seem overly functionalist. But they do have large historical warrants. So much is that so that in the dispute between them one cannot be accepted as right and the other dismissed as wrong. What they support, rather, is a picture of conflicting forces within capitalism. And what this disagreement indicates is the inability of Marxism to provide a surpassing theoretical elaboration that encompasses racism. This need not provoke a rejection of Marxism, nor should it occasion surprise if we see Marxism as confronting a specific history of liberal capitalism. That confrontation does have things to say about racism. But it could also be the case that engaging with a specific history of racism can say things about liberal capitalism. In those rare moments when critical social theory has considered racism, it has tended to be taken on as an extra, as a discrete actor in a scenario devised without it in mind. Or that has been so until recently. There are now emergent academic visions not just of the historical specificity of race but also of its current centrality and significance.[5] It is, however, difficult to establish the significance of racism in a society whose self-presentation denies that significance. Monuments to liberalism can hardly acknowledge foundations of racism. It follows that racism in its legitimate forms will not be explicit. It will be found in forms of, for example, crime and social degeneration, community and culture, nation and society. That is, the form both substitutes for explicit racism and provides a means of asserting that what is involved is not racism but something different.

The liberal denial of racism prompts certain strategies in establishing its significance. One could be seen as a root-and-branch strategy, a strategy that seeks constitutive compatibilities between liberalism and racism. This large challenge has begun to be taken up in philosophical and historical work.[6] As I interpret it, this work points to the origins of racism in the liberal Enlightenment project which, with its claims to universality, comprehensiveness and consistency, sets a fateful dimension. It can only relate to those excluded from the project through slavery or semi-slavery by saying that they are qualitatively different. This imperative, this terrifying consistency puts the enslaved and the colonised beyond the liberal equation of universal freedom and equality by rendering them in racist terms as qualitatively different. This identity in essential difference, particularly in the figure of the feckless African, becomes a counter in the making of the disciplined, 'liberal' individual in the west. Racism was, in short, basic to the creation of liberalism and the identity of the European.

Another strategy for extracting racism's significance entails a short-cut through liberalism. This could be called a strategy of telling instances. By this I mean instances, often seemingly insignificant or evanescent, which convincingly anticipate or provoke demotic responses. Jokes and politicians provide an abundance of these. Take the statement on 30 January 1978 of Thatcher as leader of the parliamentary opposition, a statement which immensely boosted both the popularity of the Conservative party and the salience of 'immigration' as an electoral issue. She said:

> ... that people are really rather afraid that this country might be swamped by people with a different culture. And, you know, the British character has done so much for democracy, for law, and done so much throughout the world, that if there is a fear that it might be swamped, people are going to react and be rather hostile to those coming in.[7]

As Martin Barker has so skillfully shown, all the elements of racism are contained in this and numerous other recent political evocations of culture, community and the miasma of unexpired imperial dreams.[8] To take one other instance, Crossman's diaries as a cabinet minister provide a candid account of anticipating a demotic response. The Labour government in the 1960s changed its policy and practice on immigration to an "illiberal" one so as to "out-trump the Tories" otherwise "we would have been faced with certain electoral defeat in the West Midlands and the South East".[9]

So far, there are two broad lines to the argument. One focuses on liberal capitalism and traces a basic conflict within it in that liberal capitalism opposes yet is maintained by racism. The other line of argument focuses on racism. It asserts the specificity and the significance of racism. That dimension intersects with the history of liberal capitalism indicating integral connections between racism and liberalism. I will now add law to the mixture.

LAW AS RACISM

Liberal cosmology provides a particular protection of law's innocence. Law is radically separate from 'material life' and can also act on and order that life: with liberal society "[p]articular self-interest must be constrained by universalistic legal and motivational structures; in this sense, the formal rationality of civil society must dominate the substantive rationality of material life".[10] In line with assertions of the centrality and significance of racism, we may ask what point is to be given to the experience of those for whom law is not separate from, much less able to order or correct that part of material life called racism. Lord Scarman could provide a celebrated confirmation that "'[i]nstitutional racism' does not exist in Britain" in a report that was an instance of it.[11] In this he was implicitly confronting and dismissing a phrase that black people used to encapsulate their experience of law and of state action.[12] That experience is not simply a contained 'different voice' which stands along with, if opposed to, liberal self-presentation. It can also be given point in founding a critical engagement with that self-presentation. An immediate problem is the powerful closure erected around liberal legality. Being radically separate from and ordering of material life, law cannot be brought into definitively complicitous comparisons with that life. Sympathetic connections between law and racism can be presented as exceptional and remediable, with the exceptional serving to contrast and confirm the great virtue of the norm.[13] Indeed, the very terms of that separation – terms of universalistic ordering, terms operatively realised in liberal legality – are ostentatiously opposed to racism. Against accusations of racism, then, law's innocence is unassailable.

If we 'respect' the terms of separation, that is, if we are not simply to reduce them to something else such as economic relations or treat them merely as a mask for something else, then the only way of integrally linking law with racism is to attack the foundation and show that those very terms of separation are racist. Law could then be seen as contradictory, as integrally opposed to and supportive of racism. I will argue that, metaphorically speaking, law positively acquires identity by taking elements of racism into itself and shaping them in its own terms. Yet law also takes identity from its opposition to and separation from racism. But this very opposition is not innocent for it operates by containing and constraining law. Law, as a result, and contrary to the principle of universality, is unable assuredly to counter racism. This is not just to say, along with assertions of critical legal scholars about the family and workplace, that by not entering areas where racism or sexism is prevalent law implicitly confers powers on those who are dominant within them.[14] Such a line of argument leaves law competent to intervene and counter that power and, of course, liberal legality is only a claim about competence, about being able to cover things, not about actual coverage. The point here is that racism marks constitutive boundaries of law, persistent limits on its competence and scope. Being so limited, law proves to be compatible with racism. I will argue, further, that it is the combination of this compatibility with law's claims to universalist competence that creates and heightens racism.

I will try to support that ambitious agenda in a way that may seem disappointingly and inaptly modest. That is, I will explore particular aspects of the operation of the Race Relations Act 1976. Although there may be a provocative persuasiveness in establishing racism in legislation aimed at countering it, there does remain the small problem of how the general assertions about law and racism that I have just indicated can be established in such a particular way. But to borrow from Foucault's "rule of double conditioning", a localised exercise of power with its "precise and tenuous relations" is effective only as a distinct but related part of a "general strategy" of power. The general strategy is, in turn, distinct but dependent for its effectiveness on the localised exercise of power.[15] The study of the localised is, in this light, necessary. It will also implicate the general. Specifically, an exploration of certain "precise and tenuous relations" involved in the Race Relations Act reveals persistent limits beyond which law will not proceed, limits erected in an overlapping of confining categories and discretions, and in the constitution of a domain of the normal. When we seek to move beyond these limits, we find on their borders "general strategies" drawing on racism, strategies which involve the power of capital and nation. This general dimension makes intelligible what would otherwise be mysterious in the limiting of localised instances. The approach from a localised instance cannot, of course, present some comprehensive, much less structured picture of the general. But I am arguing that effective general elements are invoked by it.

122

The British Race Relations Act 1976 enabled people to take civil action in respect of discrimination in certain areas of life on "racial grounds".[16] Persons discriminate if on racial grounds they treat someone less favourably than they treat or would treat others. There is also indirect discrimination which is the imposition of requirements or conditions having a discriminatory effect in that they disproportionately disadvantage racial groups, are to the detriment of the person alleging discrimination and cannot be otherwise justified. For example, educational requirements for a job that are in excess of what can be justified for the work to be done could indirectly discriminate against racial groups who are educationally 'disadvantaged'.

Almost all cases brought under the legislation concern employment. Employment cases are taken to an administrative court called an industrial tribunal. Awards which may be made in employment cases comprise damages for material loss and for injury to feelings, a declaration of the rights of the complainant and a recommendation that the employer take remedial action. Damages cannot be awarded in cases of indirect discrimination whilst there is no intent to discriminate. The Act also constitutes and empowers a governmental Commission for Racial Equality which is "to work towards the elimination of discrimination". Greatest emphasis is given to its broad power to investigate discriminatory practices, to issue non-discrimination notices and take court proceedings to have these enforced.

I will explore employment cases under the legislation, focusing on aspects of universalistic legal ordering. These are the form of universal individual right and the mode of adjudication, adjudication being the subjection of competing claims to universally applicable, impartially applied standards. I do not make the common, but infinitely contestable assertion found in critical legal studies that with legislation like this the form of right constitutes racial (or gender) oppression in terms of the action of individuals and thereby denies its wider 'social' or 'structural' determinants.[17] But this branch of critical legal studies is a source of assertions suggesting boundaries imported by the form of right, boundaries we can seek in the legislation and in the legal processes it generates. This will involve the mundane and the obvious – quotidian rules of evidence and questions about the burden of proof, for example. But, as I try to show, a multitude of oppressions are effected by the mundane and the obvious.

Right is attached to the individual legal actor who has to assert this right against the person allegedly in breach of a correlative duty. That breach is a matter of individual wrongdoing. It is something aberrant, a particular episode which disturbs the normal course. It calls for the occasional and discontinuous intervention of legal remedies. These remedies, in turn, need only reassert the normal course, need only focus on the act of the wrongdoer and correct or compensate for it. The form of right deals with deviation, and racism in liberal societies has to be a deviation. This correspondence provides a temptation to which the Race Relations Act succumbs in the basic remedy against 'discrimination'. In legal and liberal terms discrimination is a matter of intentional wrongdoing inflicted by one individual on another. The only significant remedy provided in the legislation is damages seen as redress, as affirming the norm. The complainant, the person wronged, has the onus of establishing that the norm has been disturbed. This 'burden of proof' is in practice a heavy one. As I will show later, industrial tribunals reflect the ethos of law and liberalism and take racial discrimination to be exceptional indeed.[18] There is also the banal paradox that making discrimination legally culpable has rendered it more elusive and intractable to remedial action. Unless the person supposedly discriminating is unaware or intemperate enough to provide it, it is difficult to get direct evidence of discrimination. The evidence, that is, will usually be circumstantial. Such evidence is never conclusive. It is clear from the cases that circumstantial evidence is accepted as proving discrimination, as discharging the burden of proof, only very exceptionally. Such constant rejections of complainants are facilitated by narrowing the type of knowledge that can be used in support of a claim. This narrowing is in terms of the individualistic nature of the relation and dispute between the parties. There is a concretising here of the form of right in the adversarial process. The adversaries, for example, are to be left on their own. The tribunal will only rarely help a litigant and it often explicitly refuses to do so. Evidence going beyond these individualistic dimensions will be rejected or given little weight. Instances of such evidence include social survey evidence of racial disadvantage in employment generally or statistical information about the 'racial' composition of the employer's workforce. In the same vein, the remedy of recommending that the employer take remedial action cannot extend beyond what is necessary to redress the adverse effect on the complainant. But the most potent dimension of individuality in the legal process here is that of intention. The unsurpassed aptness of a rejected applicant is not evidence of racial discrimination because she or he may have been rejected on other grounds. And such grounds, as tribunals repeatedly recognise, can include the most vague and the most irrational. Constantly, tribunals uphold employers' purported rejection of applicants in such terms as demeanour, personality, ability to fit in and even in terms of favouritism on the part of the employer. Obviously, racially-based decisions can be thus justified or obscured with ease. Tribunals also engage here in a revealing slippage, one that purports to follow on from intentionality but goes beyond legal justification in such terms. For what they assert is that such decisions are the prerogative of the employer, that they have to accept the employer's assessment and even the terms in which it is made. As a matter of course the impermeability of the employer's power is affirmed.

It is convenient now to be fair and credit the legislation with attempts to transcend the limits imported by the form of right and the related idea of discrimination. But these attempts, I now argue, end up confirming and reinforcing the original limits. The Commission for Racial Equality is given ostensibly broad powers to investigate discrimination and to issue a non-discrimination notice. Any threat that this power may be effective is avoided by its reduction in the lineaments of the form of right. Thus, a non-discrimination notice can only relate to particular acts. The Commission's power to issue a *subpoena* for information is restricted to investigations where the Commission suspects a named person of discriminatory acts, and there has already to be material supporting "a reasonable suspicion".[19] That position is reached with the aid of judicial interpretation, an interpretation which reflects a splenetic attitude to conferring judicial-type power on an administrative body thereby denying, in the view of the judges, adequate protection for the individual: "[y]ou might think that we are back in the days of the Inquisition. . . . You might think that we were back in the days of the General Warrants", thought Lord Denning. He appropriated control of this power for the judges, where it has remained. The court was "free to balance the public interests involved", those between the "immense powers" given to the Commission "to compel the disclosure of confidential information" and "the importance to the public services and industrial concerns" of preserving that confidentiality.[20] Less spectacularly, the Act in s.38(3)(a) confers a similar discretion by obliquely applying rules of evidence relating to discovery. A similar story can be told about discovery in its more general application in cases before tribunals. Discovery does have a particular significance in such cases for it is "designed to offset the probative disadvantage which the complainant would otherwise suffer" because evidence of discrimination will usually be in the hands of the employer.[21] Discovery tends to be successful when the information is narrowly focused on the applicant or the alleged act of discrimination. But 'confidentiality' almost invariably excludes discovery of more extensive information held by the employer such as details of the competitors for a job or for promotion. Inevitably, it is for the tribunal to exercise a discretion here in terms of what is "necessary for dispensing fairly of the proceedings".[22] In short, where the Act provides modes compensating for the limits entailed in the form of right, the limits are extended to confine these modes. Should this not suffice to protect the portals of capital, then adjudicators are to exercise their discretion, in both senses of the word.

The most revealing instance of this strategy is provided by indirect discrimination. Such discrimination is, in part, constituted in categories of the form of right. Action is brought by the individual who must have sustained harm. But there is no purposive wrongdoing involved. The causal element springs from the disproportionate effect the employer's "requirement or condition" has on a racial group. Tenaciously, the form of right shapes the outcome because damages cannot be awarded whilst the employer did not intend to discriminate. But the core of indirect discrimination, the salience of the effect on a racial group, goes beyond the realm of individual right. Here, legal enquiry and legal ordering cannot be confined to some episodic wrongdoing. They must now penetrate the realm of the employer, examining and assessing potentially any "requirement or condition" relating to employment. But the potency of indirect discrimination was soon countered in judicial applications of the exemption from indirect discrimination of a requirement or condition shown to be justifiable. This was rendered in terms of, variously, what was reasonable or commonsensical, or what was acceptable to right-thinking people and such, or it was simply a question of fact unique to each case. Judicial creativity enters again with an expedient balancing, the desirability of eliminating discrimination being balanced against the demands of the employer's enterprise. In this, judges and tribunals again explicitly recognise that employers are to be left with their autonomy; they ought to be able to decide what is best for business.

In looking at the two types of universalistic ordering, I have so far concentrated on the form of right and have considered the mode of adjudication only from that perspective. Adjudication sustained the form of right as a confining category and restrained extensions beyond it by the apt use of discretion and the recognition of the employer's autonomy. I will now focus more exclusively on the process of adjudication. We can start with the banality that law cannot be mechanically applied. Adjudication requires a productive impetus, a positive going-out to recognise and shape claims. We can continue with another banality: that, as it is usually put, the values of adjudicators influence their decisions. I will try to establish this not in the sense of values intruding on otherwise pristine standards and processes of adjudication, but in the sense of values constituting these standards and processes. Such standards and processes, in turn, form a particular but comprehensive perspective which quite simply includes the interests of some and excludes the interests of others. This is not a matter of remediable bias or some such. It is a matter of a whole sensibility. Adjudicators cannot be responsive to interests they cannot comprehend. Nor can they respond through standards and processes that obscure and deny these interests rather than reveal them. The productive impetus needed to recognise claims in adjudication does not operate to recognise claims founded in such interests. Where the claims are insistent and potentially disruptive, they are explained away as something else, something understood within the particular perspective, understood in the domain of the normal. I will now expand and illustrate that argument.

Adjudicative standards and processes are not pure creations. They are responsive to and draw on wider rationalities operating beyond adjudication and law. With industrial tribunals, there is an explicit mode of incorporating such wider rationalities, since, in addition to a legally qualified chairperson, tribunals are composed of two 'wing' members drawn respectively from employers' and trade union organisations. Such peope are likely to be more responsive to "good industrial relations" than to adopt a radical view towards the notorious racism of employers and trade unions.[23] They are not likely to transcend the traditional hostility of employers and unions to anti-discrimination legislation.[24] The failure, for example, of "industry machinery" to discern discrimination under the previous Race Relations Act was almost complete.[25] The point can be made dramatically by looking at cases where a wing member has some specialist background in 'race relations'. Commenting on "the experience of adjudication in the first eighteen months of the Act", Lustgarten notes that "in *every* case in which there was a split tribunal decision against the complainant, the non-specialist wingmen joined the chairman to make the majority".[26] That experience, with but few exceptions, has continued since. We are, it would seem, dealing here with two worlds. The inability of industrial tribunals to respond to one of them was starkly evident even before the Race Relations Act of 1976 in cases of unfair dismissal brought under employment protection legislation. Despite numerous such cases involving a racial element, "[i]n not one case . . . [had] there been an express finding that dismissal was for racial reasons".[27] Nor does the legally qualified chairperson inhibit the abject responsiveness of wing members to prevailing rationalities. The chairperson is more likely than these members to find against the complainant. But disagreement among tribunal members is quite exceptional. Uniformity is promoted in the chairperson's tending to be a dominating influence. This dominance is fostered in the technical nature of the process. Despite original aspirations to informality and accessibility, industrial tribunals have become increasingly legalistic. Hence, although they are never great, the chances of success are very slim without expert assistance.[28] Often tribunals assert that they are not bound by technical rules of evidence, such as the rule against admitting hearsay evidence, but almost as often this is merely a prelude to applying such rules. More generally, the crudities of such rules, of the adversarial process, of the standard tricks of advocacy designed to block the truth, all serve to exclude evidence of an often subtle and intractable racial oppression.[29] This, in sum, is a circumscribed ritual of reassertion of a world in which such oppression is non-existent or rare.

What if evidence of racial discrimination survives these exclusions? Exceptionally a complainant will succeed as a result. Much more usually, the evidence is made to conform to the domain of the normal in two ways. In one, apparent evidence of the employer's discrimination is understood by the tribunal as something else. So, a particular hostility to the applicant is understood as a communications problem, as bad management practice, or as the result of pressure or health problems. Alternatively, the domain of the normal reduces evidence of the employer's discrimination to a less challenging dimension. So, the complainant is, in terms of the common *canard*, paranoid or over-sensitive or the acts complained of are "trivial".[30] But this is the "triviality of the sand", to borrow Auden's phrase. What is happening is that the massive reality of oppression is being rejected or reduced to the insignificant, whereas the employer's reality is being accepted and elevated to the determinant. It is not so much a matter that the employer's account is believed whereas the complainant's is not. The grinding normality is that the employer's account serves to call forth and to confirm what is already there, what is already known.

Of course, industrial tribunals are not the sole occupants of the field of adjudication. But they do have something close to sole occupancy of a crucial part of it. Factual questions and questions of the weight of evidence will, as a matter of law, rarely be disturbed on appeal. Appellate courts will have a decisive influence on tribunals in determining questions of law and thereby providing precedents which tribunals have to follow. There is also the vaguer

127

question of appellate 'values' influencing tribunals. On both these counts the constant refrain has been one of restriction, reinforcing the perspective generated within tribunals. In its interpretation, race relations legislation has not been construed expansively under, say, the 'mischief rule' as befits the remedying of an acknowledged social evil. Rather, appeal courts see the Race Relations Acts as having to be interpreted strictly, especially as they restrict "the liberty which the citizen has previously enjoyed at common law" to discriminate.[31] Such judicial invocation of positive legal liberties also characterises, as we have seen, the balancing of confidentiality and the employer's autonomy against the desirability of eliminating discrimination. This line of argument may accord well with the demonstration by critical legal scholars (and others) that "the legal process at large and its discrete doctrinal components . . . are fundamentally indeterminant and manipulable", and that adjudication draws on no ultimate and principled resolution but is, rather, a "political" process.[32] The argument here is different, however. We have seen that in the process of adjudication some elements when weighed in the balance have more or less persistently been found wanting. What happens is that these seeming choices are not simply made, but themselves make the community of law. With this community, apparently disjoint or indeterminant elements do configure in hierarchies which, if not invariant, are at least usual. Judges relate to the overall ordering ethos of community in such ultimate and revealing terms as what is "sensible" and "reasonable", what conforms to "the fitness of things", and to "common sense".[33] These are not masks for an unbounded, 'political' discretion. They are, rather, borders beyond which the recognition of constraint cannot proceed in terms of the community's particular traditions and particular rationalities.

LAW, RACE AND THE LIBERAL WORLD

This community of law, like any community, is not generated purely internally. Through industrial tribunals, as we have seen, the community of law incorporates and integrally relies on a particular yet operatively comprehensive perspective. This perspective joins with the confining categories and obscuring discretions of the form of right and of the legal process to set law's bounds. These bounds restrict law but in so doing they maintain its integrity in its relation to the power of employers.[34] Law is, however, constituted not just in opposition to other types of power but also in the positive assimilation of wider, sustaining identities. There are identities predisposed toward racism with which law is intimately involved. One is the modern figure of society as a contained unit with a 'typical' membership.[35] The other is the distinct but not greatly dissimilar figure of the nation: liberal "legality . . . celebrates and elevates the law to an exalted status as the expression of unity in the nation".[36] Neither these identities nor law take on a racist dimension without its specific historical addition. Such an addition is, of course, frequent and Britain is conspicuously not an exception. In line with my

128

earlier argument, the addition of racism effects the unity of society and nation and serves to constitute the identity of its members.

I will now explore law's connections with the particularity of society and nation and relate these connections to law's universalistic pretensions. The argument will develop through instances. One is the very genius of the common law with its combination of universalistic "reason" with a "strange and . . . incoherent" (English) particularism.[37] In Dicey's seminal account of constitutional law, the combination becomes a prerogative of the 'English'. The resulting "rule of law" is not English in the sense that it should be confined to England. It is just that in less happy climes, such as Belgium, its existence is much more attenuated.[38] Adjusting Dicey's paean to our concern with a more mundane reality of legal procedure, Lord Denning recently could find a betrayal of 'England' and Empire in a small challenge posed by the European Communities (Amendment) Bill to the "English adversary system".[39] To put the argument before instances descend any further, such ethnocentric elevations of law are an inevitable reconciliation of law's palpable national connections with its transcendent universalist claims.[40] In the result, law is captured as an expression of national superiority. When that superiority incorporates racism, law is likewise captured as an expression of it.

It is hardly surprising, then, that the resort to law as a symbol of race and nation should be so facile, so common and so effective.[41] Thus, to return to the stratagem of the telling instance and to Thatcher's contribution, she precisely echoes the imperialist claim to law as a gift we gave them, gave those "people with a different culture", people who did not have law, who did not give it to the world and who in remaining essentially alien have failed to assimilate the gift adequately. Almost in passing, the not-so-distinctive contributions of the higher judiciary to this 'new racism' have also at times assumed telling dimensions.[42] But for law the most telling has probably been the immense popular response to Powell's speech in 1968, in which racial division in Britain prompted some characteristic visions: "[l]ike the Roman, I seem to see 'the River Tiber foaming with much blood'". His prop and target were provided by the then Race Relations Bill, an anti-discrimination measure even more limited and more anaemic than the current legislation. Yet Powell presented it with great effect as "a one-way privilege", as "legal weapons" which "the stranger" can now use "to overawe and dominate the rest".[43] Gilroy has acutely located a potency of Powell's appeal here in the "debasement" and "perversion" of what was pure law and English law. This "ultimate symbol of national culture" is traduced through "blacks being afforded limited legal protection".[44]

Indeed, both the critics and the supporters of race relations legislation agree that its purpose is to bring black people 'discriminated' against into society.[45] But, as the aptly named Whitelaw as Home Secretary put it: for equal rights, responsibilities and opportunities to be extended to such people, they should "demonstrate their commitment to our society" and abandon cultural and linguistic isolation.[46] The Race Relations Acts are seen not just as a powerful means for black people to achieve this, but also as a privilege given to them and as an advantage over white people. This is not just Powell's perception but a popular one.[47] It is also, incidentally, one that is wrong in that the legislation protects people of any race and cases brought by white people are not infrequent. But the error is much more extensive than that. The race relations legislation has had little reforming effect.[48] The failure of the oppressed successfully to use such powerful, privileging legal means thus confirms their essential inadequacy. Reform, in the guise of a succession of Race Relations Acts, like so much reform becomes part of the problematic, creating and sustaining that which it purports to counter.

Law, in short, is tied to a particular community which excludes those whom law would include through race relations legislation. In the liberal world-view, as we saw, law erects a universal inclusiveness, transcending and ordering material life. It is true that law as legal rules only directs what should happen and so cannot be held specifically accountable. But the liberal world-view does entail a general and a strong claim for law's competence. If the powerful and persistent ministrations of law do not bring certain racial identities into society that must be because the identities are essentially different and naturally incapable. This is but a continuation of that legacy of the Englightenment in which those constantly beyond the liberal equation have to be qualitatively different from those within it.

CONCLUSION

I started questioning the manifest opposition between liberal legality and racism by drawing on a conflict in Marxist accounts of racism. This conflict indicated that racism was incompatible yet symbiotic with liberal capitalism in Britain. This same conflict pointed towards the specificity and the enormous significance of racism. But no matter what the significance of racism, law seemed to escape any complicitous connections with it. This was because, in the liberal world-view, law was a form of universalistic ordering which transcended material life. Yet if the universalistic terms of that transcendence could, paradoxically, be held racist, then law could still be rendered accountable. To begin establishing that, I took a seemingly perverse course of looking at instances of universalistic legal ordering which were not only minutely localised but also explicitly opposed to 'racial discrimination'. These instances were the operation of the form of right and of the mode of adjudication in employment cases under the Race Relations Act of 1976.

A detailed study of such instances showed that there were certain persistent limits, certain bounds beyond which law did not proceed in countering racism. What, in an immediate sense, stood on the other side of those bounds and checked law's advance was the power and autonomy of employers. Law thus marked out areas in which the racism of employers could operate. But the relation of law to racism was seen to be more intimate. Between law and the employer, mediating and constituting the necessary distance separating them, was a comprehensive yet particular perspective generated in adjudication which 'naturally' and racially set law's limits and, in the same moment, denied

130

effect to the contrary experience of black people. This perspective inhabited the community of law which, in turn, evoked and integrally relied on a wider, racially-conceived society and nation. For these entities, law was an operative figure of great social impact. In this, law was seen to be readily involved in extensive racist strategies. Its contributions to racism were also more distinctive, however. Law's claims to universalistic ordering contrasted with its confinement in terms of specific national community. The disjunction, as we saw, is resolved by making that community and its law the incarnation of a rational universal ordering. Those of a 'different culture' are not, however, merely excluded from superior reason. When, as in the Race Relations Act, its beneficent and potent modes are extended to them in terms of universalistic ordering but then withdrawn in implicit terms of community, a gap opens which is filled by the attribution to them of an insuperable inadequacy.

NOTES AND REFERENCES

1   J.-P. Sartre, "Preface" to F. Fanon, *The Wretched of the Earth* (1967) p. 22.
2   See G. Ben-Tovim *et al.*, "Race, Left Strategies and the State" (1981) 3 *Politics and Power* p. 153.
3   M. Foucault, "Questions of Method: An Interview with Michel Foucault" (1981) 8 *I. & C.* p. 3, p. 12.
4   See A. Szymanski, "Race, Sex and the U.S. Working Class" (1973-74) 21 *Social Problems* p. 706 for an account and strange application of these Marxist views on race.
5   See, for example, Centre for Contemporary Cultural Studies, *The Empire Strikes Back: Race and Racism in 70s Britain* (1982).
6   See, for example, P. Fryer, *Staying Power: The History of Black People in Britain* (1984) chap. 7.
7   As quoted in M. Barker, "Racism – The New Inheritors" (1984) 21 *Radical Philosophy* p. 2, p. 4.
8   *Id.*
9   As quoted in J. Rex and S. Tomlinson, *Colonial Immigrants in a British City: A Class Analysis* (1979) p. 61.
10 Poole, "Reason, Self-Interest and 'Commercial Society': The Social Content of Kantian Morality" (1984) *Critical Philosophy* p. 24, p. 42.
11 *The Brixton Disorders 10-12 April 1981: Report of an Inquiry by the Right Honourable the Lord Scarman, O.B.E.* (1982; Penguin ed.) p. 209; Barker and Beezer, "The Language of Racism" (1983) *International Socialism* p. 108.
12 A. Sivanandan, "Race, Class and the State: The Black Experience in Britain" (1976) XVII *Race and Class* p. 347.
13. For example, Scarman, *op. cit.*, p. 119.
14 Cf. some targets of Rose's analysis in this collection.
15 M. Foucault, *The History of Sexuality Volume I: An Introduction* (1981) pp. 99-100.
16 The summaries in the text are supported in ss.1,2,6,17,20,43,48-51 and 54-58 of the Act.
17 For example, Freeman, "Legitimizing Racial Discrimination Through Antidiscrimination Law: A Critical Review of Supreme Court Doctrine" (1978) 62 *Minnesota Law Rev.* p. 1049.
18 Statements about legal process draw on a survey of judgments in cases before industrial tribunals and employment appeals tribunals. The records of most are kept in the Central Office of the Industrial Tribunals. I will happily supply people interested with record numbers of cases supporting or instancing the various statements. I will refer here to cases from which quotations are taken. The name of a case followed only by a number refers to its record in the Central Office.

19 R. v. Commission for Racial Equality, Ex parte Hillingdon Borough Council [1982] 1 Q.B. 276.
20 Science Research Council v Nassé [1979] 1 Q.B. 144 at pp. 172-73.
21 British Library v Palyza and Another [1984] I.C.R. 504 at p. 508.
22 Id., p. 507.
23 Francis v Newey and Eyre Limited 20743/80.
24 See, for example, A. Lester and G. Bindman, Race and Law (1972) pp. 126-130.
25 Select Committee on Race Relations and Immigration, Minutes of Evidence (Race Relations Board), Session 1973-74 (24 January 1974) p. 28.
26 L. Lustgarten, Legal Control of Racial Discrimination (1980) p. 196 (his emphasis).
27 I. A. Macdonald, Race Relations: The New Law (1977) p. 122.
28 V. Kumar, Industrial Tribunal Applicants Under the Race Relations Act 1976: A Research Report (1986).
29 On tricks of advocacy see Paynter, "Presenting Your Case: A Guide to Effective Advocacy Before the Industrial Tribunal: Part Two" (1984) The Lawyer p. 14. Other points were dealt with earlier.
30 Shah v Richards Longstaff Ltd. 26623/84. On the canard see D. J. Smith, Unemployment and Racial Minorities (1981) p. 158.
31 Per Lord Diplock in Dockers' Labour Club and Institute, Ltd. v Race Relations Board [1974] 3 All E.R. 592 at p. 598.
32 Hutchinson and Monahan, "Law, Politics and the Critical Legal Scholars: The Unfolding Drama of American Legal Thought" (1984) 36 Stanford Law Rev. p. 199 at pp. 211-12.
33 P. Goodrich, Reading Law: A Critical Introduction to Legal Method and Techniques (1986) p. 152.
34 The point is developed more generally in Fitzpatrick, "Law and Societies" (1984) 22 Osgoode Hall Law J. p. 115.
35 P.Hirst and P. Woolley, Social Relations and Human Attributes (1982) chaps. 2 and 3.
36 C. Sumner, Reading Ideologies: An Investigation into the Marxist Theory of Ideology and Law (1979) p. 293.
37 D. Little, Religion, Order and Law: A Study in Pre-Revolutionary England (1969) p. 172.
38 A. V. Dicey, Introduction to the Study of the Law of the Constitution (1885) chap. 4.
39 480 H.L. Debs., cols. 249-51, 265 (8 October 1986).
40 Law's inter- and sub-national existences do not detract from its powerful national configuration.
41 For an enthralling account and analysis of instances see P. Gilroy, 'There Ain't No Black in the Union Jack': The Cultural Politics of 'Race' and Nation (forthcoming) chap. 3.
42 Barker and Beezer, op. cit., and Lester and Bindman, op. cit., pp. 90-91.
43 E. Powell, Freedom and Reality (1969) pp. 286, 289.
44 Op. cit., chap. 3.
45 For example, Sivanandan, op. cit., and Home Office, Racial Discrimination (1975; Cmnd. 6234) p. 6.
46 "Whitelaw Seeks to Reassure Immigrants on Equal Rights" The Guardian, 12 July 1980.
47 See, for example, A. Phizacklea and R. Miles, "Working-class Racist Beliefs in the Inner City" in Racism and Political Action in Britain (1979; eds. R. Miles and A. Phizacklea) p. 113.
48 C. Brown and P. Gay, Racial Discrimination: 17 Years After the Act (1985).

Women in Confinement: Can Labour Law Deliver the Goods?

JOANNE CONAGHAN* and LOUISE CHUDLEIGH*

In June 1985, the government Green Paper on social security, containing proposals now nearing the stage of implementation after the passing of the Social Security Act 1986, described maternity pay as "a form of reward for continuous service with one employer for a period of years".[1] Thus, in just ten years the maternity provisions introduced in 1975 as part of a package of 'minimum standards' for the protection of employees have been transformed from the status of basic rights to rare rewards – or have they?

With the maternity provisions and indeed employment protection generally openly under attack as part of the present government's policy of deregulation, the question arises as to what extent these provisions are worth preserving.[2] It may appear obvious that feminists should engage in the struggle to preserve these hard-won rights especially given the increasing percentage of women, particularly married women, entering the labour market and attempting to combine home and work responsibilities.[3] However, feminists may be in danger here of becoming locked in a struggle which will produce little in the way of results. The debate over maternity rights raises the crucial question of strategy in a particularly revealing form. Feminists engaged in promoting women's interests are constantly faced with the question of what exactly those interests are. Sometimes women's immediate interests do not correspond with their long-term strategic interests when informed by an understanding of the nature and causes of women's oppression. For example, feminist campaigns in the inter-war years to improve maternity services arguably did as much to strengthen the ideology of motherhood as to promote women's rights. As Jen Dale observes:

> ... the 'woman question' had been largely collapsed into the 'mother question' as women's individual needs were subordinated to those of the mother-child diad.[4]

Thus feminists must ask what benefits, if any, the maternity provisions provide for working women and at the same time must consider whether or not their long-term effects do more to increase women's responsibilities than reduce them.

It is to these questions of strategy that this paper is addressed. Within this context, we will look first at the philosophy which shaped the emergence of employment protection in the 1970s including the maternity provisions in

* Department of Law, University of Kent, Canterbury, Kent CT2 7NY, England.

their original form. The paper will then look at the development of New Right philosophy and politics in the 1980s and its implications both for labour law and for women. It is hoped that this exploration will throw light on the dilemma of feminists drawn into the struggle to preserve a set of provisions which are themselves inadequate both in form and content.

THE EMERGENCE OF EMPLOYMENT PROTECTION

Until the 1960s the legal approach to labour relations in Britain was traditionally characterised as 'abstentionism', that is, the stated policy of successive governments from the passing of the Trades Dispute Act 1906 was to abstain from close legal regulation of industrial relations and to facilitate 'voluntary' regulation by the parties themselves through the medium of collective bargaining. However, during the 1960s growing industrial disorder increasingly focused legislative attention on the employment area. What began as a piecemeal legislative strategy in the 1960s continued with an unprecedented statutory onslaught in the 1970s. In particular the return of a Labour government in 1974 and the subsequent 'social contract' struck between government and the unions resulted in a plethora of legislation aimed both at the protection of individual employees and the promotion of collective bargaining. Within this context emerged the employment protection framework of which the maternity provisions form a part. Originating in the Employment Protection Act 1975 and consolidated in the Employment Protection (Consolidation) Act 1978, the maternity provisions formed part of a package of rights concerned with security of earnings. However, the framework established was not viewed either by the legislators or the unions as a departure from the previous emphasis on voluntary arrangements but was regarded as a means of facilitating collective bargaining by providing a statutory 'floor of rights' which could form the starting point for union-management negotiations. Thus, from their very conception the statutory maternity provisions, as with the other rights secured for employees during this period, were regarded as a bare minimum.

The original maternity provisions came into effect in 1976 and 1977. *Very* basically, under the new legislation an employee expecting a baby acquired at least three rights. First, a pregnant employee acquired the right to complain of unfair dismissal because of pregnancy – under s.60 of the Employment Protection (Consolidation) Act 1978 dismissal for any reason connected with pregnancy was automatically unfair in most circumstances.[5] Secondly, she acquired the right to receive maternity pay[6] – this entitlement, lasting for six weeks, gave an employee the right to nine tenths of each week's pay less any maternity allowance payable under the Social Security Act 1975 (whether or not she was entitled to the whole or any part of that allowance).[7] Thirdly, she acquired the right to return to work with her employer after a period of absence due to pregnancy and confinement (maternity leave).[8] This right was exercisable any time after eleven weeks before the expected date of confinement. Moreover, an employee was not obliged to return until twenty-nine weeks after the week of confinement. She was obliged to notify her employer three weeks in advance of her intended absence and intention to return, and was required to notify her employer one week beforehand of the date of her return.

Apart from her new rights under the Employment Protection Act 1975 a pregnant employee was also entitled, under the social security scheme, to a maternity grant to help with the immediate expenses of having a baby (fixed at £25 in 1969 and still £25) and to maternity allowance (subject to contribution requirements), payable for eighteen weeks from the eleventh week before the expected week of confinement.[9] The standard rate at the moment is about £29. Taken together the social security and employment provisions may appear to confer no significant benefit on pregnant workers. But, as we shall see, reality does not always correspond with appearance.

EVALUATING THE MATERNITY PROVISIONS
HOW WELL DO THEY WORK?

Any attempt to evaluate the maternity provisions immediately raises the issue of criteria: according to what standards should the maternity provisions be assessed; what ends do they serve to promote? This is not as unproblematic a question as it at first appears.

Insofar as the employment protection framework is characterised as 'instrumental', that is, exemplifying the use of law as an instrument for the promotion of certain objectives, it is not always clear what in fact those objectives are. For example, one can identify at least three particular ends attributable to the maternity provisions. The most obvious is, of course, improving women's job status in the labour market by compensating them for the biological fact of child-bearing. However, a second and equally significant aim is "to protect the health and physical welfare of mother and baby".[10] A concern with infant mortality has always accompanied debates about the employment of women and has been of major significance in stimulating welfare reforms. The regulations restricting women's working hours in factories, first introduced in 1844, are an early example.[11] Likewise the introduction of the maternity grant in the National Insurance Act 1911 can almost certainly be related to concern over the high rate of infant mortality. Thus, it is possible to view the maternity provisions as embodying a state policy designed to supplement the reproductive function of the family. A third apparent end of the maternity provisions is the accommodation of changing economic conditions and in particular the changing gender-composition of the labour market. We have already referred to the great increase in married women entering the workforce in the postwar years.[12] Such a change in the composition of labour arguably rendered maternity provisions of some sort inevitable. Thus, in a symposium on maternity benefits published in 1971 (before the maternity provisions were introduced), much of the focus is on the new phenomenon of the working mother and her economic implications. The symposium presents child-care and maternity provisions as a positive benefit

135

to employers because it enables them to recruit and retain a highly mobile, committed and efficient labour force.[13] This economic perspective is reinforced by Lewis and Simpson's suggestion that "the maternity provisions had as much to do with the efficient operation of the labour market as with the rights of women".[14]

It is thus clear that any assessment of the provisions must take account of the variety of ends which they appear to serve. To some extent a failure to recognise this explains the different conclusions as to the value of the provisions reached by sympathetic commentators on the one hand and the government on the other.[15] For while the former are mainly concerned with their value as an equal opportunities strategy, the latter are clearly measuring their worth by reference to the efficient running of the labour market. Thus equal opportunities advocates argue that the maternity provisions are at present inadequate in scope and ought to be extended.[16] In contrast, the government views maternity rights as a heavy burden on employers – particularly small employers – which should, therefore, be reduced. This apparent deadlock is highlighted by the findings of a series of studies on the maternity provisions carried out at the end of the 1970s which appear to support the view of equal opportunities advocates and undermine the arguments of the government.[17] The Policy Studies Institute (P.S.I.) study conducted by Bill Daniel provides evidence to suggest that little over half of women who work during pregnancy (fifty-four per cent) qualify for maternity rights due to the stringent nature of the qualifying conditions; and of those even fewer actually exercise their rights.[18] The low take-up rate has been variously explained as resulting from the ignorance of employees, the complicated nature of the legislation and the fact that for most women the arrival of a baby creates financial and care responsibilities which the provisions simply do not accommodate. For example, returning to work after the birth of a baby is inconceivable if the mother cannot find or afford adequate day-care provisions. It is clear that the presence of a small child particularly at pre-school age has a major effect on a woman's availability for paid work.[19]

Research studies not only lend support to the equal opportunities contention that the maternity provisions are too narrowly drawn and should therefore be extended, but also suggest that government arguments for the reduction of maternity rights are ill-founded. In answer to the government claim that maternity rights impose a heavy burden on small employers, both the P.S.I. study and a Department of Employment survey suggest that small employers have had very little experience of the legislation.[20] Moreover, despite government arguments that the provisions are unpopular with employers, a survey conducted in 1980 found that eighty-three per cent of employers in their sample thought that the provisions were working well and those who expressed dissatisfaction invariably had no experience of them.[21] However, despite this countervailing evidence the government went ahead with their plans to cut the maternity provisions in 1980 and still echo the same tune in relation to further pending cuts. Meanwhile, equal opportunities

136

supporters continue to urge the extension of the maternity provisions and, most recently, the implementation of the E.E.C. Directive on Parental Leave (providing both parents with a right to leave for child-care purposes over and above existing maternity provisions), which our government, predictably, is fervently opposing in the European forum.[22]

At this point of the debate it is necessary to step outside the deadlock which the government's attack on maternity rights creates and look at the struggle taking place from a broader perspective. Such a perspective throws into focus two separate but related questions. First, given the evidence of studies conducted before government cuts were implemented that the maternity provisions were not in fact having a significant impact, we need to ask why the maternity provisions have failed as an equality strategy? Secondly, given the evidence of the same studies that government fears of employer costs and inconvenience were groundless, why have they continued to pursue a policy of restriction nevertheless? We will now address the first of those questions.

THE FAILURE OF MATERNITY PROVISIONS AS AN EQUALITY STRATEGY

The maternity provisions are unique in expressing both women's equality with men and their difference. They are designed to promote equality by creating the conditions for equal competition between women and men as individual workers. At the same time the method by which this object is to be achieved involves singling out women for 'special treatment' as child-bearers. Why has this strategy failed to secure women's equality? We would argue that the key to answering this question involves recognising that the 'form' of the maternity provisions embodies a masculine conception of work. Current conceptions of employment reflect a male norm: they are built upon a notion of the male worker who is full-time, long-term and unionised. Women workers tend to deviate from this norm: first, their working patterns are often interrupted and part-time;[23] secondly, many women workers are not unionised because as a 'secondary' sector labour force they find it difficult to organise.[24] Thirdly, and perhaps most importantly, while legal conceptions of work focus upon the public arena of the workplace as a divorced and separate entity from the private sphere of the home and family, the reality of women's lives reflects no such separation. Thus, labour law both embodies and conceals the gender division of labour and, by focusing exclusively on the world of paid work, ignores the differing responsibilities which men and women have in the home. These assertions require further exploration.

1. Male Conceptions of Work and Workers

Like other aspects of the employment protection framework, the maternity provisions require a worker to be engaged as an "employee", that is, under a "contract of employment".[25] Various studies on the nature of women's paid work demonstrate that women often fail to fit this category by virtue of the "casual" nature of their work, for example, as child-minders or home-

137

workers.[26] Moreover, many women are employed upon a sub-contractual basis which excludes them from employee status,[27] particularly in newly privatised areas such as cleaning. To qualify for maternity rights a woman must also be continuously employed for two years at the eleventh week before the expected date of confinement.[28] For many women this requirement is too long, either because domestic responsibilities dictate an interrupted work pattern, or because women as a low-paid, badly-protected sector of the workforce are more likely to find themselves on short-term contracts which prevent the accumulation of statutory rights. Moreover, the requirement of "continuous" employment for sixteen hours or more per week tends to exclude many part-time workers, the majority of whom are women.[29] Clearly, therefore, the conception of work upon which the maternity provisions are based does not accommodate the wide and varied working patterns of women.

2. Maternity Provisions and Collective Bargaining

As has been observed, the maternity provisions were conceived of as a minimum standard designed to form a starting point for collective negotiation. Indeed, Gill and Whitty have suggested various ways in which statutory rights could be improved by collective bargaining.[30] For example, workers could negotiate a reduced service qualification, the extension of coverage to all part-time workers, longer maternity pay (Gill and Whitty suggest eighteen weeks), arrangements permitting the part-time return of new mothers and paternity leave provisions.

We would argue that such suggestions do not go nearly far enough, but even as they stand they appear unmistakably 'pie in the sky' when one considers the existing extent of negotiated maternity arrangements. A survey in 1980 revealed that only eighteen per cent of employers in their sample made more generous maternity arrangements than the law provides and, in general, concluded that progress to improve benefits by collective negotiation had been slow.[31] Clearly, as Drake and Bercusson point out:

> ... the future of maternity benefits will depend in practice on the extent to which trade unions ... fight for provisions to be made in collective agreements safeguarding them.[32]

Inevitably, this in turn depends upon the influence of women in the trade union movement. Although women make up thirty per cent of total union membership at present, by virtue of the occupational segregation existing in the labour market they are confined to a narrow range of platforms and continue to be under-represented in the higher echelons of the movement. At the T.U.C. conference in September 1986, for example, less than fifteen per cent of the total 1,100 delegates were women. Moreover, not only do women find it difficult to find a voice in the union movement due to job segregation, the burden of domestic responsibilities and sexist attitudes by male union members, but many also find it impossible to organise at all. Women workers are commonly employed in small disparate workplaces – catering, cleaning and shop assisting, for example, where unionisation has always been difficult. As a result, two thirds of the female workforce are non-unionised and therefore unlikely to benefit from union negotiation to improve maternity rights.

3. Maternity Provisions and the Public/Private Dichotomy

Maternity provisions are exclusively concerned with women at work. They focus on the pregnant worker, facilitate her departure from and return to the labour market, but take no account of the transformation in her life which has occurred through the facts of pregnancy and childbirth. In other words, the maternity provisions reflect the traditional liberal dichotomy between the public world of the market and the private world of the home and family. A view of the market and the family as separate and distinct spheres fails to perceive the interaction between the two; how, for example, woman's role in the public sphere is limited and influenced by the domestic burdens she has to carry in the private sphere while her dependent position in the private sphere is reinforced by her low-paid marginal status in the public sphere.[33] Because the maternity provisions conceive of the labour market as 'public', positing its isolation from the private sphere of home, they do not question the assumption that the primary role of women is as mothers. Maternity rights do not lift the domestic burden of child-care from women: they merely facilitate the carrying of an additional burden should a mother choose to enter the labour market. But it is clear that this choice is already circumscribed by the existence of family responsibilities. Not only does a true equality strategy require a dramatic increase in the existence of day-care facilities and nurseries for pre-school children but it also requires a radical transformation in the ideology of motherhood and the family. The maternity provisions in their present form do not begin to bring about this transformation.

4. The Limits of Equal Opportunity

The maternity provisions are predicated upon two fundamental but flawed concepts: equality and individualism. From a feminist perspective the concept of equality is flawed because it constantly requires women to compare themselves with a male norm. Equality becomes 'sameness with men' and where women are clearly *not* the same as men, the concept of equality demands an eradication of the difference – so pregnant workers are permitted to leave and return to the labour market as if nothing had happened. Thus, the equality principle continually directs women to strive for the male norm, to participate equally in the male world and to conceive of any deviation – part-time commitment, interrupted work patterns – as marginal. The male conception of the full-time, long-term, unionised breadwinner becomes central, unchallenged and consequently reinforced. Therefore, it is arguable that the maternity provisions as part of such an equality strategy do more to increase the ideology of the world of work as a world of men than to change it.

Individualism is the second flaw upon which the maternity provisions depend. Crucial to an equality strategy is an insistence that women be treated as 'individuals', that is, that they are assessed for the purposes of competition

139

in the marketplace on factors other than sex. The maternity provisions attempt to secure women's status as individuals by ensuring that where the consequences of gender differences are unavoidable, as in the case of pregnancy, women suffer no disadvantage as a result. Such a strategy is problematic for a number of reasons. First, it creates for women a dual status whereby they carry both the responsibilities of equal citizenship in the public sphere and the burden of dependence in the private sphere.[34] Second, and consequently, attempts to guarantee women's equal status in the world of work fail to take account of factors which prevent women from entering or fully participating in that world, for example, child-care. Thirdly, by conceiving of the labour market solely in terms of the individuals who occupy it and by placing as a goal the ideal marketplace populated by freely-competing individuals, this strategy is premised on a false picture of the social world because it focuses on and deals only with individual acts and not with the structures of power which continue to reinforce hierarchical gender relations. As a result, attempts to transform women into 'individuals' through the maternity provisions do not threaten those underlying power structures.

THE POLICIES OF THE NEW RIGHT[35]

So far our critique of the maternity provisions has focused on their operation before the changes made by the Conservative government. Our focus now turns to the nature and impact of Tory cuts in the maternity provisions: do they mark a significant departure from previous government policies and, if so, what implications for women do they create?

1. The Cuts: Past, Present and Future

We will begin by exploring exactly what changes in the maternity provisions the Thatcher administration has made and intends to make. To date the most significant changes are embodied in the Employment Act 1980, but further changes in the Social Security Act 1986 sections 46-50 will come into force in April 1987. Moreover, a recently published government White Paper has invited comment on proposed additional cuts.[36] The changes wrought by the 1980 Act are as follows. First, the Act imposes further complicated notice requirements on a woman intending to return to work.[37] These notice requirements, which if not followed to the letter result in the loss of the right to return, have been decried by judges and academic commentators alike for their complexity and also because in many cases they leave a pregnant worker dependent on the scruples of her employer to communicate to her her rights and how they may be exercised. The 1980 Act also limits a woman's right to return to her job. The right will not arise if she works for an employer who employs five or less employees and who demonstrates that her re-employment is not "reasonably practicable".[38] A woman also loses her right to return if an employer, demonstrating that her re-employment in the same job is not "reasonably practicable" offers her alternative employment, the terms and conditions of which are "not substantially less favourable to her" and she

140

"unreasonably refuses".[39] The 1980 Act, most uncharacteristically, is also the source of a new maternity right – time off work for ante-natal care – but arguably this right was motivated not by a concern for women's equality but by the existence of a high incidence of perinatal mortality in this country.[40] In any case, the right hardly compensates the pregnant worker for the loss of her right to return to her job.

Further significant changes are now in the Social Security Act 1986. The object of the changes is claimed to be the simplification of present maternity benefits but it is feared that the result will be a more complex system. Essentially the changes involve the abolition, for most purposes, of the old maternity allowance, payable by the Department of Health and Social Security (D.H.S.S.) in favour of a new system whereby both maternity pay and allowance become the responsibility of employers. The new system, to be known as 'statutory maternity pay', will create three tiers of entitlement. The first and most beneficial will entitle a pregnant worker to the present six weeks' maternity pay followed by twelve weeks of flat-rate payment more or less equivalent to the present maternity allowance. The qualifying conditions for this entitlement are those currently subsisting for maternity pay – two years' continuous employment.[41] Women failing to meet these conditions may be entitled instead to eighteen weeks of the flat-rate payment if they are continuously employed for six months at the fourteenth week before confinement and meet the necessary contribution requirements. Women who fail to fulfil these conditions may be entitled to the old maternity allowance, claimable from the D.H.S.S., if they satisfy a further set of complicated conditions dependent upon National Insurance contributions. Essentially, then, the strategy is to bring the social security and maternity pay provisions together under the administration, in most cases, of employers. Commentators maintain that these new arrangements will not benefit women for a number of reasons. First, they create a system infinitely more complicated. A pregnant worker seeking financial help may be subject to long delays while her entitlement is determined. Secondly, the new payments will be subject to tax and National Insurance and will, therefore, be worth less in real terms. Thirdly, the scheme will be administered by employers and thus, apart from imposing an extra burden of administration on them, will create greater possibilities for employer abuse. Finally, these changes must be set within the context of the government's policy on social security as a whole. The Green Paper on social security generated much protest from women's rights organisations when it was published in June 1985. Apart from the plans to reorganise maternity allowance it proposed, *inter alia*, the abolition of the universal maternity grant, a freeze on child benefits, an end to the state earnings related pension scheme, a state pension scheme particularly advantageous to women, and the phasing out of family income supplement.

Not surprisingly, the National Council for Civil Liberties decried the proposals as reflecting "a Victorian view of women as subservient, dependent and unequal".[42] Set against this backdrop, the government's new maternity scheme hardly inspires optimism. However, as if the picture were not bleak enough, a further set of restrictive proposals has just been announced.[43] First, it is proposed that the right to return be denied to women working for employers of ten or less – a further concession to the small business lobby. Secondly, the government wants to raise the number of hours constituting continuous employment from sixteen to twenty. The government's defence of this indefensible attack on the rights of part-time workers is a most disingenuous expression of concern for them. Arguing that the employment protection legislation discourages employers from recruiting (a claim that the P.S.I. study found to be without foundation), the White Paper continues:

> This is particularly true of legislation intended to protect part-time workers and consequently there are fewer opportunities for part-time work than there might otherwise be. Flexible part-time work is particularly welcome to women and therefore regulations which tend to reduce its availability tend to place women workers at a disadvantage. (para. 7.1)

Ironically, the government is presenting its assault on women workers as a strategy in their favour.

2. Understanding the Cuts: Building Barriers Not Bridges

One way of explaining the Tory attack on maternity rights is in terms of economic policy: the government is pro-market and anti-regulation. It maintains that regulations such as those embodied in the employment protection legislation restrict the operation of the market by imposing a heavy administrative and financial burden on employers which results in reduced profit and thus deters recruitment. The government is, therefore, for "cutting the red tape" by reducing the degree of regulation.[44]

Free market ideology also throws light on New Right conceptions of the employment relationship by regarding the buying and selling of labour as a transaction which works best as an agreement between free and equal individuals. The employment relationship is conceived as contractual and regulation, in the form of statutory employment rights, is eschewed as a restriction on the freedom of the parties. Contractual ideology is, therefore, a crucial part of the government's deregulation perspective:

> ... in each case the Government has to consider why it is necessary to depart from the basic principle that terms and conditions of employment are matters to be determined by the employer and employee concerned.(para. 7.2)

Thus, to some extent, cuts in the maternity provisions may be regarded as part of an economic policy directed at employment protection as a whole.

Such explanations of the fate of the maternity provisions imply a government strategy which, although indirectly disadvantaging women as a group, is not intended specifically to do so. In other words, women suffer incidentally rather than by design. Feminist accounts of the New Right, on the other hand, suggest that such gender-blind analysis offers only a partial understanding of the New Right approach. A true understanding requires, as one writer observes, "an account of the New Right which puts women rather than men at the centre of the stage".[45] Feminists argue that the economic

142

vision of New Right philosophy corresponds with a social and moral vision which places women in a particular role within the family. A conception of government which denies its responsiibility for services presently assumed by the welfare state, raises directly the question as to who is to undertake these services. If the state is to cut public child-care facilities, benefits to the old, the sick and the disabled, who is to assume responsibility for them? There is much evidence to suggest that the government sees the family as the primary carrier of these duties. The Family Policy Group, set up by the Thatcher administration, clearly envisaged a shift from public to family responsibility.[46] It is equally clear that the government is pursuing such a strategy *via* cuts in the social services. It is implicit in the proposals contained in the 1985 Green Paper and quite apparent in other policies they have implemented – for example, the institution of an 'availability' test to be satisfied by women with pre-school children before they can qualify for unemployment benefit. Increased family responsibility really means reliance upon the domestic role of women in the home. It is not, therefore, unreasonable to suggest that part of this strategy involves limiting women's role in the labour market. The reductions in the state maternity provisions must be understood, therefore, not just in terms of economic policies: they reflect a social and moral perspective which reinforces the sexual division of labour and assigns to women a subordinate social role.

These gender-specific implications are not apparent in New Right philosophy, but they are nevertheless inherent in it. Just as a conception of social interaction between free atomistic individuals disguises the existence of class so, also, does it ignore the significance of gender. New Right conceptions of a free market, untrammelled by government interference, correspond with a vision of the family as a sphere of relations beyond state control. At the same time, just as the 'abstentionism' which characterises a *laissez-faire* approach to economics conceals the state's real interest in a promotion of particular economic forms, so also are New Right claims about the privacy of family life belied by the growing involvement of government in family issues: the Gillick case, the Powell Bill and the controversy surrounding the Warnock Report all exemplify state concern with and interest in family life.[47] The present administration's commitment to preserving and policing the family is further illustrated by the Sex Education Bill with its built-in emphasis on family morality. Clearly, then, despite a philosophy that professes state abstention from the 'private' sphere of the family, the maintenance of a particular conception of family life is central to New Right strategy. For feminists the crucial question becomes how to respond.

TOWARDS BUILDING BRIDGES?

The picture thus confronted appears to be bleak. Current government policy seems bent upon annihilating a set of provisions which in themselves are far from satisfactory. How should feminists approach this dilemma?

It is tempting to conclude that both New Right and liberal instrumental approaches should be rejected by feminists as part of the same overall strategy

– a strategy based on economic need. There is much to suggest that differences between them can be understood as necessary responses to changing economic circumstances. When the state needs women in the labour force it is more than able to provide the facilities to accommodate them as the greater number of public day-care and nursery facilities during the Second World War demonstrated.[48] On the other hand, when the state wishes to shed labour it adopts a policy which assigns to women a primary domestic role; hence, the reduction in day-care facilities which accompanies a post-war policy which regarded women's rightful place as in the home. Thus, it is arguable that the emergence of the maternity provisions were a product of the changing gender composition of the labour market which accompanied the entry of married women into the labour force in the 1960s. Likewise, with the onset of recession and the high rate of inflation, the need to shed labour focused on women as an obvious target particularly because, as Lewis and Simpson observe, their return to the home disguised the true extent of unemployment.[49]

If an economic perspective throws some light on a coherence between New Right and liberal approaches, an exploration of their underlying philosophies also reveals marked similarities. Both depend upon a concept of state which focuses on the centrality of the individual as the bearer of rights and duties. Both reinforce the separation between home and work, between the public and private spheres, recognising the civic equality of both sexes in the public sphere but continuing to reaffirm their inequality in the family. Even the welfare state, the reduction of which is seen to be a major attack on women's interests, continues to be informed by a conception of women as economic dependents. Thus, strategies which rest upon the extension of maternity rights, including increased public day-care facilities, for example, are deficient in their failure to challenge underlying gender relations. Moreover, arguments which call for a state commitment to child-care arrangements by emphasising the important social function of reproduction are double-edged: recognition of the importance of child-bearing and child-rearing is not incompatible with the conception of society which assigns these functions to the family. Indeed, this perspective underlies the philosophy of the Beveridge report in its recognition of the important status of women as "home-makers".[50]

These problems suggest that the way forward lies not by focusing on motherhood but by emphasising parenthood. Strategies such as the present E.E.C. Parental Leave Directive at least challenge the ideology of motherhood and create a climate for shared parental responsibilities. Moreover, the implementation of effective parental leave legislation would arguably extend current equality strategies from the public to the private sphere and at the same time create a demand for alternative working patterns which respond to and accommodate parental needs. However, the progress to date of the Parental Leave Directive has not been encouraging. Awaiting approval since 1983, the Directive has gradually been diluted to take account of members states' objections, coming in particular from the U.K.[51] Proposals to reduce leave, to make concessions for small businesses and to allow the right transferable as between parents (thus enabling in practice a father to transfer his leave entitlement to the mother) are likely to render the Directive, if implemented, all but impotent.

Such reflections present a way forward as riddled with obstacles. Nor do we pretend to be equipped with any blueprint for a solution. However, we would suggest that the questions which this paper raises create a climate for strategy-building which is in the long term more likely to succeed because it is founded on a less blinkered perception of the issues involved. Such a perception recognises the limited value of maternity rights as an aid to individual women and as at least a minimal social symbol of their right to work, but at the same time it demands that the merits of a maternity strategy be placed in the context of its limitations, and, more broadly, it reveals that the challenge for feminists lies not just in *reversing* current political trends but in developing and directing a *new* political programme.

NOTES AND REFERENCES

[1] D.H.S.S., *Reform of Social Security, Volume Two* (1985; Cmnd. 9518) para. 5.22.
[2] On deregulation see, for example, Department of Employment (D.E.), *Building Businesses Not Barriers* (1986; Cmnd. 9794).
[3] The British workforce increased by about two million between 1961 and 1981 largely due to the increased economic activity of married women. See V. Beechey, "Women's Employment in Contemporary Britain" in *Women in Britain Today* (1986; eds. V. Beechey and E. Whitelegg) chap. 2.
[4] J. Dale, "Feminism and the Development of the Welfare State: Some Lessons from Our History" (1986) 16 *Critical Social Policy* p. 57 at p. 61.
[5] Except where an employee's condition makes her unfit for work, s.60(1)(a), or contravenes any statutory enactment, s.60(1)(b).
[6] Employment Protection (Consolidation) Act 1978 ss.33-44.
[7] Entitlement to maternity allowance is dependent upon a mother's National Insurance record: Social Security Act 1975 s.22 and schedule 3.
[8] Employment Protection (Consolidation) Act 1978, ss.33, 45-48.
[9] *Op. cit.*, n. 7.
[10] E. Ellis, "Parents and Employment: An Opportunity for Progress" (1986) *Industrial Law J.* p. 97 at p. 101.
[11] These regulations in their modern form, have just been abolished by the Sex Discrimination Act 1986.
[12] *Op. cit.*, n. 3.
[13] "Maternity Benefits and Day-Care Provisions" 15 *Industrial Relations Rev. and Reports* p. 23.
[14] R. Lewis and B. Simpson, *Striking a Balance? Employment Law After the 1980 Act* (1981) p. 12.
[15] By 'sympathetic commentators' we mean writers who, while critical of the present scope of maternity rights, nevertheless promote their retention and extension, for example: Ellis, *op. cit.*; J. Mayhew, "Pregnancy and Employment Law" in *Gender, Sex and Law* (1985; ed. S. Edwards); F. Winch, "Maternity Rights Provisions – A New Approach" (1981) *J. Social Welfare Law* p. 321.
[16] For example, the National Council for Civil Liberties (N.C.C.L.) and the Equal Opportunities Commission (E.O.C.).
[17] Relevant studies include W. W. Daniel, "Maternity Rights: The Experience of Women", Policy Studies Institute (P.S.I.), No. 588, June 1980 and "The Experience of Employers",

P.S.I., No. 596, August 1981; R. Clifton and C. Tatton-Browne, "The Impact of Employment Protection on Small Firms", D.E. Research Paper No. 6 (1979); "Maternity Leave – the I.R.-R.R. Survey; Part One: The Act's Provisions in Practice", *Industrial Relations Rev. and Reports*, No. 217, February 1980.

18   Daniel, *op. cit.* For details of the qualifying conditions see *infra*, nn. 25-30.
19   A recent D.E. survey found that ninety-three per cent of childless women were economically active compared with thirty-one per cent of women with pre-school children. Moreover, only seven per cent of women with pre-school children work full-time. Beechey, *op. cit.*, pp. 82-83.
20   Daniel, *op. cit.*; Clifton and Tatton-Browne, *op. cit.*
21   I.R.-R.R. Survey, *op. cit.*
22   The Draft Directive on Parental Leave and Leave for Family Reasons was produced by the E.E.C. Commission in 1983. An amended version is still awaiting approval by the Council of Ministers. Ellis, *op. cit.*
23   For an account of women's working patterns, see Beechey, *op. cit.*, pp. 79-85.
24   See R. S. Barron and G. M. Morris, "Sexual Divisions and the Dual Labour Market" in *Dependence and Exploitation in Work and Marriage* (1976; eds. D. Barker and S. Allen).
25   Employment Protection (Consolidation) Act 1978, s.153.
26   Although recent cases suggest that homeworkers may be employees: *Airfix Footwear Ltd. v Cope* [1978] I.C.R. 1210; *Nethermere (St. Neots) Ltd. v Taverna* [1983] I.R.L.R. 103. For an account of employer exploitation of "casual" women workers see C. Freeman, "The 'Understanding' Employer" in *Work, Women and the Labour Market* (1982; ed. J. West).
27   See A. Coyle, "Going Private: The Implications of Privatisation for Women's Work" (1985) 21 *Feminist Rev.* p. 15.
28   Employment Protection (Consolidation) Act 1978, s.33(3)(b).
29   *Id.*, schedule 13. If an employee works between eight and sixteen hours per week for five years her employment will be treated as continuous.
30   T. Gill and L. Whitty, *Women's Rights in the Workplace* (1983) chap. 14.
31   "Maternity Leave Survey Part Two: Company Maternity Provisions", *Industrial Relations Rev. and Reports*, No. 218, February 1980.
32   C. Drake and B. Bercusson, *The Employment Acts 1974-1980* (1981) p. 28.
33   *Supra*, n. 19.
34   A conception of women as dependants still dominates, for example, social security legislation. See the E.O.C.'s *Green Paper: Reform of Social Security, Response of the Equal Opportunities Commission*, August 1985.
35   We use the term 'New Right' broadly to denote political, philosophical and moral positions associated with far right ideology and practice.
36   *Supra*, n. 2.
37   Employment Protection (Consolidation) Act 1978, s.33(3)(c) and (d); s.33(3A) and (3B) inserted by Employment Act 1980, s.11.
38   Employment Protection (Consolidation) Act 1978, s.56A(1)(a), (b) inserted by Employment Act 1980, s.12.
39   *Id.*, s.56A(2)(a), (b), (c).
40   *Id.*, s.31A (inserted by Employment Act 1980, s.13).
41   *Supra*, nn. 28-29.
42   *The Guardian*, 10 June 1985.
43   *Supra*, n. 2.
44   *Id.*, para. 1.8.
45   T. ten Tusscher, "Patriarchy, Capitalism and the New Right" in *Feminism and Political Theory* (1986; eds. J. Evans *et al.*) p. 61 at p. 67.
46   *The Guardian*, 17 February 1983.
47   Although the Gillick case was a private civil action and the Powell Bill was a private Member's Bill, both called upon the state to express a position on the matters involved.
48   In 1944 there were 1,450 day nurseries. In 1981 the figure was 540. Winch, *op. cit.*

49 "...it is not disingenuous to suggest that the government was happy to alleviate or disguise the extent of unemployment by encouraging women to withdraw from the labour market", Lewis and Simpson, *op. cit.* p. 46. Michele Barrett comments, " . . . the application of the 'reserve army' model for female wage labour should not be regarded as an adequate explanation of the general characteristics of women's work under capitalism". M. Barrett, *Women's Oppression Today* (1980) p. 159. We agree but would still, nevertheless, maintain that the maternity provisions can be understood at least in part in terms of labour mobility.

50 Dale, *op. cit.*, p. 62.

51 *Supra*, n. 22.

The Conceptual Foundations of Modern Company Law

PADDY IRELAND,* IAN GRIGG-SPALL* and DAVE KELLY**

Critical legal studies should be primarily concerned with exploring the ways in which law constitutes and reinforces relations of domination and subordination in society. It is, therefore, surprising that it has given so little attention to company law, given that incorporated companies – now the dominant legal organisational form of capital – are a major site of those relations. To date the only alternatives to traditional, expository approaches to company law have been broadly contextualist in nature.[1] These have undoubtedly widened our knowledge and understanding of the subject, providing useful analyses of its relevance and technical rules. But being essentially atheoretical, contextualism has accepted the company as a given legal object. It has consequently offered little, if anything, by way of analysis or explanation of the key concepts which constitute the basic structures of modern company law.

We hope that this paper will lay the foundations for a more critical approach to company law. Limitations of space force us to concentrate largely on the central concept of separate personality, but we believe that our analysis opens up further areas for study, both within company law itself and beyond. The crux of our argument is that company law, and in particular the joint stock company as an economic organisational form,[2] can be properly understood only in the context of an analysis of the various forms taken by capital. And, more specifically, that it is the emergence of the joint stock company share as a new form of fictitious capital that underlies the doctrine of separate personality and, therefore, the basic conceptual structure of contemporary company law.[3]

THE DOCTRINE OF SEPARATE PERSONALITY

Few would dispute that the doctrine of separate corporate personality is one of the cornerstones of modern company law. As one leading treatise says, the distinction between the company and its members is "fundamental", "[lying] at the root of many of the most perplexing questions that beset company law".[4] In its modern version, the doctrine posits what L. C. B. Gower

* Department of Law, University of Kent, Canterbury, Kent CT2 7NY, England.

** Department of Law, North Staffordshire Polytechnic. College Road, Stoke on Trent ST4 2DE, England.

describes as "the complete separation of the company and its members".[5] The incorporated company is usually conceptualised not merely as an entity with an independent legal existence from its shareholders, but as an object which is cleansed and emptied of them. It is this depersonalised conception of the company that enables it to be 'completely separated' from its members. The company is, so to speak, reified. Traditionally, this 'complete separation' is seen as flowing from the legal act of incorporation, a point which is usually illustrated by reference to *Salomon v Salomon & Co. Ltd.*.[6] Correspondingly, a sharp line is drawn between incorporated companies, objects in themselves whose members stand in a completely external relationship to them, and *un*incorporated companies which are "mere collection[s] or aggregation[s] of individuals", in which the members *are* the company.[7]

This view as to the origins of the 'complete separation' of companies and their members is untenable. An examination of eighteenth and early nineteenth century cases and texts makes it clear that incorporation did *not* at that time entail such a separation. Incorporation did create an entity, the incorporated company, which was legally distinguishable from the people composing it, but there was no suggestion that this entity was 'completely separate' from its members. On the contrary, up to the middle of the nineteenth century incorporated joint stock companies were consistently identified with their component members and were conceptualised not as depersonalised objects but as entities composed of those members merged into one legally distinguishable body. In other words, an incorporated company was its members, albeit those members "united so as to be but one person in law . . . ."[8]

The contrast between this conception of the incorporated company and that prevailing today – and a fairly precise idea of when the change in conception took place – can be grasped by considering a subtle difference in the wordings of the 1856 and 1862 Companies Acts. Section 3 of the 1856 Act stated that: "Seven or more persons . . . may . . . *form themselves* into an incorporated company", clearly indicating that the people were the company; that it was made up *of* them. Perceived as such, the incorporated company could hardly be 'completely separate' from its members. However, the corresponding provision of the 1862 Act (s.6) omitted the words 'themselves into'. People formed companies, they no longer formed 'themselves into' companies. A company was made *by* them but not of them. While the 1856 Act clearly identified the company with its members, the 1862 Act suggested that it had an existence *external* to them. Seen as a thing made by, but not of, people, the incorporated company was depersonalised and thus 'completely separated' from its members. The form of words adopted for the first time in the 1862 Act persists today.[9]

The prevalence in the early nineteenth century of the view of the incorporated company as people merged into one body is further revealed, with particular clarity, linguistically. Nowadays an incorporated company is usually referred to in the singular, as an 'it', confirming its depersonalised, reified status. In the early nineteenth century, however, when they were

150

perceived as associations of people merged into one body, joint stock companies – incorporated and *un*incorporated – were frequently referred to in the plural, as 'theys'. For example, in *Ex parte the Lancaster Canal Co.*, an 1828 case concerning an incorporated canal company, Sir Lancelot Shadwell remarked: "The company was formed for the purpose of making a canal; and for that purpose *they* were, as of necessity, *they* must be, empowered to purchase lands."[10] And in *Myers v Perigal* (1851) Lord Truro observed: "It appears that the company carried on *their* concerns through the agency of *their* directors, and *were* empowered to invest *their* capital . . . ."[11] Similar examples can also be found when reference is being made to corporations rather than to companies. For instance, in *Bligh v Brent*, decided in 1837, Baron Alderson emphasised the separate personality of the incorporated company and its distinctiveness from its members, but still persistently referred to the corporation as a 'they': " . . . the corporation may do what *they* like with [the money], and may obtain their profit in any way *they* please from the employment of *their* capital stock . . . ."[12] In *Baxter v Newman* (1845) counsel is reported as arguing: "In *Bligh v Brent* the corporation *were* the legal owners, as well as the *persons* entitled to the profits."[13] In fact, corporations of all kinds, and not just incorporated joint stock companies, were regarded as people merged into one legally distinct body and were thus identified with their members. In his 1793 treatise Stewart Kyd defined a corporation as " . . . a collection of many individuals united into one body . . . .'[14]

Those who adhere to the conventional view that 'complete separation' is a function of the legal act of incorporation sometimes recognise that up to the mid-nineteenth century incorporation did not have this effect. However, they dismiss this, attributing it to the confusing influence on the law of *un*incorporated joint stock companies, or to contemporary misapprehensions about the 'true' nature and effects of incorporation. According to the latter view, it was not until *Salomon* in 1897 that the "implications" of incorporation "were fully grasped even by the courts", since which time "the complete separation of the company and its members has never been doubted".[15] Neither of these explanations stands close scrutiny. Many of the rules identifying companies with their members were formulated in relation to incorporated, not *un*incorporated, companies. And far from being inadequately grasped by contemporary lawyers, the meanings attached to incorporation in the early nineteenth century were perfectly well understood, but different from those attached to it today. Company lawyers who fail to recognise this are guilty of a teleological reading of the past which, as Foucault and others have argued, turns it into "a confused and stuttering version of the present".[16] The 'complete separation' of companies and their members, which emerged *for the first time* in the nineteenth century, was *reflected* in the changed consequences attributed to incorporation, but incorporation was not its source. This must be sought elsewhere, in the changing economic and legal nature of the joint stock company share.

THE CHANGING LEGAL NATURE OF THE SHARE[17]

Throughout the eighteenth and early nineteenth centuries, the term 'share' was "used in its natural sense, namely as an appreciable part of [a] whole undertaking".[18] To possess a share in a joint stock company implied ownership of a share of the totality of the company's assets. Legally, shares in joint stock companies, incorporated and unincorporated, were viewed as equitable interests in the property of the company. "Shareholders", says D. G. Rice, "were regarded as owners in equity of the company's property."[19] In incorporated companies the legal interest in the property was vested in the corporation; in *un*incorporated companies, constituted through deeds of settlement, the legal title was vested in trustees. Both held the property on trust for the shareholders. Thus, in *Child v Hudson's Bay Co.*, decided in 1723, Lord Macclesfield declared that: "The legal interest of all the stock [assets] was in the company, who are trustees for the several members."[20] It followed that, as property, shares were directly related to and co-extensive with the assets of the company and that their legal nature depended on the nature of those assets. Shares could be either real or personal estate depending on whether or not the company owned land. When the courts had to decide whether shares (in both incorporated and *un*incorporated companies) were realty and, therefore, within the Statutes of Mortmain or Frauds, they uniformly held that the matter turned on the nature of the company's assets.[21] In the early 1830s it was still consistently being held that company shares were realty if "the corporation were seized of real estate".[22] Crucially, while the share was legally perceived as an equitable interest in the company's assets, shareholders – the equitable co-owners of those assets – were necessarily closely identified with their companies. They could not be 'completely separate'.

From the 1830s, however, the legal nature of shares began to be reconceptualised, and by the mid-nineteenth century the close link between shares and the assets of companies had been severed. The crucial case, *Bligh v Brent*, was decided in 1837 and concerned shares in an incorporated waterworks company. The issue before the court was whether the company's shares were realty and within Mortmain. In accordance with the prevailing view, counsel argued that the nature of the company's shares as property depended on the nature of the company's assets. In every joint stock company, he asserted, "the shareholder has an estate of the same nature as the company". Despite the overwhelming weight of the authorities, the court rejected this view. They argued that the case turned on "the nature of the interest which each shareholder is to have", and in their view shareholders in incorporated joint stock companies had interests only in the profits of companies and no interest whatsoever in their assets. The shares were personalty, irrespective of the nature of the company's property.[23]

Bligh v Brent was the turning point, although uncertainties remained for some years after, particularly in relation to the nature of shares in *un*incorporated companies and in companies whose business activities were closely connected to land. By the mid 1850s, however, these had largely‧

disappeared. In *Watson v Spratley*, decided in 1854, the court had to determine the nature of the shares of an *un*incorporated mining company. It held that the matter turned on "the essential nature and quality of a share in a joint stock company", and declared its shares to be interests only in profits.[24] Henceforth, shareholders, even in *un*incorporated joint stock companies, had no direct interest in the physical assets of their companies. Shares were personalty irrespective not only of the nature of the company's assets but also of its legal status. They were an entirely separate form of property: legal objects in their own right. They had been freed from their direct link to the property of joint stock companies. By 1861 Sir John Romilly was asserting that "shares in joint stock companies . . . are, in fact, in the nature of property".[25] Critically, as the share became property in its own right, a legal space emerged between incorporated and *un*incorporated joint stock companies – owners of the assets – and their shareholders – owners of the shares.

The recognition of the share as a new form of property was not, however, without problems. The exact legal nature of this new form of property eluded and continues to elude company lawyers. As L. C. B. Gower openly admits, the question "What . . . is the exact juridical nature of the share?" is more easily asked than answered.[26] Lawyers know what a share is not – a direct interest in the company's assets – but not what it is. For example, in defining the share, one leading company lawyer got into the following tangle:

> A share is, therefore, a fractional part of the capital. It confers upon the holder a certain right to proportionate part of the assets of the corporation, whether by way of dividend or of distribution of assets in winding up. It forms, however, a separate right of property. The capital is the property of the corporation. The share, although it is a fraction of the capital, is the property of the corporator. The aggregate of all the fractions if collected in two or three hands does not constitute the corporators the owners of the capital – that remains the property of the corporation. But, nevertheless, the share is a property in a fractional part of the capital . . . .[27]

Although this passage is cited with approval by one contemporary company law treatise,[28] it is neither coherent nor helpful.

In short, what company lawyers seem to have had great difficulty accommodating is the major change, recognised by writers such as C. B. Macpherson, that has taken place over the last two hundred years in the preponderant nature of property. As Macpherson observes, property no longer predominantly takes the form of rights in specific material things – land, factories, machines and so on – but the form of rights to revenues.[29] Since the eighteenth century there has been an explosion in these new, abstract, intangible forms of property. Law not only enforces these rights of property – things such as government bonds, loan stocks, mortgages and other instruments of credit – law actually constitutes them as property on a par with property in actual material things. Of these new forms, the joint stock company share is one of the most important.

To understand the emergence of the modern doctrine of separate personality, with its reified conception of the company and 'complete separation' of company and members, we need to trace the historical processes whereby the share and other similar titles to revenue emerge as legally recognised autonomous forms of property. We will, therefore, first consider the economic nature of these titles to revenue and then outline the conditions necessary for them to emerge as forms of property in their own right.

RIGHTS TO REVENUE AS FORMS OF MONEY CAPITAL

The most appropriate starting point is Marx's analysis of these titles to revenue as forms of what he calls interest bearing or money capital. The ideal typical money capital transaction is a loan in which, in return for an increment in the form of interest, money is temporarily transferred from its legal owner to another person who uses it in the production process. Analytically, the transaction involves the transformation of money into money capital: a move from money as a means of facilitating exchange to money as a commodity in itself which commands a price. As Marx explains, this transformation can only take place under certain historical conditions – conditions in which labour power has become a commodity. It is the class relation between capitalist and wage-labourer which permits the transformation of mere money into capital. Interest, the return that accrues to money capital, is part of the surplus value produced by wage-labour.[30]

This transformation of money into money capital is not, however, apparent in the basic motion underlying the capitalist mode of production:

$$M - C \underset{MP}{\overset{LP}{<}} - P - C_1 - M_1$$

The capitalist spends money (M) to purchase certain commodities (C), means of production (MP) and labour power (LP). These are utilised in the production process (P) to produce other commodities (C_1) whose value is greater than those used in their production. The latter commodities are then sold for a sum of money (M_1) which is greater than the original money expended. The difference in magnitude between M and M_1 constitutes surplus value or profit and accrues to the capitalist. Money here is merely a means of facilitating exchange, although it operates as "capital *in* the production process".[31]

For this movement to occur, however, capitalists must have sufficient money to start production. Even in the labour intensive, low technology production processes that predominated in Britain during early industrialisation, where the amount of money required was generally small, capitalists were often compelled to borrow money. When the technology involved was more advanced and the fixed costs higher – as in areas such as insurance, canals, public utilities and, later, railways – the sums needed were often much larger and borrowed money was absolutely indispensible.[32] From an early stage in the history of capitalism, therefore, the development of a credit system, in which money was transformed into money capital, was essential to

154

enable the centralisation of sufficient capital for production to commence. The 'normal' circuit of capital becomes:

$$(M -)\, M - C \Big\langle{{\text{LP}}\atop{\text{MP}}} \quad - P - C_1 - M_1 \Big\langle{{\text{I} \quad (\text{Interest})}\atop{\text{PE} \quad (\text{Profit of enterprise})}}$$

In this process, the functions of contributing funds and of utilising those funds in the production process come to be performed by different people. 'money capitalists' contribute funds, 'industrial capitalists' utilise them. The former ensure that surplus value is produced, but as they borrow the capital they operate they have to surrender part of the surplus value created. The surplus value generated in production thereby comes to be divided into two qualitatively distinct parts: profit of enterprise which accrues to the industrial capitalist and interest which accrues to the money capitalist. Interest represents a relationship between two capitalists and, as such, necessarily entails antagonism between them as they contest the division of surplus value.[33]

Historically, then, the credit system and money capital in its many guises emerge as integral parts of the capitalist mode of production. Capitalists are forced by "the logic of the overall circulation of capital . . . to create new financial instruments and a sophisticated credit system which pushes money and interest bearing capital into a prominent role in relation to accumulation".[34]

RIGHTS TO REVENUE AS PROPERTY; THE NATURE OF FICTITIOUS CAPITAL

Part of the process whereby a sophisticated credit system develops is the legal constitution and recognition of these 'new financial instruments' - these new forms of money capital – as autonomous forms of property. In this section we will be concerned with the 'logic of the overall circulation of capital' that generates this development. We will look first at the 'pure' phenomenal form of money capital, the loan, and return later to the share.

At common law these titles to revenue were initially classified as 'choses in action'. This category – which by the eighteenth century covered instruments such as bills, notes, cheques, government stock and joint stock company shares – was used to describe all personal rights of property enforceable only by action and not by taking physical possession.[35] Titles to revenue were, therefore, conceptualised as rights personal to the parties bound by the obligation. As such, they were non-assignable and incapable of being independent forms of alienable property. At common law choses in action could not even be stolen and legislation was needed to take them out of this rule.[36] Similarly, in early incorporated companies, the instrument of incorporation had to specifically provide for the transferability of shares, which were otherwise considered to be non-assignable.[37] Gradually, however, as

Sir William Holdsworth observes, "some of the choses in action . . . changed their original character and [became] very much less like merely personal rights of action and very much more like rights of property".[38] Marx outlined the conditions in which this happened in his analysis of what he called 'fictitious capital', when he showed that in certain circumstances titles to revenue develop a capital value of their own separate from the value of the productive assets from which their value is derived.[39]

The key to understanding this development is the barriers that inhibit the circulation of money capital and the need to overcome them. When capital exists as money it is exchangeable, liquid and mobile. Once 'loaned' against future surplus value production, however, it becomes tied to specific assets, and problems arise if lenders are not willing to give up control of their money for sufficient time for borrowers to finance their operations. Historically, the most important solution to these problems was the establishment of developed markets for titles to revenue, permitting money capital to preserve its flexibility and liquidity. It is under these conditions that these titles develop a capital value of their own and become a form of capital in themselves. They emerge as 'fictitious capital' and come to be legally recognised as new autonomous forms of property.

The separate capital value of these titles is established in the market through the process we call the 'capitalisation of revenues'. A periodic income is capitalised by calculating it, on the basis of the prevailing rate of interest, as an income which would be realised by a capital loaned at this rate of interest. So, for example, if one had an annual income of £50 and the prevailing rate of interest was ten per cent, that income would represent the annual interest on £500. That £500 would be the fictitious capital value of the legal title to the annual £50.[40]

Money capital comes to be invested in many different titles to future surplus values and money capitalists become indifferent to the ultimate source of their revenue. They invest in government debt, stocks, shares and so on. As markets develop in these titles, they emerge as autonomous forms of property. Marx noted that as this happens, "capital more and more acquires a material form, is [increasingly] transformed from a relationship into a thing". This thing, "which embodies . . . the social relationship . . . acquire[s] a fictitious life and independent existence".[41] It is in this form that the social relationship comes to exist in our consciousness. Moreover, as this occurs, "the conception of [such] capital as a self-reproducing and self expanding value, lasting and growing eternally by virtue of its innate properties, is thereby established".[42] In short, the circuit of money-capital appears as $M - M_1$, money-capital seeming to possess the inherent ability to command interest. Interest seems to accrue merely as a result of legal agreement between two individuals and the circuit of money-capital assumes a phenomenal form that appears quite separate from, and external to, the circuit of productive capital.

One of the major purposes of Marx's analysis of fictitious capital was to expose the 'fetishisation of money' that underlies the legal recognition of these titles to revenue as new forms of property, as self-expanding 'things'. In the

156

eighteenth and early nineteenth centuries, when titles to revenue were still usually regarded as choses in action rather than as property in themselves, revenues were generally seen as connected to specific social relations, as reflected in classical political economy. The reification and fetishisation of these titles broke the direct link between revenues and productive activity, and was the basis for the development of new forms of economic, political and social consciousness. These new forms of consciousness abandoned the notion of labour as the source of value and declared capital – a thing – to be equally productive. The fetishisation of money capital through the legal constitution of its phenomenal forms as property in themselves led inexorably, therefore, to the dominance of exchange and market ideologies from the mid-nineteenth century.[43]

THE SHARE AS FICTITIOUS CAPITAL

The share form of money capital cannot become fictitious capital in exactly the same way as, say, government bonds or loan stock, for there is a much closer relationship between the value of shares and the functioning industrial capital of companies. Nevertheless, the periodic income which shareholders receive in the form of dividends is capitalised in the same way as that for government bonds. The capitalised value of the share is the sum of money which would command at the prevailing rate of interest a return equivalent to the income actually accruing to the share. So, for example, given a prevailing rate of interest of ten per cent, a share whose nominal value was £100 and which paid £20 per annum, would have a market value of £200 because when capitalised at 10 per cent it would represent a fictitious capital of £200. On the other hand, a £100 nominal value share paying only £5 per annum would represent a fictitious capital of only £50. Thus, fictitious share capital exists as a capitalised claim on the surplus value generated by a company's productive capital. The price of shares, therefore, is determined not by the value of the company's assets, but by the volume of profit generated by those assets and by the prevailing rate of interest.[44] As Paul Sweezy notes: "One difference always remains, namely, that the shareholder runs a greater risk of loss than the pure lender and hence the yield on shares can be expected to exceed interest on money by a variable risk premium."[45]

The share-market, then, apparently doubles the capital of companies. On the one hand, there is the concrete, productive capital. In law this is the sole property of the reified 'company', now a phenomenal form of industrial capital. On the other hand, there is also the fictitious share capital, a new phenomenal form of money capital and the property of the shareholders. The same sum of money thus comes to function as capital for two people. Industrial capitalists use it as capital *in* the production process and money capitalists use it as capital *outside* the production process. As Hilferding says, "the second capital is an illusion". Only the industrial capital and its profit 'really' exists, "but this does not prevent the fictitious [share] capital from existing in an accounting [and, we might add, legal] sense", although "in

157

reality it is not capital, but only the price of a revenue". Critically, shareholders can now recover their capital in money form at any time by simply selling their titles to revenue. The share market thus "endows [shares], which the individual can now always realise, completely with the character of money capital". Dividends crystallise out as just another form of 'interest'.[46]

As with other forms of money capital, the basic condition for joint stock company shares to emerge as separate forms of property with capital value in themselves is the development of a generalised market in them. We now turn to the historical development of this market.

THE HISTORICAL EMERGENCE OF THE JOINT STOCK COMPANY SHARE AS A NEW FORM OF FICTITIOUS CAPITAL[47]

The first British joint stock companies began to emerge in the sixteenth century. They were *not*, however, "public in the full modern sense of the term", but were "more in the nature of 'extended partnerships'".[48] The relatively few joint stock companies in existence were divided into very few large denomination shares, and clauses restricting and regulating their transfer were common. Although from the outset shares were sold outside personal acquaintances, there was no basis for a developed public market in them. In the eighteenth century, when the stock exchange grew rapidly, the basis of its growth was increasing government debt, trade in company shares forming a negligible part of its business. The number of companies quoted in Castaing's *Course of Exchange* actually fell from seven in 1753 to six in 1775 and to five in 1800.[49]

The numerous joint stock canal, insurance and other companies formed in the late eighteenth and early nineteenth centuries generated few changes in this respect. Studies of canal companies reveal limited numbers of relatively large denomination shares, few shareholders and considerable stability of shareholding.[50] The prices of canal, dock, insurance and water works shares were included in the official list for the first time in 1811, followed later by those of other miscellaneous companies, but "there was no really widespread interest in them as an outlet for savings . . . .[T]here are no statistics on daily share turnover, [but] indirect evidence suggests that it was very limited."[51] Exchange business continued to be concerned almost exclusively with government stock. So far as the legal nature of the share was concerned, the undeveloped state of the market was crucial.

By this time the great majority of shareholders were simple *rentiers* who played little active part in management and treated their shares as mere rights to revenue. However, in the absence of a public share market, shares could not develop as fictitious capital with a value in themselves. As a consequence, they inevitably retained a direct link to a company's productive assets and were legally conceptualised not as property in their own right but as equitable interests in those assets, realty or personality. In short, while the share incorporated a title to revenue, it was considered to be so inextricably connected to the assets of companies that it could not yet be constituted as a

158

separate form of property. It was a rather peculiar legal amalgam of money and industrial capital, which had not yet been juridically separated within the joint stock company. Such a legal distinction had already been drawn in respect of other titles to revenue, such as loans.[52] In these circumstances shareholders could not be 'completely separated' from their companies. This was reflected in the contemporary view of joint stock companies, incorporated and *un*incorporated, as entities composed of shareholders merged into one body; as aggregates of people; as 'theys'. People still 'formed themselves' into companies.

In the period after 1825 the nature of the share was transformed. The principal cause was the rapid development of the railway system.[53] Railways involved massive outlays on fixed capital, requiring the aggregation of large amounts of money capital. The smaller denomination, freely transferable share was the chosen form of centralisation. The railways brought, therefore, a dramatic increase both in the number of shareholders and in the number of shares available for trading. Dealings in railway shares involved an "extraordinary volume of transactions by previous standards".[54] By the second railway boom of the 1840s the stock exchange had been "perfectly revolutionised",[55] and was "geared . . . to handle a growing range of company securities".[56] Stock exchanges even emerged in provincial centres, and gradually a national investment press developed. Joint stock company shares had become much more widely held: " . . . a class of property had been, if not created, then vastly expanded".[57]

The effects of these developments on shares, however, were qualitative as well as quantitative. Shares were not only much more numerous, they were now marketable commodities, liquid assets, easily converted by their holders into money. They were titles to revenue capable of being capitalised; a form of fictitious capital, separate from the productive capital of the company. Legally, they were judicially redefined as objects of property in themselves. Shares, said Bacon C.J. in 1871, "are not things in action at all but are as much part of [a] bankrupt's estate as if they had been freehold property".[58] Most important of all for the future development of company law, with the legal constitution of this new form of property a gulf emerged between companies and their shareholders and between shareholders and their shares. Companies owned the productive capital, the actual assets; shareholders owned the fictitious share capital, the shares, which they could now sell at will. Shareholders were now 'completely separate' from their companies.[59] They no longer formed 'themselves into' companies, but formed companies, objects external to them. A company was no longer a plural entity, a 'they', people merged into one body; it was now a singular entity, an 'it', an object emptied of people. Both the company and the share had been reified.

The conditions now existed for the emergence of the modern version of the principle of separate personality, and gradually the meaning attached to incorporation changed. In the 1870s Seward Brice, reflecting on Kyd's 1793 definition of a corporation as "a collection of many individuals united into one body", commented: '[It is] fairly accurate . . . but sufficient stress is not laid upon that which is its real characteristic in the eye of the law, viz. its existence separate and distinct from the individual or individuals composing it."[60] Modern company law was emerging.

RECONSIDERING COMPANY LAW

We have shown that, contrary to the orthodox view, the source of the modern principle of separate personality is not incorporation but the historical processes whereby the joint stock company share emerges as a form of fictitious money capital. In so doing we offer a methodology for the study of company law which involves an excavation of the specifically historical conditions and social relations which lead to the emergence of joint stock companies as a phenomenal form of industrial capital and the share as one of the phenomenal forms of money capital. This method "reasons from the forms in which economic phenomena present themselves on the surface of society to the material network of essential relations peculiar to the mode of production in question which explain why the phenomena should take such forms".[61] Such a 'transcendental analytic' enables us not only to grasp that exploitation and class struggle between wage-labour and capital and between fractions of capital (industrial and money) are the essential relations underlying the joint stock company and the share, but also to explain how the latter serve to obscure those relations. It casts considerable light on many aspects of company law, of which we would like to briefly consider a few.

First, it enables us to understand the reasons for the difficulties that jurists have encountered in legally conceptualising the share. The joint stock company share is a form of property whose basis lies in the statutory contract between the shareholder and the company, the terms of which are contained in the company's Memorandum and Articles. These normally provide for, *inter alia*, some provision as to repayment of capital on a solvent winding-up and a title to dividend. Although this title is readily saleable and easily capitalised – constituting the share as a form of property in its own right – it is contingent upon, and varies according to, profitability. As a result, shares inevitably retain a much closer link to productive capital than loan capital. It is the contingent and variable nature of the return that prevents the share from being a 'pure' money capital form like the loan.

Secondly, it illuminates the sources and purposes of the doctrine of *ultra vires*, whose emergence can now be seen as a part of the process whereby legal protection was afforded the joint stock company share. The doctrine, by restricting a company to the objects of its memorandum and declaring that even the unanimous shareholders cannot ratify an *ultra vires* transaction, constituted the share as a *specific* form of freely transferable property: a railway share, an insurance share and so on. In thereby stabilising the share the doctrine sought to enable more 'rational' decisions to be taken in the market by investors. It also reflected and reinforced the increasing reification of the company.[62]

Thirdly, we can make sense of the difficulties that company lawyers have with the concept of capital – described by Farrar as "ambiguous and confusing"[63] – and with that "baffling branch of the law"[64] dealing with dividends and capital maintenance. As originally formulated, the doctrine of capital maintenance essentially entailed the protection of a company's productive capital, and failed to grasp the difference between this and fictitious share capital. Later revisions were based on a recognition of the share as fictitious capital and a desire to protect its integrity as such, as represented by its value on the stock exchange. The crucial distinction between the value of a company's productive capital and the value of its fictitious share capital also helps us to comprehend the legally neglected and, to lawyers, rather mysterious notion of 'goodwill' which surfaces when businesses are valued.

More generally, we can comprehend the essential basis of the legal distinctions drawn between public listed companies and private companies, and the problems that arise from their both having the same basic legal form and status. In brief, only joint stock company shares can properly become forms of fictitious capital, property in themselves; only joint stock company shareholders can become 'pure' money capitalists. Whatever the established legal consequences of incorporation, the shareholders of private companies can never 'completely separate' themselves from their companies in the same way as shareholders in public, joint stock companies.[65]

It also becomes apparent that the overriding contextualist concern with the so-called separation of ownership and control within modern joint stock companies is premised upon, but fails to properly understand, changes in the phenomenal forms of capital. The development of the share and other forms of credit enables capitalists to withdraw from the production process, which comes to be supervised by managers. Contextualists fail to theorise the resulting reification of the company and 'externalisation' of shareholders, and this leads them to the mistaken claim that the 'separation of ownership and control' has fundamentally altered the nature of the joint stock company. For the same reasons, claims that worker participation can 'democratise' companies are misconceived.[66]

Finally, in demonstrating the centrality of law to the development of the circuits of money capital, our analysis has some important implications for critical legal studies in general. Recently, a number of critical legal theorists have correctly emphasised the ways in which law, as well as being constituted by capitalist social relations, is actually constitutive of them. For example, Karl Klare, in forwarding such a "constitutive theory of law", suggests that the legal process is "one of the primary forms of social practice through which actual relationships embodying class power [are] created and articulated".[67] Having made this important point, however, they tend to focus specifically on people: on the legal dimensions of their personal relationships and on their legal constitution as individual legal subjects. In so doing, they fail to recognise that capitalist social relations come to be reified and depersonalised; that is, that class relations under developed capitalism cease to be personal but

161

come, to a significant extent, to be embodied in things, some of which – like the joint stock company share – are constituted *in law* as autonomous forms of property. To oversimplify, a pre-condition of the full development of the notion of the individual legal subject existing in apparent isolation – the premise of fully developed bourgeois theory – is the disconnection of revenues from social relations. Crucial to this process is the legal reification and mystification of titles to revenue; that is, their constitution as things in themselves, as self-expanding, autonomous forms of property.

CONCLUSION

The historical process whereby the share and the joint stock company are contemporaneously reified is but a part of the general historical process which occurs with the development of capitalism, whereby persons cease to relate to persons except through the ownership and exchange of things. Things come to relate to other things. This reification of social relations is an inseparable aspect of developed capitalism. Its root lies in the commodification of labour power, wherein living, creative energy is treated as just another thing to be bought and sold at a price. It is this reification of living labour which is the initial basis for the complete reification and mystification of all social relations.

The processes of production – the means of human life – come to be controlled by abstract relationships between things, relationships expressed in the economic terms of price, profit, interest, rent and wages. Modern political economy merely formulates the laws of alienated labour. Thus, it is not a person but a thing, capital (often in the form of 'the company'), which possesses the power to set the production process in motion. Or more contemporarily, it is the failure of this thing to yield adequate profit which occasions the dismissal of masses of workers and the increased exploitation of others worldwide. Similarly, it is the relationship of the share (and of loan stock) to the joint stock company – of object to object – which defines the basic relationship between finance and production and which thereby regulates productive activity and with it our means of existence. People come to be mere adjuncts or agents of these objects, either as their temporary owners or as directors, employees or customers of the reified entity, the company. And they relate to these objects, of course, only as buyers or sellers of other things, including themselves. People become mere personifications of things over which they have lost control. They are "alienated from their real conditions of existence"[68] and their lives come to be governed by the relationship of fetishised object to fetishised object. Participants in capitalist production live in a bewitched world in which their own relationships appear to them as properties of things.

So it is with stock, shares, mortgages and overdrafts – all of which confront us as forms of self-expanding autonomous property. Things whose demands over our lives lead, at best, to intensified incorporation and exploitation, and, at worst, to catastrophe and crisis. These forms of property – of 'interest-

162

bearing' capital – and their necessary adjunct wage-labour – come to be crucial aspects of what Fromm calls "the insanity of our normality".[69] An insanity which declares that money must have its price in our energy, our lives, our very conditions of existence. These claims of money capital, whether as demands at work or demands at home, come to be accepted as natural and inevitable features of our everyday lives. And the destruction of whole peoples – of whole cultures – by such demands come to be merely part of the necessary working of the international monetary system.

Marx's critique shows that "capital's seemingly natural and eternal forms rest on relations that are social and historical", relations constructed by human beings and capable of being changed by other human beings. In so doing it has the capacity, both in theory and in practice, to "blow that world apart".[70]

NOTES AND REFERENCES

[1] See, for example, T. Hadden, *Company Law and Capitalism* (2nd ed. 1977). Also D. Kelly, Book Review, (1986) 20 *Law Teacher*.

[2] The distinction between the joint stock company as an *economic* form and the incorporated company as a *legal* form is crucial to this paper; see P. Ireland, "The Rise of the Limited Liability Company" (1984) 12 *Int. J. Sociology of Law* p. 239. Our analysis is essentially concerned with joint stock companies (very roughly, public companies) and their shares. Originally, company law was specifically formulated to regulate such companies.

[3] This essay is an abridged summary of the work we are doing on company law, capital fetishism and the reification of social relations. We have footnoted some of the detailed papers on which this essay is based, and would be happy to provide copies and further references to those interested.

[4] F. B. Palmer, *Company Law* (21st ed. 1968; ed. Schmitthoff and Thompson) p. 134.

[5] L. C. B. Gower, *Modern Company Law* (4th ed. 1979) p. 100.

[6] (1897) A.C. 22.

[7] F. B. Palmer, *op. cit.*, p. 124.

[8] J. W. Smith, *Mercantile Law* (3rd ed. 1843) p. 81.

[9] Joint Stock Companies Act 1856 s.3, 19 & 20 Vict. c.40; Companies Act 1862 s.6, 25 & 26 Vict. c.89.

[10] Mont. & Bligh 94; 1 Deac. & Chitty 411.

[11] 2 De G. M. & G. 599.

[12] 2 Y. & C. Ex. 268.

[13] 14 L.J.C.P. 193.

[14] S. Kyd, *On Corporations* (1793) Vol. I, p. 13.

[15] L. C. B. Gower, *op. cit.*, pp. 97, 100.

[16] M. Cousins and A. Hussain, *Michel Foucault* (1984) p. 37.

[17] For a detailed discussion see P. Ireland, I. Grigg-Spall and D. Kelly, "The Legal Reconceptualisation of the Share" (unpublished). Throughout this paper we will be focusing on ordinary shares.

[18] W. R. Scott, *The Constitution and Finance of English and Irish Joint Stock Companies to 1720* (3 Vols. 1909-12) Vol. I, p. 45.

[19] D. G. Rice, "The Legal Nature of the Share" (1955, unpublished dissertation) p. 2.

[20] P. Wms. 207.

[21] See *Howse v Chapman* (1799) 4 Ves. 542; *Buckridge v Ingram* (1795) 2 Ves. Jun 652.

[22] Sir John Leach in *Ex parte The Vauxhall Bridge Co.* (1821) 1 Glyn. & Jac. 101.

[23] *Supra*, n. 12.

[24] 10 Ex. 222.

25 *Poole v Middleton* 29 Beav. 646.
26 L. C. B. Gower, *op. cit.*, p. 397.
27 Lord Wrenbury in *Bradbury v English Sewing Cotton Co. Ltd.* (1923) A.C. 744 at 767 (H.L.).
28 J. Farrar, *Company Law* (1985) p. 134.
29 C. B. Macpherson, "Capitalism and the Changing Concept of Property" in *Feudalism, Capitalism and Beyond* (1975; eds. Kamenka and Neale) p. 104.
30 See K. Marx, *Capital*, Vol. II, chap. 1; and *Capital* Vol. III, chap. 21.
31 K. Marx, *op. cit.*, Vol. III, p. 375.
32 See D. Landes, "The Structure of Enterprise in the Nineteenth Century" in *The Rise of Capitalism* (1960; ed. D. Landes); also P. Ireland, "The Rise of the Joint Stock Company" (unpublished).
33 K. Marx, *op. cit.*, Vol. III, chaps. 21 and 23.
34 D. Harvey, *The Limits to Capital* (1982) p. 254.
35 See W. Holdsworth, *A History of English Law* (2nd ed. 1937) Vol. VII, p. 516.
36 For example, 2 George II c.25, dealing with, *inter alia*, South Sea bonds, bank notes and East India bonds.
37 W. Holdsworth, *op. cit.*, Vol. VII, pp. 531-32; see also A. B. Dubois, *The English Business Corporation after the Bubble Act 1720-1800* (1938).
38 W. Holdsworth, *op. cit.*, Vol. VII, p. 543.
39 K. Marx, *op. cit.*, Vol. III, chaps 25 and 29; Harvey, *op. cit.*, pp. 266-70.
40 See K. Marx, *op. cit.*, Vol. III, chaps. 25 and 29. The idea is best illustrated by government stock.
41 K. Marx, *Theories of Surplus Value* Book III, (Progress ed. 1972) p. 483.
42 K. Marx, *op. cit.*, n. 30, Vol. III, p. 394.
43 See S. Clarke, *Marx, Marginalism and Modern Sociology* (1982).
44 See R. Hilferding, *Finance Capital* (R.K.P. ed. 1981) pp. 107-116; see *Short v Treasury Commissioners* [1948] A.C. 534.
45 P. Sweezy, *Theory of Capitalist Development* (1968 ed.) p. 238.
46 R. Hilferding, *op. cit.*, pp. 109-10.
47 For detailed coverage see P. Ireland, I. Grigg-Spall and D. Kelly, "The Legal Reconceptualisation of the Share" (unpublished).
48 W. R. Scott, *op. cit.*, Vol. I, pp. 45-46; K. G. Davies, "Joint Stock Investment in the Later Seventeenth Century" in *Essays in Economic History* (1954; ed. Carus-Wilson) Vol. II, p. 273.
49 See W. R. Scott, *op. cit.*; E. Morgan and W. A. Thomas, *The Stock Exchange* (1962); P. G. M. Dickson, *The Financial Revolution in England* (1967).
50 G. H. Evans, *British Corporation Finance* (1936).
51 A. D. Gayer, W. W. Rostow and A. J. Schwarz, *The Growth and Fluctuation of the British Economy 1790-1850* (1953) p. 376.
52 In contemporary partnership law loans varying with profits were held to constitute the lender a partner. See P. Ireland, I. Grigg-Spall and D. Kelly, "Usury and Transitional Forms of Money Capital" (unpublished).
53 M. C. Reed, "Railways and the Growth of the Capital Market" in *Railways in the Victorian Economy* (1969; ed. Reed) p. 167.
54 A. D. Gayer, W. W. Rostow and A. J. Schwarz, *op. cit.*, p. 409.
55 D. Morier Evans, *The City, or the Physiology of London* (1845).
56 M. C. Reed, *op. cit.*, p. 163; see also M. C. Reed, *Investment in Railways in Britain 1820-1844* (1975).
57 B. R. Mitchell, "The Coming of the Railway and U.K. Economic Growth" (1964) 24 *J. Economic History* p. 331.
58 *Ex parte Union Bank of Manchester* 12 Eq. 354.
59 The emergence of the share as a fully independent form of property and the concomitant separation of the share from shareholders was not completed until the introduction of general limited liability and the market dominance of fully paid-up shares.

60 S. Brice, *Ultra Vires* (1st ed. 1875) pp. 1-2.
61 D. Sayer, *Marx's Method* (2nd ed. 1983) p. 17; since the 1930s in Britain the 'group' or holding company-subsidiary form has become more dominant than the single joint stock company form. See P. Ireland and I. Grigg-Spall, "Managerial and Legal Forms of Industrial Capital" (unpublished).
62 See D. Kelly, "Rethinking Ultra Vires" (unpublished).
63 J. Farrar, *op. cit.*, p. 125.
64 L. C. B. Gower, *Modern Company Law* (3rd ed. 1969) p. 115.
65 See P. Ireland, *op. cit.*, n. 2.
66 See I. Grigg-Spall, "Worker Directors and the Joint Stock Company" (unpublished).
67 K. Klare, "Law Making as Praxis" (1979) 40 *Telos* pp. 128-30.
68 L. Althusser, *Lenin and Philosophy* (1971) p. 163.
69 E. Fromm, *The Sane Society* (1955).
70 D. Sayer, *op. cit.*, p. 149.

New Directions in European Community Law

FRANCIS SNYDER*

European Community law is firmly established as part of the law syllabus, yet as a subject of teaching and research in Britain it is barely fifteen years old. This unusual conjunction of accepted status and relative youth offers teachers and students of European Community law a great opportunity. Such is the possibility of exercising a potentially decisive influence on the development of European Community law, not only as an intellectually fascinating subject of study, but also as a significant element in the dominant ideologies and practices of the contemporary world. But how and where can we best devote our attention? In answering this question, we may choose to build or not on certain basic foundations. Two points are crucial, however, to the continued vitality of our common project: first, that we develop a more critical understanding of European Community law, and second, that we move in new directions.

FRAGMENTS OF A BASELINE

1. Elements of the Context

European Community law represents, more evidently perhaps than most other subjects an intricate web of politics, economics and law. It virtually calls out to be understood by means of a political economy of law or an interdisciplinary, contextual or critical approach. Nevertheless, it has often been regarded (and taught) simply as a highly technical set of rules, a dense doctrinal thicket into which only the ignorant or the foolish would "jump in and scratch out their eyes",[1] still less try to understand in terms of social theories of law. This is partly because European Community law has been incorporated to some extent into the English textbook tradition.[2] It is also due, partly, however, to the ways in which the study of European Community

* School of Law, University of Warwick, Coventry CV4 7AL, England; from 1 October 1987 at Faculty of Laws, University College London, 4-8 Endsleigh Gardens, London WC1H 0EG, England.

I wish to thank the Nuffield Foundation for its support of the research on which this paper is based; participants in the European Law workshop at the Critical Legal Conference, University of Kent, September 1986 for stimulating discussion of some of the issues; and Siân Miles and Mark Gould for helpful comments on an earlier draft.

law in Britain has been shaped by other features of its historically specific content.

European Community law as a subject of study in Britain began in particular political circumstances. The accession of the United Kingdom (U.K.) to the European Community was hotly contested and still remains controversial. It elicited sharp disagreements between and within political parties and other groups which to some extent continue today. The teaching of European Community law in Britain pre-dated but was greatly stimulated by and gained its main *raison d'être* from U.K. accession. Consequently, the development of the subject has reflected the continuing political controversy concerning Britain's European Community membership, albeit usually indirectly and often in complex ways.

European Community law has also been influenced significantly by its teachers. European Community law has been taught in the U.K. by a handful of specialists. Most are male; most began their careers in teaching or law practice in constitutional and administrative law; and most have served as legal secretaries at the European Court of Justice. Moreover, European Community law conforms to the well-known general rule that the teaching of comparative and international law in England and Wales has been and remains largely the province of scholars born in other countries. It would be surprising, in these circumstances, if many teachers of European Community law were not pro-European, at least in one of the many – and contradictory – senses of the term. These and similar features are relevant to any attempt to chart new directions, because future developments in European Community law, as in other fields, depend to a great extent on the individuals and groups involved and on the relations between them.

A further influence on European Community law has been what we can describe as a particular combination of teachers and audiences. The European Community's distinctive features, even before U.K. accession, have often been considered to lie not in substantive law but rather in institutions and procedures. Following the logic of this rather artificial distinction between substance and procedure, and struck by the relative unfamiliarity of European Community institutions to budding common lawyers, teachers of European Community law in Britain initially often considered that if a choice were necessary, substantive law should be given less emphasis than institutions and procedure. In addition, European Community law has generally been viewed in Britain through a peculiar, unnecessarily parochial lens, which focuses either on law students and teachers (the academic tradition) on law or practitioners (the craft tradition)[3] but rarely on both together. Much of European Community substantive law has been seen primarily as a practitioner's subject.

As a result, the typical pattern of study and teaching of European Community law in Britain formed a curious amalgam until recently. Law undergraduates were introduced to the distinctive features of European Community institutions and procedures, while European Community substantive law, with some exceptions, was reserved for more advanced courses or practice. Even though European Community law may technically be part of English law, it was rarely discussed in any detail in courses such as English legal system, constitutional law or administrative law. Student textbooks, again with exceptions, generally mirrored the particular image of European Community law seen through this complex cultural kaleidoscope, an image which most teachers, students, textbooks and publishers continued to reproduce. They gave special attention to constitutional and administrative law; even competition and commercial law, though of special interest to many practitioners, were only subsidiary, secondary themes. Contextual or critical work on European Community law was virtually unknown.

2. Towards Critical Analysis

It is surprising, therefore, curious that at the same time European Community law has often appeared to be especially accessible to critical analysis. The history of the European Community seems to mesh neatly with the main trends in the development of capitalism since the Second World War. The post-war period, according to this view, encompasses the long boom of capitalism in the 1950s, during which the European Community was established, and continues through the 1970s world recession, marked in Europe by growing agricultural surpluses, declining enthusiasm for any European ideal, apparently ceaseless budget quarrels and increasing economic nationalism.

In addition, the general principles on which the European Community was founded, and which are consecrated in its basic legal texts, appear both to the beginner and sometimes also to the specialist merely to restate in legal language and in treaty form the underlying assumptions of contemporary capitalist economies. Consider, for example, the 'four freedoms' enunciated in the European Community's constitution, the Treaty of Rome. They include the free movement of goods, workers, services and capital. These fundamental legal principles, the backbone of the European Community, seem to be simply a capsule summary of Marx's description in *Capital* of the general circulation of labour power and other commodities.

Moreover, a parallel is frequently drawn, by writers as diverse as those in policy studies and those in neo-Marxist sociology, between the operation and legitimation of the European Community and apparently similar processes at the level of the nation state. National and supra-national state structures in contemporary western Europe thus participate in a particular division of economic and political labour, in which each performs different roles or what Murray calls state or public functions.[4] They differ fundamentally, however, in that national governments are subject, both in theory and in practice, to replacement by popular election, whereas the staff of European Community institutions, with the exception of the weak Parliament, are bureaucratically recruited or politically appointed. Consequently, European Community law is sometimes viewed as a threat, not just to national sovereignty or even to the possibility of a genuinely socialist government, but also to the values and practices of locality, local organisation and individual participation in the

169

making of political decisions which compose and thus continually reconstitute democracy.

Furthermore, within the broad context of the international economy, the European Community is often considered to be inherently neo-colonial. Acting for the rich and north in its manifold relations with the poor and south, it represents at best an unfortunate if inevitable legacy of the past, at worst a new form of foreign, capitalist domination. The Lomé Convention, European Community food aid and the role of the European Community in international commodity agreements, for example, thus are frequently viewed as integral parts of a slightly modified, updated, international division of labour, indelibly marked by history and simply perpetuating unequal relations between Europe and the Third World.

These broad assertions contain at least a kernel of truth, but nevertheless they are both reductionist and simplistic. They posit too close a connection between law and political economy and they focus our attention too narrowly on particular facets of general issues to the exclusion of crucial elements of their wider context. For our purposes, however, their importance is four-fold. First, they challenge us to make explicit the underlying assumptions about law, the state and society which as teachers and students we bring to European Community law. Secondly, they direct our attention to the necessity of understanding European Community law in its social, economic and political context. Thirdly, they remind us that facts, including facts about the nature and operation of European Community law and institutions, exist and make sense only within particular theoretical frameworks: an important element in any critical study of European Community law is a social theory of law. Finally, they open up the possibility of developing alternative topics and proposing new directions in the teaching and study of European Community law.

SOME THEMES IN EUROPEAN COMMUNITY LAW

Teaching and research on European Community law in Britain and other countries therefore provide the foundation for a two-fold development. On the one hand is the continuation of certain established lines of enquiry. This includes the tradition of highly sophisticated scholarship concerning legal doctrine in fields such as European Community institutions, procedures and competition law. On the other hand, building on this basis, is the study of European Community law in its social and economic context and from the perspective of critical theory. This second aspect would integrate the study of European Community law more fully into the principal, highly fruitful lines of enquiry which during the past several decades have marked the best legal scholarship in other fields. Special emphasis needs to be given to four different themes, each of which embraces several areas of substantive law. They are (i) institutions, rules, ideologies and processes; (ii) law, economy and society; (iii) the international political economy; and (iv) state forms and legal pluralism, including the relationship between European Community law, the law of the member states and the laws, customs and practices of local communities, firms and other organisations.[5] Here it is possible, for reasons of space, to consider only the first three themes.

1. Institutions, Rules, Ideologies and Processes

Legal scholarship in Britain has traditionally focused especially on the courts. The study of European Community law has generally been no exception. While building on this base, we need to extend our concern not simply to other institutions but more broadly to the interrelationship of institutions, rules, ideologies and processes. Of special importance among the institutions, in addition to the Court, are the Commission, the Council, the Parliament, the Committee of Permanent Representatives and the management committees and other sites of European Community micro-politics and rule-making. We must also go beyond the analysis of legal doctrine and be concerned with the ways in which European Community institutions work in practice. Consequently, we need to make use of the methods, theoretical insights and findings of other social sciences. Our work, thus, may potentially contribute not only to our common understanding of European Community law as a subject of intellectual enquiry, but also to the development of new social practices in policy-making and in politics.

How, for example, is European Community law actually made? Even though almost thirty years have passed since the European Community's formation and almost fifteen since the U.K.'s accession, we are still unable to answer this question. The answer is important, however, both for academic study and for practical politics. In trying to understand the European Community legislative process, we might begin by noting that one of its distinctive features is the overt interconnection between politics, policy and law-making. This point can be illustrated by a specific instance.

Among the central features of the European Community's most costly, most controversial common policy, the Common Agricultural Policy (C.A.P.), are the schemes of regulatory legislation known as common organisations of the market or agricultural commodity regimes. The most recent regime concerns lamb and mutton, known officially as sheepmeat. The making of the sheepmeat regime was stimulated by the accession to the European Community of two major lamb-producing countries, the U.K. and Eire, in 1973. It also coincided with important changes in the early 1970s in the European and international food and agricultural economy. First were significant shifts in peasant and agricultural union politics in France, previously the European Community's principal lamb producer. Second was the restructuring by the French government of its national food marketing system, especially the replacement of Les Halles in Paris by the market in Rungis. Third were several crucial macro-economic processes in the international meat trade: the early 1970s slump in certain world market prices, for example, encouraged multinational British and American trading companies to diversify into U.K. domestic distribution and to emphasise intra-European

171

Community trade. These and other processes at the local, national, supra-national and international levels occurred just at the onset of the recession in Europe, which was marked increasingly by economic crises, centrifugal political trends and nationalist protectionism. After British and Irish accession, however, the European Community Commission proposed the first agricultural commodity regime since the heady 1960s, designed not only to promote intra-European Community trade and protect European producers, but also to use supranational law as a potentially potent symbol of western Europe's continuing economic unity.

The ensuing negotiations centred on a bitter trade dispute, the 1978-80 'lamb war' between Britain and France. They provoked three formal European Community Commission proposals for draft legislation. They also embraced three cases before the European Court, including the only instance since the creation of the Common Market in which a member state (France) refused on socio-economic grounds to follow a European Court of Justice decision. Moreover, though apparently concerned only with putative, narrow national interests, the sheepmeat negotiations involved a wide range of local, national and supranational forces in Europe, New Zealand and the U.S.A. as well as virtually the entire gamut of European Community institutions. Even the adoption of compromise legislation in 1980 did not end the dispute. Subsequently the European Court of Justice recognised that the sheepmeat regime was subject to renegotiation, and the Franco-British trade conflict continued at least until 1982, both in complex legal disputes and in violent protests.[6]

This particular example illustrates some general characteristics of European Community law. Of special significance are the operation of most European Community law without overt sanctions, the wide range of interests involved in law-making and the extent to which European Community regulatory legislation always remains renegotiable. It also reveals several of the principal features of European Community legislative processes. One is the close relationship between legal and economic structures, in this instance the interconnection between local, national, supranational and international levels of the sheepmeat marketing chain and the influence of different interests in the legislative process. Another feature is the sharply contrasting concep-tions of the legislative process and the issues at stake which are held by different actors and the ways in which these conceptions shaped the various proposals for legislation and the eventual outcome. Further, the making of this particular regulation was intricately connected with other disputed issues during the same period. These other issues, part of a complex configuration of elements, influenced the politics of both the price and market and the agricultural structural aspects of successive draft regulations leading up to the regime.

We can formulate these observations on the way a specific European Community law was made in terms of four hypotheses. The first is that the nature and outcome of European Community legislative processes and the political and socio-economic structures within which these processes occur are

172

intimately related: each constitutes, shapes and potentially transforms the other. Both process and outcome in the making of the sheepmeat regime are related, for example, to changes in the sheepmeat marketing chain at the local, national, supranational and international levels. The sheepmeat marketing chain embraces the role of the state and the socio-economic and ideological aspects of production, distribution, exchange and consumption.

The second hypothesis is that the sheepmeat regime, at least superficially, differs fundamentally from previous European Community commodity regimes. It expressly includes not only a price and market policy, like other regimes, but also an agricultural structures policy, which was previously distinct. This apparently unique conjunction is due primarily to the regime's specific historical context, the particular features of French politics during the period, the importance of regional policies in U.K. agricultural politics and the symbolic importance throughout Europe of the family farm. It must be viewed, however, in its broader context. Seen in this light, the sheepmeat regime has two related purposes: (i) to provide a legal framework for free trade in lamb and mutton within the European Community while simultaneously permitting different national support policies towards producers in Britain and France; and (ii) to serve as a counterbalance to the increasing industrialisation of European Community agriculture under the aegis of agro-industrial trading firms and national governments.

The third hypothesis is that the 'lamb war' involved a specific, ideal type (in the Weberian sense) of legislative process. This distinctive type is 'stone-walling', which we can define as "the threatened or actual, partial or complete withdrawal of co-operation in Community affairs by a Member State until its demands on a disputed issue are met to its satisfaction".[7] Protracted, politically risky and therefore rare, 'stonewalling' is often considered to be merely an obstructive tactic. In fact, however, it represents an ideal type of legislative process, one which in an economic integration scheme such as the European Community may be inevitable.

A final hypothesis is that the sheepmeat regime, despite its distinctive features, exemplifies much contemporary European Community legislation. It does not unify the European economy by means of uniform laws. Instead, it serves primarily as a supranational umbrella, beneath which the European Community increasingly recognises the validity of diverse national policies. Common Market law, in a fragmented Europe, is, therefore, mainly a co-ordinating device.

2. Law, Economy and Society

A second theme is the European Community's economic law. It is often considered to comprise mainly competition law and policy, but in fact it includes a wide range of substantive areas. One important domain is the European Community's agricultural and food policy. It accounts for over eighty per cent of European Community legislation and judicial decisions. Moreover, it extends far beyond the agricultural sector. It involves the relations between agriculture and industry, economic regulation, competition policy, consumer protection and numerous other areas of domestic European Community law as well as the European Community's international relations.

Some of the central features of European Community economic law can be illustrated by a significant decision of the European Court of Justice, reviewing the legality of a particular economic policy. Case 114/76 *Bela-Muehle* was one of the 'skimmed milk powder cases'.[8] It came before the European Court in 1976. Under the provisions of Rome Treaty Article 177, a West German state court, the *Landgericht* Oldenburg, asked the European Court of Justice for a preliminary ruling on the validity of a European Community Council regulation.The regulation in question was Regulation 563/76 of 15 March 1976,[9] the first in a series of measures, including the co-responsibility levy and the dairy quotas, by which the Commission has tried (unsuccessfully) to control the European Community's increasing flood of milk production.

Regulation 563/76 was the product of complex and protracted negotiations. In December 1975 the Commission proposed a scheme for disposing of skimmed milk powder, which with butter and some cheeses is the main C.A.P. intervention product in the dairy sector and, therefore, a major form of dairy surplus. Under the scheme producers of animal feedingstuffs were to be legally required to buy surplus skimmed milk powder from national intervention agencies (such as the Intervention Board for Agricultural Produce at Reading), and incorporate it in the proportion of two per cent into their products. This proposal was vociferously opposed, however, by a powerful group of interests, including livestock producers, the dairy trades, animal feed manufacturers, importers and crushers of oilseeds and U.S.A. soya producers and traders. Consequently, it was abandoned and replaced by the proposal that eventually became Regulation 563/76.[10]

Regulation 563/76 established what was known unofficially as the skimmed milk powder deposit scheme. It entered into force on 15 March 1976 and applied until 31 October 1976. It created a complex chain of obligations and conditional entitlements. At one end of the chain, Article 1 of the Regulation established "an obligation to purchase skimmed milk powder held by intervention agencies for use in feedingstuffs for animals other than young calves". At the other end, the granting of aids for certain vegetable protein products or the issue of a protein certificate allowing free circulation in the European Community of certain imported animal feed protein products was subject to the submission of a standard European Community document (or a deposit, which was to be released on production of the document). The document constituted proof of the purchase and denaturation (making unfit for human consumption, a practice now abandoned) of a certain quantity of skimmed milk powder.

Compared to this complex political and legal background, the facts and the European Court's decision in *Bela-Muehle* were relatively straightforward. The applicant's factory produced concentrated feedingstuffs; the defendant operated a battery-hen unit. The defendant refused to pay the cost of the deposit for the issue of protein certificates, which had been passed on to it by the applicant, who had been charged the amount by its own suppliers. The defendant argued that Regulation 563/76 was incompatible with the principles of non-discrimination and proportionality. As defined and distinguished in *Bela-Muehle* by the Advocate-General:

> ... non-discrimination is concerned with the relationship between various groups of persons and takes the forms of equality of treatment by bodies vested with public authority, whereas the principle of proportionality means that the burdens imposed on the persons concerned must not exceed the steps required in order to meet the public interest involved.[11]

The defendant's argument was accepted by the Court.

The Court held, on the one hand, that Regulation 563/76 was discriminatory in the way in which it distributed the costs of the scheme between various agricultural sub-sectors. The financial burden of disposing of the surplus skimmed milk powder, as the Advocate General pointed out, [12] was in fact borne not by milk producers but primarily by poultry farmers and pig breeders. On the other hand, the Court held that the regulation contravened the principle of proportionality. The purchase price of the surplus skimmed milk powder was three times higher, for equivalent protein value, than that of imported soya, the substance it replaced. The obligation to purchase the skimmed milk powder at such a disproportionate price was not necessary, in the Court's view, to attain the objective of disposing of surplus stocks; less onerous means could have been used. The Court therefore held the regulation to be null and void.

Bela-Muehle exemplifies some principal features of European Community economic law. Among them are its imbrication of the European Community's complex institutional distribution of power, the intimate relationship of law, politics and policy, and the interconnection between domestic and international economic relations. These elements were combined in the dispute in an especially intricate set of social practices. They were both reproduced and transformed by the judicial decision. The case also illustrates certain underlying assumptions which are implicit in European Community economic law, especially as interpreted and applied by the European Court of Justice. These presuppositions concern the state's role in the economy and the distinction between law, the economy and politics.

Bela-Muehle concerned a highly controversial aspect of European Community policy: the delimitation of the legally permissible ways in which the agricultural surpluses can be controlled. On this general issue the Commission, the Council and the Court held different views. Measures proposed by the Commission, approved by the Parliament and adopted by the Council were challenged in the courts. Following the Article 177 preliminary ruling procedure, this challenge occurred first in a national court and then in the European Court. Because of the European Community's institutional structure, the European Court of Justice would seem to have had the last word.

In evaluating the Regulation, the Court did not mention other proposed surplus disposal measures. Nor did it question the general framework of

175

European Community policy concerning the dairy sector. Indeed, such a wide-ranging enquiry was expressly ruled out by the Advocate-General. In his opinion he stated that "an appraisal of whether or not the regulation is consistent with Articles 39 and 40 of the Treaty cannot involve consideration of the whole of the Community's economic policy in milk and milk-products", especially the level of intervention prices.[12] The Court's decision was based on this abstraction of specific legal issues from broader European Community economic policy. It presumed that such a distinction was both possible and valid. It thus could not consider whether the skimmed milk powder deposit scheme, though perhaps second best, might not have been an adequate policy.

By narrowing its focus in this way, the Court also excluded any discussion of the relationship between European Community agricultural surpluses and the international economy. Its legal logic severed the close connection which actually exists in the European food chain between C.A.P. law and policy, agricultural production and food marketing and the operation of multi-national companies. In *Bela-Muehle*, however, these relations were of crucial importance. They were directly relevant to the legal principles of non-discrimination and proportionality.

Comparing the prices of animal feedingstuffs, the Court stressed that the price of skimmed milk powder was high compared to that of the alternative. This was so only, however, because soya oil cake was imported into the Community free of any variable import levy. It was a major and controversial exception to general European Community international agricultural trade agreements. The Court took for granted, however, the existing framework of international economic relations.

Moreover, the exemption of soya oil cake from the European Community's variable levy is a tribute to the political and economic power of the European Community's oilseed crushing industry. This group includes Unilever, the world's largest food and agricultural multinational company. Through numerous subsidiaries, multinational firms buy oilseed cake from producers in the U.S.A. and Brazil, transport it and import it into the European Community, process it within the Community, especially in the Netherlands, and then sell it in compound feedingstuffs to the Community's dairy producers. These social relations cut across national and European Community boundaries. They shape and determine the main features of the European Community's animal feeds market, including the ways in which the market is regulated. In *Bela-Muehle* the Court focused. however, on the outcome of European Community legislative processes, not on their content, and on specific price indices, not their broader meaning. It took for granted the social organisation of the economy and its political consequences.

Furthermore, the Court considered to be discrimination the imposition on some poultry farmers and pig breeders of the high cost of disposing of surplus products produced by some dairy farmers and processors. In reaching this conclusion it did not mention two widely recognised, legally significant features of the European food and agricultural economy. First, a (if not the) major reason for the ever-increasing production of surplus milk is the use of

176

compound feedingstuffs. They are used in the greatest proportions by larger enterprises. Secondly, with the internationalisation of capital the European food economy is becoming increasingly integrated. Superficially different subsectors, whether called 'agricultural' or 'industrial',[14] are often highly interdependent, linked not just by general market relations but by the law of contract and property. The Court took for granted, however, that all dairy farmers, considered as units of production, were equal and autonomous. It apparently gave little attention to the possibility that its decision – assuming it had a wider effect – might favour high technology over low technology agriculture, multinational companies over small producers, international trade over local production, import dependency over self-sufficiency, or links with the U.S.A. and Brazil over those with other trading partners.

These taken-for-granted elements embody two sets of assumptions. The first assumption concerns the distinction between public and private and the economic role of the state. The Court held that Regulation 563/76 was contrary to the general principles of non-discrimination and proportionality. It considered these principles, at least in the *Bela-Muehle* case, to be almost inextricably intertwined. Implicit in both principles are a series of presuppositions. These are that the economy, *ab initio*, comprises entirely private, apolitical actors; the public, politically organised state is absent. Thus, the state is far from being a basic, constituent element in the creation of a capitalist economy. At least initially, it stands outside this set of socio-economic relations.[15] Its sporadic, irregular, albeit sometimes necessary incursions into the economic domain need to be controlled. Both of these general principles, non-discrimination and proportionality, are purportedly concerned (and ostensibly used by courts) to limit the ways in which, and the extent to which, the state intervenes in the economy.

A second set of assumptions concerns the distinction between law, policy and politics. This distinction posits politics and policy as partisan and law as neutral. In this view, law is outside and above policy-making and politics; and the framework of policy-making and the boundaries of politics are established by law. This same distinction is often applied to the European Community (and other) institutions. It categorises the Commission, the Parliament and the Council as political institutions, and the Court as legal (counterposed to political). Law is a powerful, politically neutral instrument of social control, and in the European Community it is applied in the last instance by the Court.

To state these presuppositions is not only to depict a particular vision of an ideal world. It is also to sketch the main outlines of a powerful ideology, which, though not shared by all European Community institutions, nonetheless underlies many of the decisions of the European Court. Yet, as *Bela-Muehle* demonstrates, the European Court of Justice, plays a very important role in European Community policy-making and in both micro- and macro-politics. It should be clear that in the same social practices in which it seeks to operate as a check on other European Community institutions, the European Court is also making economic policy. Moreover, as the saga of the European Community dairy surplus demonstrates, discussions and negotiations on

177

specific issues of economic policy do not end with a particular judicial decision. The Court's decision in *Bela-Muehle* needs to be viewed in this broader perspective. It thus may be seen to be simply one element in a continuing political process.

These sets of assumptions underlay the European Court's *Bela-Muehle* decision. The Court in this case ruled on the validity of a specific regulation. More broadly, it considered the legal limits of administrative action concerned with the implementation of a specific economic policy. More broadly still, it confronted the vexed question as to how to dispose of the European Community's agricultural surplus and who should bear the cost. The elements which the Court took for granted not only shaped its final decision. They are among the basic premises of European Community economic law. Though usually in the form of legislation, at least initially, the European Community's economic law also comprises judicial decisions. It is for this reason that the taken-for-granted elements in the Court's *Bela-Muehle* decision are especially significant. For the European Court is not just an especially important interpreter of European Community economic law. It is also a major creative force in European Community law-making, policy-making and politics.

3. The International Political Economy

A third theme is the European Community's role in the international political economy. Legal scholarship on the European Community's external relations has focused largely on the Common Commercial Policy. Clearly, however, the European Community's importance in the world economy and in international political and legal relations encompasses other elements. Among the most important so far as Third World countries are concerned is food and development policy. European Community law exercises a significant but often little appreciated influence on the nature and scope of food and agricultural policies in the Third World. Moreover, numerous aspects of European Community law which are frequently regarded as disparate and distinct are in fact interrelated in their common relationship to Third World food policy. This face of the relationship between the European Community and African, Caribbean and Pacific (A.C.P.) countries forms a major area of future work.

The European Community is the largest importer of agricultural products in the world, and an important share of its imports come from Third World countries. In addition, the European Community follows the U.S.A. as the world's second largest agricultural exporter. Conversely, numerous developing countries are affected, directly or indirectly, by the C.A.P. Most form part of the intricate web of the European Community's external relations. Almost all are influenced by the European Community in matters as diverse as the activities of non-governmental organisations or the extension of western models of food production. The European Community thus plays a major role in shaping international and national patterns of food production and distribution.

178

Since the Second World War multinational companies, states, international organisations and regional groupings such as the European Community have virtually transformed the world's food economy.[16] The "set of activities and relationships that interact to determine what, how much, by what method and for whom food is produced"[17] is today largely international rather than national in scope. Correlatively, the food chain now tends to be viewed as broader than simply production. It is recognised, rightly, as being composed of the provision of inputs, agricultural production, processing, distribution and trade, and consumption. These changes can be described as two socio-economic processes: integration and internationalisation. Both have been stimulated and encouraged by European Community law.

Both integration and internationalisation have occurred in two apparently separate spheres, the circulation of commodities and the organisation of power. These spheres have often been treated as different and distinct, but in fact they are intimately related. Their conjoint elaboration and development in the past three decades has formed an important, albeit incompletely realised element of the European project, reflected to a great extent in European Community law. It also underlies the contemporary world food order, an important segment of which is the network of relationships between the European Community and Third World countries.

These socio-economic processes have also had another important ramification. The partial but gradual industrialisation of European Community agriculture and the transformation of food production, processing, distribution and consumption in the world economy since the 1950s have been closely linked with a new political project, a novel conception of food policy. Contemporary food policy is not directed simply at achieving a satisfactory balance between food imports and domestic production or only at improving nutrition and protecting the consumer. It is concerned instead with the formulation of coherent national and international policies regarding the food economy as a whole. It thus embraces agricultural production, food manufacturing and retailing and household and extra-household consumption. Accordingly, it takes account of the systematic nature of the food chain, the increased integration of agriculture and industry and the connection between domestic and international forces. It also considers the links between the agri-food sector and the rest of the national and international economy.

The implications of this conception of food policy are only beginning to be examined seriously at an international level, especially with regard to relations between the European Community and Third World countries. Yet, as recent events have demonstrated, such an examination is long overdue. The world food order, built up between the 1940s and the 1970s, is now in crisis. Nowhere is this crisis more apparent than in the Third World, particularly in Africa. The severe famines in many countries during the 1970s and 1980s have had extremely serious consequences, both short-term and long-term, for thousands of human beings and for world food production and trade. The crisis is also evident, however, in the U.S.A. and western Europe. The ever-increasing stocks of surplus agricultural commodities and pressures for reform of the

179

C.A.P. are only two among many signs of the distorted priorities in the world food economy. Clearly, it is time to reconsider the basic principles of the world food order, including relations between the European Community and the Third World.

The socio-economic aspects of these relations have been widely discussed, but their legal elements have received little attention. Yet the frequently intense debates concerning possible reforms have continually demonstrated the political and ideological importance of European Community law. Among its relevant elements are, first, the parts of European Community law which in principle are concerned wholly with food and agricultural policy within the Community, but which nevertheless have important implications and consequences for the Third World. They include the legal framework of the European Community food policy for self-sufficiency; the C.A.P. and its implications for Third World food policy, especially with regard to cereals, dairy products, sugar and beef; potential reforms of the C.A.P.; European Community food law and its international implications; and the industrialisation of European Community agriculture and its integration with trade.

The second group of elements are the relationships between the European Community and the African, Caribbean and Pacific countries which are linked to the Community by the Lomé Convention. They embrace the Lomé Convention and its predecessors in relation to food and agricultural policy and rural development; the right to food and the human rights provisions in the Lomé Convention; the adoption of European Community-sponsored food strategies in certain Third World countries; and the implications of the Community's special relationship with the A.C.P. countries for non-Lomé countries.

The third group of elements are the more general external relations of the European Community in so far as they concern Third World food and agricultural policy. They include the effects of European Community arrangements with mediterranean countries; the Generalised System of Preferences (G.S.P.); relevant provisions of the General Agreement on Tariffs and Trade (G.A.T.T.); international commodity agreements, especially regarding wheat and sugar; the import by the European Community of so-called cereals substitutes, such as soya and manioc; the spread of the European model of food production and its effects on Third World social and physical environments; the role of European Community-based non-governmental organisations; relations between the European Community, the U.S.A. and Third World countries regarding food policy; legal aspects of the transfer of food and agricultural technology, including pesticides, seeds, fertilisers and biotechnology; the legal aspects of European Community food aid, including the Food Aid Convention and the management of Operation Flood in India; and the legal arrangements regarding European Community provision of famine relief and the principal legal issues, such as the extent of national sovereignty, which have been raised by famine relief operations. These are among the central political and economic issues in the contemporary world, and they need to be incorporated into our study of European Community law.

180

CONCLUSION

A critical approach to teaching and research in European Community law is likely to build to some extent on already established foundations. It also, however, must develop on at least three different levels. The first level is to explore new areas of study: not just those which, using mainly food and agricultural law examples, I have outlined in this paper, but also many others, such as legal pluralism, gender relations and immigration and labour. The second level is to develop new approaches, particularly by bringing the methods and findings of the other social sciences to bear on different aspects of European Community law. The third level is to begin, in both teaching and research, to analyse European Community law using social theory and critical theories of law. Why, for example, have particular aspects of European Community law been given so much attention – and others so little – by teachers, practitioners and students? What legal ideologies and other related social practices have contributed since the mid-1950s to the legitimacy (or lack of legitimacy) of the European Community, and how and by what institutions, interests and processes have they been generated? To what extent are the ideas of indeterminacy, antiformalism, contradiction and marginality developed by critical theorists in the U.S.A., which focus mainly on the United States Supreme Court, useful in providing new insights into European Community law? It is now time to open the study of European Community law to broader perspectives and to move in these new directions.

NOTES AND REFERENCES

[1] This was the advice given by Karl Llewellyn to first-year law students in *The Bramble Bush* (1930 rep. 1951).
[2] See Sugarman, "The Making of the Textbook Tradition" in *Common Law and Legal Theory* (1985; ed. W. Twining).
[3] On this distinction, see M. Weber, *Law in Economy and Society*, (1966; trans. E. Shils and M. Rheinstein) pp. 198-223.
[4] Murray, "The Internationalisation of Capital and the Nation State" (1967) 67 *New Left Rev.* p. 84. See also H. Radice (ed.), *Multinational Firms and Modern Imperialism* (1975) and (1983) 11 *International J. Sociology of Law*, special issue on 'The International State'. On policy studies, see H. Wallace, W. Wallace and C. Webb (eds.), *Policy-Making in the European Community* (2nd ed. 1983).
[5] On legal pluralism, see Snyder, "Anthropology, Dispute Processes and Law: A Critical Introduction" (1981) 8 *Brit. J. Law and Society* p. 1; Griffiths, "What is Legal Pluralism?" (unpublished); Fitzpatrick, "Law, Plurality and Underdevelopment" in *Legality, Ideology and the State* (1983; ed. D. Sugarman); Santos, "Modes of Production of Social Power and Law", Working Paper No. 1, Institute for Legal Studies, University of Wisconsin, Madison, (1985).
[6] For further discussion, see Snyder, "Whose Common Market? The Making of the E.E.C. Sheepmeat Regime", presented at the Wenner-Gren Foundation for Anthropological Research Symposium on 'Ethnohistorical Models for the Evolution of Law in Specific Societies', Bellagio, Italy, August 1985; Snyder, "Law-Making in the European Community: Preliminary Notes on Structures, Processes and Interests" in *Law, History and Society: New Directions in the Anthropology of Law* (forthcoming, 1987; eds. J. Collier and J. Starr).

181

7   F. Snyder, *Law of the Common Agricultural Policy* (1985) p. 49.
8   The full name of the case was Case 114/76 *Bela-Muehle Josef-Bergmann KG v Grows-Farm GmbH & Co. KG* [1977] E.C.R. 1222. The other 'skimmed milk powder cases' were Case 116/76 *Granaria BV v Hoofdproduktschap voor Akkerbouwprodukten* [1977] E.C.R. 1247; Joined Cases 119 and 120/76 *Oelmuehle Hamburg AG v Hauptzollamt Hamburg Waltershof* and *Firma Kurt A. Becher v Hauptzollamt Bremen-Nord* [1979] E.C.R. 1269; Joined Cases 83 and 94/76, 15 and 40/77 *Bayerische HNL Vermehrungsbetriebe GmbH & Co. KG v Council and Commission* [1977] E.C.R. 1209; Case 101/78 *Granaria BV v Hoofdproduktschap voor Akkerbouwprodukten* [1979] E.C.R. 623.
9   O.J., C.E.,1976, L67/18.
10 For further details, see Norris, Pickard and Young, "Three Case Histories in Agriculture" (unpublished), Centre for European Agricultural Studies, Wye College, University of London, pp. 40-59. They report the suggestion that the compulsory incorporation scheme was proposed by the then Agricultural Commissioner Lardinois primarily to make the modified scheme, which was subsequently adopted, acceptable as a softer alternative.
11 *Per* Advocate-General Capotorti [1977] E.C.R. 1222 at 1232.
12 *Id.*, at 1231.
13 *Id.*, at 1227.
14 See Snyder, "L'Agriculture et l'Industrie dans le Droit de la C.E.E." (1987) 5 *Droit et Société*.
15 See the very useful article by the former President of the Court of Justice, Professor J. Mertens de Wilmars, "The Case-Law of the Court of Justice in Relation to the Review of the Legality of Economic Policy in Mixed-Economy Systems" (1982) *Legal Issues of European Integration* p. 1.
16 See Y. Ghai, R. Luckham and F. Snyder (eds.), *The Political Economy of Law: A Third World Reader* (1986).
17 Organisation for Economic Co-operation and Development, *Food Policy* (1981) p. 10.

182

Critical Legal Education in Britain

ALAN THOMSON*

While the terms 'critical legal studies' and 'critical legal education' are frequently heard in legal academic discussion in Britain today, there exists a widespread uncertainty, felt by both those who identify with these terms and by curious outsiders, about what they refer to. In the first section of this paper I consider, particularly in relation to education, what the critical movement is and where it came from, concluding with a few remarks on the relation of that movement to the critique of the Enlightenment at large. In the second section I offer some thoughts on the distinctive nature of critical education in general, which I follow up by discussing in the third section some possibilities and problems in the development of a critical education through law.

CRITICAL LEGAL STUDIES AND EDUCATON

1. What Is It?

The difficulty in providing a simple answer to this question is that although there have been numerous movements in legal studies and education in Britain over the last twenty years or so, many of them claiming progressive or radical credentials, it is only relatively recently that the umbrella term 'critical', imported from the U.S.A., has come into widespread usage in this country. However, while the term itself may be of recent application to legal studies in Britain, it would be mistaken to think that what has now acquired an identity by adopting the U.S.A. label is simply an American import, or that it is only as old as the usage of that label. In attempting to answer the question "What is critical legal studies and education in Britain?" I will therefore be pointing to a stream or movement in legal academia, which has been developing for some two decades under a variety of labels, and which I will suggest draws its coherence from the critique of the Enlightenment in a double sense.

Though my concern in this paper is primarily with critical legal education, I do not think it is possible to separate that from a consideration of the critical legal studies movement as a whole, for I would suggest that one of the most striking features of that movement has been the central part which a concern over education has played in generating its momentum, making critical legal studies as much a movement in the classroom as in the learned publication.

* Darwin College, The University, Canterbury, Kent CT2 7NY, England.

In the traditional approach of legal academia, research and scholarship are perceived as operating at the frontiers, while education is seen as the process of transmitting relatively well established truths and skills; thus, education appears as a secondary and derivative activity. Furthermore, to the extent that education becomes an issue at all in this approach, it appears to pose predominantly technical problems of how to make the transmission of knowledge and skills more effective, or of what areas of legal doctrine are appropriate for training lawyers. In this tradition the truth claims of legal knowledge are not only treated as unproblematic but are rarely raised in education at all.

By contrast, in the critical legal movement not only does education tend to be taken more seriously, but the boundaries between research and teaching and between frontier and well established territory become increasingly blurred as, and I would suggest this is a general feature of the critical movement, the truth claims of traditional legal knowledge are rendered explicitly problematic.

I would suggest that the relative importance attached to education in the critical legal movement, particularly clearly shown in the U.S.A., is not a purely accidental feature, but flows from certain general orientations of the movement as a whole, in particular its understanding of the relation between knowledge and politics, its deep suspicion of abstract truth and its view that legal education is necessarily a political process. I will attempt to clarify these points later. However, I think they only become fully intelligible when one understands the historical development of the critical movement, for, in my view, as the word 'movement' implies, critical legal studies and education are not so much characterised by adherence to a set of positions, or having a theoretical orthodoxy, but by a continuing 'struggle to break up the rigidity to which understanding has reduced everything'. The critical movement is, then, a dialectical movement which establishes its identity in opposition. Since each critique which momentarily becomes a position engenders its own critical opposition, we might say of the critical legal movement 'it does not have a nature but only a history'.

2. Where Did It Come From?

Like the emergence of most movements, what we can now retrospectively call the critical legal movement arose in Britain out of a diffuse dissatisfaction with, and opposition to, the existing order of things. That order of things in legal education was the equation of legal education with 'learning the law'. In this expository or dogmatic tradition, legal education is confined to the exposition of the currently operative legal rules. This exposition is pursued through the reading of legal texts to disclose what 'the' law in the singular is (an activity which this tradition assumes to be possible) and through seeking 'correct' legal answers to hypothetical problems. Indeed, Glanville Williams' little book bearing the title *Learning the Law*, in which the author even doubts whether students may criticise the law, symbolised for some the old order against which a new order sought to establish itself.

From the 1960s onwards, as older law teachers (many of whom were full or part-time practitioners) began to retire, a new generation of younger law teachers began to emerge who generally had little experience of or contact with legal practice. For many of this generation, touched by the radical inconoclasm of the 1960s and seeking to establish their identity and respectability in an academic rather than a legal context, the expository tradition appeared not only intellectually barren but to occupy a peculiar middle ground between the genuinely academic and the truly practical: an inadequate way of relating theory and practice. What I think principally motivated those teachers to seek a way of vacating that territory was a sense of the unreality of law as it appeared through the legal texts. Thus, the gap between legal appearance and reality became, and in my view remains, a central theme of the critical legal movement in its attempt to establish a new relationship between theory and practice.

Inspired in part by the earlier realist movements in Scandinavia and the U.S.A., but more importantly by observing the vast growth of state intervention in the post-war years, many law teachers became aware of the increasing gap between law in the books and in reality, and began to see teaching law in isolation from its social, political and economic context as an heroic folly. Books like Friedman's *Law in a Changing Society* published in 1959 represented early attempts to mobilise critically the idea of this gap and to commit legal study and teaching towards practical change.

At that period one gap in particular attracted the attention of a more radical element in an emerging critical movement: the gap in legal services, or the so-called 'unmet legal need' problem. This not only brought the issue of the provision of legal services onto the legal academic agenda but it also responded to the growing desire of some law teachers to identify with the poor and underprivileged. Poor people's law, in the shape of such courses as welfare law, labour law and consumer law were added onto the traditional curriculum of subjects such as property, contract and trusts, which came increasingly to be seen in reality as rich people's law.

Up to the mid 1970s the emerging critique of law dominantly took the form of exposing the social reality beneath the appearance of law as it presented itself through reading the legal text. Reflecting this approach one might mention the growing interest in legal process as opposed to substance, particularly in criminal law; the increasing concern with policy in the law and the emphasis on empirical studies, particularly efficacy studies, which characterised the 'socio-legal' or 'law and society' movements. Thus, when the publishers Weidenfeld and Nicolson introduced a new form of legal text in the 'Law in Context' series in 1970, they were entirely in tune not only with the spirit of the time among progressive academics but importantly also with the increasingly dominant perception of law in government and among administrators.

In the 'law in context' approach, law appears as an instrument or means of realising extra-legal policy objectives, and, revealing its liberal pedigree, reality is identified with that which a direct empiricism reveals. In this

185

approach the critique of law shifts from the internal concern with coherence, determinacy and non-contradiction *in* the rules shown by the expository tradition to an external critique *of* the rules in terms of their practical effects and efficiency in realising policy objectives. While various social scientific techniques and concepts may be deployed to get at the empirical reality, it is a mixture of law and common sense which is generally used to define the context in which law is explored, thus allowing theory little part in the identification of the issues through redefinition of the conceptual map.

Though it may be said that the law in context books, by not critically distancing themselves from the viewpoint of the modern administrator, provide not so much a critique of law but are merely the texts of a new more purposive form of law, they have had an enormous impact in the exposure of law to critical examination in the educational process.

Another expression of the attempt to mobilise in legal education a critique of law in terms of social reality was the experiment with clinical legal education which began to emerge alongside the neighbourhood law centre movement in the 1970s. The animating idea, which diverged somewhat from the emphasis on practical lawyering skills in models from the U.S.A., was that by identifying with the client's situation the student would learn what law 'really' meant. Though potentially radicalising, clinical legal education has so far failed to develop as a significant component of critical legal education.

In each of the approaches so far considered, what I have suggested is a key mobilising theme of the critical movement, the gap between legal appearance and reality, is interpreted as the gap between legal appearance and *legal* reality, for each approach uses law in some sense to define the reality to be considered. In short, they implicitly assume the autonomy of law as well as the possibility of a direct empiricism. The critical reaction to these approaches, which challenged both these assumptions, was to turn not to empiricism or legal practice but to theory in order to identify the reality beneath the law which would become the basis of a critique of law.

From this there has emerged a whole succession of 'of law' subjects, an anthropology of law, numerous sociologies of law, an historical materialism of law, an influential economics of law, social histories of law and most recently a semiotics of law. However, in each case the quest is essentially the same, the discovery of the reality behind law's appearance, and in each case the method is essentially the same, namely using the conceptual apparatus of a theory to construct a map of reality within which to locate law. This approach, which could be called the 'law as' approach since it seeks to understand law as the effect or expression of something else, some deeper reality, to a greater or lesser extent challenges the idea of legal autonomy by seeking to account for it. Despite recent criticisms of its inherent reductionism, in Britain it is significantly through such 'law as' approaches that new theoretical ideas have found a place in law school curricula.

Although all such approaches claim in some sense to be disclosing a reality hidden by law's appearances, two quite distinct variants can be discerned. First, those in which the underlying reality is hidden only in the sense that it is not immediately obvious, like the laws of motion beneath the apparent motion of objects, and, secondly, those in which the very fact that something is hidden (that the truth is in some way, though not necessarily consciously, concealed or repressed) is considered of critical importance. In the former category one might include the law and economics approach and the semiotics of law, each of which seek to reveal a hidden structure beneath the law. In the latter category one might include those social histories such as E. P. Thompson's account of the Black Acts,[1] which seek to show how the appearance of law conceals the history through which it came to appear, for example, by revealing the hidden interests that law or particular laws served. In this case the disclosure of a hidden history serves not simply as an historical explanation but to deligitimate some aspect of law's present appearance.

Overwhelmingly the most influential body of theoretical ideas which have been deployed in this second approach has been that drawn from the Marxist tradition which experienced a general upsurge in the 1970s. For those who were made increasingly uneasy by the growing awareness of the gap between law's appearances and claims and the social realities of capitalist society, and who also sensed a deep structural bias in the entire legal enterprise, a Marxist analysis of law offered an appealing unifying theory, through which the hitherto isolated examples of 'law against the people' acquired a new significance and coherence.

In the early 1970s the received interpretation of Marxism in relation to law was to see law primarily as an instrument of class domination, with the emphasis falling on those areas of public law where this was most obvious. In this approach, attention was directed to what law did, and more particularly to what functions it fulfilled in maintaining the relations of exploitation in capitalism, with the relation between legal appearance and reality being conceived as that between false mask and truth. In short, the truth behind the legal appearance was discovered in the functions law performed for capitalism.

Somewhat later, influenced by Gramsci's notion of hegemony, one particular function of law, that of ideological domination, became prominent. This led to the conceptualisation of law as a legitimating ideology. Seen through the concepts of hegemony and legitimation, the relation between legal appearance and reality came to be seen less in terms of mask and reality and increasingly in terms of reality and necessary appearance. This led in turn to the recognition that legal relations were in some sense real social relations. The rediscovery in the 1970s of Pashukanis' attempt[2] to show that the legal form was the necessary form of capitalist social relations gave substance to this idea and, as well as providing a way into a critique of private law, led to the reconceptualisation of the relation between law and reality as that between form and real content. More recently criticism of the ahistorical nature of Pashukanis' approach has led to a rethinking of that form/content distinction in terms of the distinction between abstract appearances and their historical conditions of possibility.

While Marxist currents remain strong in the modern critical legal movement, in more recent years Marxist approaches to the study of law have become increasingly unfashionable, particularly among many critical scholars in the U.S.A. who, having identified Marxism with rather simplistic instrumental and functional accounts of it, reject it for its functional reductionism. Before passing on to consider why today there is an increasing disenchantment with Marxism and what has moved to centre stage, I think it is important to stress one characteristic feature of the critical legal movement which it has inherited from its encounter with Marx. This is the idea of critique as a form of understanding which rejects the separation between theory and practice and denies the possibility of neutral truth in the abstract. Thus, for the critical legal movement, revealing the reality behind law's appearances is not to be seen as a purely academic exercise, the recovery of a positivist truth, but an exercise in subversion directed against domination, in which the true and the good cannot be separated as they are in the liberal tradition and the dominant western epistemology.

Ironically, it is this anti-positivist message, which many in the critical legal movement learnt from Marx, which has today made many of its adherents critical of orthodox Marxism. Thus, of the two strains in the Marxist tradition, one which stresses Marx's contribution in providing a theory of history and an analysis of the political economy of capitalism, and the other which stressed Marx's method of ideology critique, it is probably the latter, mediated *inter alia* through the Frankfurt School of critical social theory and Habermas in particular, which has had the greater influence on the critical legal movement today. Thus, while ideology critique remains a central medium of critical legal study and education on both sides of the Atlantic, the possibility of reducing ideology, including legal ideology, to the social relations of production has been subject to increasing doubt within legal studies and much more generally.

This doubt has taken two different forms. First, there is the doubt that it is sufficient to provide a critical account of domination in the modern world exclusively through class and production relations. Most significantly feminism, while generally adopting a Marxist inspired notion of critique as theory linked to and emerging from practical social transformation, has more or less radically challenged the Marxist primacy of class and production relations and insisted on the centrality of gender and sexuality on any critical agenda. Similarly, the perceived failure of Marxist analysis to encompass racial oppression, the position of the Third World, the destructive power of technology and the rise of the nation state, with the threat which that entails for human survival, reveals to many that the Marxist critique is at best a partial critique.

While to some extent the above concerns can be accommodated by adding on to Marx's critique of political economy a critique in terms of gender, race, technological reason, etc., the second form of doubt about the Marxist project is much more far-reaching. It is the self doubt of a civilisation which must call itself 'post-modern' when it puts into question the faith of modern society, the

Enlightenment belief in the possibility of progressive transformation through reason, of which Marxism is such a brilliant expression. The intellectual expression of this doubt, which unravels the western word, is, because it rejects the idea of underlying structures, what is usually known as post-structuralism,and it is this, particularly through the writings of Foucault and Derrida, which has more or less consciously shaped the style and language of the contemporary critical legal movement. I say style and language because post-structuralism is the denial of the possibility of a discourse whose truth claims can be grounded, a denial of the correspondence between an order of words and the order of things, and a consequent recognition that there is nothing but discourses, discourses which while they might talk to each other are ultimately untranslatable. Thus history, as an order to which any discourse can sustain a claim of privileged access, is dissolved and indeed in Foucault's writing the whole project of writing grand histories of the past such as Marxism, with their metaphors of surfaces and depths, and appearances and realities, is seen as but one moment in the history of discourses. For Foucault we can know the past only as genealogies, origins of the present, a present which has no centre or coherence but is merely the field in which the discourses of power compete as rhetorics. While Foucault concedes that it may be possible to discover a reality behind the text in the limited sense of the conditions of possibility of particular discourses, and it is that which opens up occasional spaces to resist power, Derrida denies even that link between discourse and reality, by insisting that it is possible to reveal that what any text rests upon can be shown to be unable to support the propositions the text itself makes.

The reception of these ideas has had a very significant impact on the critical legal movement, particularly in the U.S.A. where it has combined with and reinforced an attempt to 'trash' liberal legality from within. First, it has led to a rejection of the 'law as' approach to get at the reality beneath law. Secondly, rejecting such reductionism, it has led scholars to take legal doctrine more seriously as an apparently discrete form of discourse and to subject it to an immanent critique to demonstrate the incoherence, contradictoriness and indeterminacy of the claims implicit in law's appearance. This can be seen as an attempt to fracture legal autonomy from the inside, for example, by showing that the claim of legal discourse to be distinct from other discourses such as politics and ethics cannot be supported on the basis of what the legal text itself rests upon; that basis frequently being presented as a series of fundamental contradictions endemic to western liberal societies. In short, the gap between appearance and reality, though it must now be a metaphor, is found and opened up in law itself, rather than between law and something else and it is opened up with the aim of creating possibility spaces for a new social order.

3. The Critical Legal Movement and the Critique of the Enlightenment

In the preceding pages, through the idea of the gap between legal appearance and reality, I have tried to sketch the development of a movement that has now acquired identity under the label 'critical'. Maybe in trying to answer the question "What is critical legal studies and education?" I should stop there and let that history speak for itself. However, at the risk of over-generalising, I feel it might be useful to try and draw out from that story what I see as some general characteristics of the critical legal movement before briefly pointing to its relationship with the critique of the Enlightenment at large.

First, I would suggest that the critical legal movement is based upon a recognition of the partial nature of the account of law as it appears through the expository tradition, not simply in the sense of it being incomplete, but in the stronger sense of being politically loaded, in that it silently reinforces certain assumptions, and covertly communicates certain values. More generally, the critical legal movement denies the possibility of any politically neutral account of law.

Secondly, the critical legal movement seeks not only to question such hidden assumptions and values but recognises the crucial role that holding such ideas plays in maintaining the social order. Thus, the concept of ideological domination, the idea that we are dominated by not seeing how we see, becomes a crucial critical concept, and ideology critique, which seeks to thematise the invisible structures of thought, becomes a dominant methodology. While such ideology critique is pursued in different ways, in each case the aim is to demonstrate the contingency of dominant ideas in and about law by accounting for how or why they come to be held.

Thirdly, I would suggest that the critical legal movement is characterised by a commitment to the ideal of individual liberation coupled with a recognition of the limitations of liberal legality to achieve this. Thus, the critical legal movement is necessarily a political movement in that, in the name of human emancipation, it aims to subvert the legal in order to transcend it.

Fourthly, flowing beyond the recognition that all forms of knowledge about law are necessarily political, I believe that in the critical legal movement there is a suspicion felt more or less strongly of all abstract forms of truth and a doubt about the possibility of any pure objective knowledge. Certainly, accompanying a rejection of legal positivism there are strong currents of general anti-positivism.

Fifthly, and in a sense drawing together the above elements, is the critical legal movement's more or less conscious rejection of the distinctions between theory and practice and fact and value, which are characteristic of the liberal world view, in favour of a view that denies the possibility of pure theory and sees the measure of a theory in terms of its potential for affecting practical social transformation.

To identify the main themes in the critical legal movement in this way is to show how it draws its inspiration from the project of the critique of the Enlightenment at large, the attempt to create the possibility of human freedom by the penetration of dogmas and authority through reason. However, while positivism in both its legal and its scientific forms, which both owe much to Kant, represents one interpretation of this project, an interpretation which insists on the separation of the true and the good and the possibility of

190

objective truth in the abstract, the inspiration that the critical legal movement draws from the Enlightenment is found in that stream of critical thought that ran through Marx and Freud, and runs *inter alia* through the Frankfurt School and critical hermeneutics. In this latter stream, albeit in very different ways, we find an attempt to develop a counter vision of truth, to create a version of truth in terms not of abstract correctness but of appropriateness, appropriateness for its human subjects, as opposed to the disinterested truth established by the cold and hard detachment from human needs, sufferings and purposes we call objectivity.

The critical legal movement in its assault on the expository or dogmatic tradition in law and legal education, and in its emphasis on law as ideology, identifies with the first great and brilliant theme of the Enlightenment: the belief in the potential of thought to cut through humanly produced distortions and illusions (the negative moment of critique) and to see this as the precondition for human emancipation. Yet, it is precisely a consciousness of domination through universal claims, a consciousness of the dialectic of the Enlightenment, in which reason itself becomes the source of domination, that engenders a scepticism about the possibility of an emancipatory positive critique that is based either on universal pure reason as in Kant, or on universal reason in history as in Marx.

As the reflexive meaning of the critique of the Enlightenment gains currency in which universal reason becomes the object rather than the method of critique, for example, in the post-structuralist movement, we find in the critical legal movement a rejection of the idea of a positive and transcending critique and an essentialisation of the negative moment of critique, through which, like Foucault's genealogies, it merely hopes to open up occasional spaces in which to overcome the structures of power.

Although the critical legal studies movement may have gone some way on this reflexive path that may lead to a despairing nihilism, I believe it still retains a strong commitment to the Enlightenment faith in constructing emancipatory forms of understanding, though denying the adequacy of an objective and detached form of truth. It is, of course, precisely the claim of critical Enlightenment thought in general that it is not merely academic but can become practical, which is the source of its attraction to law teachers, for it offers the possibility of overcoming the tension between the theoretical and the practical that has for so long dominated legal education.

THE IDEA OF CRITICAL EDUCATION

To recognise that the critical legal movement is concerned with a distinctive and non-positivist form of knowledge has important implications for establishing critical educational programmes. Most crucially, since the measure of critical knowledge is not given by its abstract correctness but by its effect in unmaking and remaking the world through establishing a practical countervision of it for real people, education no longer appears as the transmission of a commodity but enters into the constitution of critical knowledge itself. Berthold Brecht captured the importance of communication in critical thought brilliantly when he said:

> You cannot just 'write the truth', you have to write it *for* and *to* somebody, somebody who can do something with it . . . .You must address yourself not merely to people of a certain disposition, but to those people whom this disposition benefits on the basis of their social position.[3]

To subscribe to this view is to recognise that education is not merely a secondary or derivative activity but an essential and creative one; as I suggested earlier, this recognition is a characteristic feature of the critical legal movement. Furthermore, the concern that finds expression in Brecht's remarks for the subjects of education and the real world in which they find themselves, marks off critical education from other forms of education, with which it stands in critical opposition, and with which it necessarily engages in a political rather than a purely academic struggle.

Critical education, like all critical activity, initially establishes itself through negative critique. So in order to reveal a countervision of critical legal education one must begin with a critique of the dominant models of education currently operating in legal education. Education in general, I would suggest, can be seen as a process involving three elements. First, knowledge, in which I include theory, information and recipes; secondly, the consciousness of the subject, both student and teacher; and thirdly, the practical reality, the 'real' world in which those subjects have to live their lives. Different models of education can be distinguished in terms of how these three elements of knowledge, subjects and reality are articulated. Through a critique of these models of education a model of critical education emerges.

1. The Technical Model

In this model, which has been the dominant one in legal education, education appears as the one-way transfer of knowledge, seen as a commodity, to a passive subject, who then applies that knowledge to an apparently independently existing reality with the aim of technically modifying or manipulating that reality in practice. In this model the subjects, both students and teachers, are passive rather than active subjects in relation to knowledge, for knowledge is presumed to have an independent and objective existence and, like any commodity on the market, it does not matter whose it is. Like law itself it is everybody's because it is nobody's. Corresponding to this passive relation between knowledge and subject is an external relationship between knowledge and reality, in which the model for the relationship between theoretical knowledge and practice is technology. Legal education in this model is essentially a matter of acquiring a kit of tools.

2. The Liberal Arts Model

In this model the student appears not as a passive carrier of knowledge but as an active subject, for she or he is perceived as engaged with theoretical understanding in a personally involving or active way. Thus, the emphasis is

192

on discovery, self-improvement and awareness aimed at the realisation of a personal 'critical' consciousness. This approach, which arises from the humanist and liberal concern not to treat people as mere means but as ends in themselves, treats the student as important for her or his self. Education in this model is not justified in relation to the outer reality but is thought of as an end in itself. Crucial to this approach, which seeks to respect the individual, is to allow a relatively large validity to students' interpretations, values and opinions, and thus to view education as an open trusting dialogue between adults.

As to the relationship between, on the one hand, knowledge and the subjects involved in the educational process and, on the other hand, the outer reality, there is essentially none; that link is severed as clearly as it is maintained in the technical model, and it is severed precisely to overcome the denial of the active subject implicit in the technical model. This finds expression in such slogans as 'education for education's sake'.

3. The Scholastic Model

In this model priority is given to truth, seen as something to which the scholarly mode gives a privileged access, and education assumes a religious quality as an encounter with a sacred and pure understanding, in relation to which the student is to be a witness. Education, which is primarily geared to the creation of future scholars, is totally subservient to the theoretical project. In its Enlightenment form it is the glorification of intellectualism and an engagement with pure theory. Paradoxically, it finds expression today in certain approaches inspired by post-structuralism, in which the pursuit of the denial of the possibility of truth replaces the pursuit of truth as the pure theoretical project.

4. The 'Instruments of Change' Model

This model, whose contents can range from a mild reformist to an outright revolutionary programme, is essentially a variant of the technical model in that it treats students as means to real world ends, with the difference that the theory that is to inform practical action is more or less critical of existing arrangements In its ideal typical form it involves transmitting to students a body of received truth, to be followed by a technical application. In adopting a technological conception of the relation of theory and practice it becomes a theory *for* practice as opposed to a theory *of* practice. As with the simple technical model and unlike the liberal arts version, 'correct' understanding becomes central, and the assumption that education is a process of discussion between equal adults must be strenuously denied, for the actual project, the transformation of the real world, like the theoretical project in the scholastic model, cannot be sacrificed for some vague liberal notion of equality of respect. Within the reaction of legal education to the technical model, we find approximations to this model in certain positivist versions of Marxism.

To relate these four models back to my earlier conceptualisation of education as involving the three elements of knowledge, subject and reality, I would suggest that in each of these models we find a tendency to give priority to one of the three elements. In the technical model and its 'instruments of change' variant it is the practical outer reality, in the liberal arts model it is the individual subject and in the scholastic model it is the element of knowledge. Furthermore, with one exception, the three elements appear as independent, and in that one exception, the linking of the subject with knowledge in the liberal arts version, this is achieved at the expense of excluding practical reality. I would argue that the aim of critical education is simultaneously to overcome these separations by combining the concern for practical transformation shown in the 'instruments of change' model with the concern to relate knowledge and subject in the liberal arts model and to subordinate the scholastic project to these concerns. Another way of putting it is to say that critical education aims to establish a congruence between the student's self-understanding and her or his theoretical understanding of the possibilities of change in the outside world. By understanding the conditions of her or his own alienation, a critical education seeks to enable the student to assume a responsibility in overcoming them. To achieve that would be for knowledge to become the self-understanding of real people capable of informing their practical actions in their real situations.

CRITICAL LEGAL EDUCATION:
SOME POSSIBILITIES AND PROBLEMS

One of the implications of the importance necessarily attached to education in any critical movement as I have identified it is that the emphasis in critical legal education shifts from a concern about what to say *about* law to how one can provide a critical education *through* law. As I have tried to show at the most general level, critical education aims to provide an enabling perspective, that is to say a form of understanding which enables students to overcome their experience of powerlessness through recognising the sources of it. The primary mode of critical education is then to recognise what is taken for granted, for by negating the taken for granted we come to recognise what it is.

Seen in this light, providing a critical education through law involves bringing to consciousness the taken for granted in and about law so that we can recognise what it means. Most importantly, for this to become more than a merely academic exercise and become practically enabling, we must address the student as herself or himself. Equally, the student must never lose sight of the fact, even when the topic looks most abstract and theoretical, that that issue is the 'real' world, seen as the situation in which the student finds herself or himself, and that the critical goal is to reveal the possibility of that situation being otherwise.

In my view there is no single approach or body of theory which can uniquely accomplish this task in relation to law, for what gives the critical project identity is its intent, not any particular intellectual position. Thus, for

194

example, despite the limitations I have referred to earlier, the 'law in context' approach may frequently achieve a critical purpose by exposing the illusoriness of certain legal appearances, or the relativity of the formal legal version of justice.

However, although I am denying the existence of a critical orthodoxy, two general points might be made. First, although the cry for more theory was a marked feature of the development of the critical movement, it is not the mere existence of theory in legal education which makes it critical but the appropriation of theory for practical transformation. Secondly, despite the above *caveat*, it may nevertheless be possible to point to certain ideas or bodies of literature which may have a particular utility in developing a critical education through law. For example, the ideas of cultural and historical relativism applied to ideas such as the rule of law, individual rights, private property and individual responsibility may enable students to grasp the artificiality as opposed to the naturalness of their own conditions of existence, and a similar task may be performed by phenomenology and interpretative sociology. Historical materialism has, of course, an extraordinary potential in revealing the apparently necessary and right as only contingent, and thus of showing the way law chokes off the possibilities for the individual. However, because of its attempt at theoretical closure it poses a considerable danger of closing off the very critical space it has itself opened. Perhaps one of the most useful general approaches in creating a critical legal education is the historical understanding not of the past but of the present. Historical materialism, much modern feminism and anti-imperialism and the work of and inspired by Foucault can be seen as examples of this. In grasping the hidden history of the present appearances, one has a powerful tool to reveal how things could be otherwise and thus to overcome powerlessness. One should also mention the critical contribution of those forms of discourse analysis which show how law's appearances, such as its authority and ability to provide determinate answers, arise from the nature of legal discourse itself, for these open up the possibility of reading law subversively.

Finally, one might mention the important contribution to critical legal education which has been made, particularly in the U.S.A., by attempting to grasp law in terms of liberalism, precisely because liberalism is the dominant disposition of most law students. In the early stages of legal education, the experiences about law and legal ideas on which one can draw in an attempt to make the educational process personally meaningful, although extremely important, for they include very general perceptions of law, order and justice, are necessarily limited. As students acquire an increasingly detailed and technical knowledge about law, the problem of anyone who seeks to make education critical is how to continue to relate this knowledge to the students' experience of the real world outside the classroom, so that one continues to talk to them as people and as responsible for that world. To expose the sense in which law is a liberal institution by demonstrating the liberal assumptions and values not only in the idea of law itself but in legal institutions, concepts and

195

forms of reasoning provides a way of relating often highly technical aspects of law to the living experience of liberal capitalism and to the everyday political issues it generates. It thus provides a way in which students can recognise themselves in and, therefore, assume responsibility for legal doctrine.

Despite the possibilities that these and many other alternatives have opened up, there are two overrriding problems which must be overcome if critical legal education is to establish itself securely. First, there is the problem of extending critical education from the periphery of introductions, separate 'theory' courses and trendy options, to inform the blackest of black letter areas. This matters not only because of the intrinsic importance of many of these areas, but also because they constitute what most students' dispositions lead them to consider the 'real' and 'relevant' law. One of the achievements of the critical movement in the U.S.A. has been to get stuck into these areas in its attempt to take law seriously. However, it has generally done so by restricting itself to a negative critique or rubbish-clearing exercise and by restricting itself to an immanent critique of law's claims as opposed to a transcendent critique, which I would argue is necessarily based on an understanding of the real conditions of the possibility of ideas. It restricts itself in these ways because it limits the idea of ideology critique to a critique of ideas as they appear in discourse as opposed to the social reality in which that ideology is realised.

The second and even more pressing problem, on the solution to which I would suggest the success of the critical legal movement depends, is for that movement to fulfill its promise to provide a theory that informs practical action, in the Aristotelian sense of the pursuit of the good, as opposed to purely technical action. In so far as I have suggested that it is in the nature of critical thought that it is practical in this sense, in my view it is not, as some have suggested,[4] the problem of establishing theoretical coherence which will determine whether the critical legal movement has a future, but whether that movement can inform practice in relation to law. To view education as a moment of such practical action is a necessary preliminary step, and it is taken as soon as we recognise and accept the political nature of the educational process. However, in the final analysis the aspect of the real disposition of students which we must address is not just what to think about law and legal practice but what to do about it. One of the merits of the orthodox Marxist explanation of law as the ideology of bourgeois society was to identify a possible practical politics in relation to law, namely what Mathiesen calls a "politics of abolition".[5] However, apart from any theoretical questions about this position, it is difficult to see how this view can be shown to benefit those who we are training to make their living out of law. By contrast, one of the major reasons for the vitality of feminism in critical legal studies today has been its ability not only to indicate what should be done, but what can be done to benefit at least some of the actual people one is talking to.

Other critical approaches tend to offer little in the way of a practical agenda in relation to legal practice. For example, while the specification of the problem in terms of transcending the legal by establishing a new form of normative discourse is shared by both Habermas and many theorists in the

U.S.A., as in Unger's deviationist doctrine, there is a large gap between that aspiration and our ability to tell future and present practitioners what to do. Most importantly, as with much critical writing generally, it fails to identify those who have a real interest in acquiring the understanding that critical thought offers. To fail at this level means that thought becomes purely theoretical, and if critical thought cannot inform practice then surely it is not critical at all.

NOTES AND REFERENCES

1   E. P. Thompson, *Whigs and Hunters* (1977).
2   E. Pashukanis, *Law and Marxism* (1983).
3   B. Brecht, *Gesammelte Werke* XVIII (1967) p. 230.
4   A. Hunt, "The Theory of Critical Legal Studies" (1986) 6 *Oxford J. of Legal Studies* p. 1.
5   T. Mathiesen, *Law, Society and Political Action: Towards a Strategy Under Later Capitalism* (1980).

As befits a discussion of a discourse against authority, citation of authority has been kept to a minimum, however, the author would be happy to provide details of the sources relied upon to anyone interested. Indicative general references would include:
R. Unger, "Critical Legal Theory" (1982) 96 *Harvard Law Rev.* p. 561.
D. Kennedy, *Legal Education and the Reproduction of Hierarchy* (1983).
P. Freire, *Pedagogy of the Oppressed* (1972).
R. Geuss, *The Idea of a Critical Theory* (1981).
P. Connerton, *The Tragedy of Enlightenment* (1980).
J. Habermas, *Knowledge and Human Interests* (1974).
M. Foucault, *The Order of Things* (1970).
J. Derrida, *Positions* (1972).
T. Mathiesen, *op. cit.*.